From the Battle of Britain to Hitler's Berchtesgaden

From the Battle of Britain to Hitler's Berchtesgaden

Wing Commander James 'Jim' Bazin, DSO, DFC
Fighter pilot, bomber pilot

Fenella and Michael Bazin

First published in Great Britain in 2023 by
Pen & Sword Military
An imprint of
Pen & Sword Books Ltd
Yorkshire - Philadelphia

Copyright © Fenella and Michael Bazin, 2023

ISBN 978 1 39906 690 7

The rights of Fenella and Michael Bazin to be identified as the Authors of this work has been asserted by them in accordance with the Copyright, Designs and Patents Act 1988.

A CIP catalogue record for this book is available from the British Library.

All rights reserved. No part of this book may be reproduced or transmitted in any form or by any means, electronic or mechanical, including photocopying, recording or by any information storage and retrieval system, without permission from the Publisher in writing.

Typeset in INDIA By IMPEC eSolutions
Printed in the UK on paper from a sustainable source by CPI Group (UK) Ltd, Croydon, CR0 4YY

Pen & Sword Books Ltd. incorporates the Imprints of Pen & Sword Archaeology, Atlas, Aviation, Battleground, Discovery, Family History, History, Maritime, Military, Naval, Politics, Railways, Select, Transport, True Crime, Fiction, Frontline Books, Leo Cooper, Praetorian Press, Seaforth Publishing, Wharncliffe and White Owl.

For a complete list of Pen & Sword titles please contact

PEN & SWORD BOOKS LIMITED
47 Church Street, Barnsley, South Yorkshire, S70 2AS, England
E-mail: enquiries@pen-and-sword.co.uk
Website: www.pen-and-sword.co.uk

or

PEN AND SWORD BOOKS
1950 Lawrence Rd, Havertown, PA 19083, USA
E-mail: uspen-and-sword@casematepublishers.com
Website: www.penandswordbooks.com

Contents

Foreword by Air Marshal Sir Ian Macfadyen KCVO CB OBE   vii
Acknowledgements   x
Preface   xiii

Chapter 1   Pre-war   1
Jim Bazin's education in England, his early career, and his introduction to 607 (County of Durham) Squadron

Chapter 2   3 September 1939 to 20 May 1940   10
The 'Phoney War', 607 Squadron in France, and the Battle of France

Chapter 3   June 1939 – December 1940   37
Rebuilding the squadron, June to mid-July 1940, and the Battle of Britain

Chapter 4   December 1940 to November 1943   60
'Resting': Training Controllers in GCI, Controller in HQ 14 and HQ 13 Groups in Inverness

Chapter 5   Mid-November 1943 – 31 August 1944   67
Conversion to bombers, 49 Squadron and CO of IX Squadron

Chapter 6   September 1944   89
Operation Paravane, the first *Tirpitz* raid

Chapter 7 1 October – 12 November 1944 115
The Walcheren Campaign, the Sorpe Dam and
Operation Obviate: the second *Tirpitz* raid

Chapter 8 13 November – 31 December 1944 130
Operation Catechism: The final raid on *Tirpitz*,
more operations, and a curious incident

Chapter 9 January and February 1945 153
A disastrous New Year, a VC for George Thompson,
Bergen U-boat pens, synthetic oil refineries, railway bridges
and viaducts

Chapter 10 March to November 1945 173
Bombing operations continue, Berchtesgaden, Victory in Europe

Chapter 11 Postwar 201
1946-1951, a return to 607 Squadron, and his civilian career

Appendix Jim Bazin's operations with 49 and IX Squadrons
and the men who flew with him 209

Bibliography 212
Endnotes 217
Index 225

Foreword

Air Marshal Sir Ian Macfadyen KCVO CB OBE

James (Jim) Bazin was drawn to a love of flying, indeed it was in his veins. He was fortunate to have joined the then Auxiliary Air Force well before the Second World War and had thus amassed a degree of flying experience prior to 1939 which was to put him in good stead when fighting broke out. Much has been written about the Battle of Britain. Much less is known about the Battle of France. His fine wartime flying career began in France in 1939 with 607 Squadron, flying outdated Gladiators and later Hurricanes before the fighting began. The graphic account of events in May 1940 well demonstrates the chaos of the time. There followed his participation in the Battle of Britain. As this book brings out, both were battles of intense aerial combat which put great strain upon any young pilot. His experience and flying skills, and not a little luck, saw him emerge safely from both battles. Furthermore, he deservedly won a DFC for leadership and some courageous flying.

After fighting in the Battle of Britain, his relative old age as a junior officer (twenty-seven!) was going against him and he was selected to become one of the first RAF Fighter Controllers. This was a new RAF role that directed fighter aircraft onto their target using radar. He was ideally suited to this pioneer ground-based work as an experienced fighter pilot and with a more mature outlook than most of the very young men who had fought in the air battles of 1940. There was nothing like this role anywhere else in the world as Britain was at the time a world-leader in radar technology. He must have done well in the role as promotion quickly followed. However, it is clear from his flying logbook that he got into a cockpit as often as possible despite being on a 'ground tour'.

He would have realised, in late 1943, that to get command of a fighter squadron was unlikely, not only because age was again against him, but for him gone were the days of the great fighter air battles in and around England, or indeed Malta. Jim Bazin was a man who wanted adventure and action. He was well placed for a change in role to fly bombers because of the desperate need for more and more bomber pilots, particularly those with many hours of flying in their logbooks. So began a new RAF life: flying with a crew was an entirely new experience and required new skills. Only relatively few made such a change. To his enormous credit, he quickly mastered these skills and took command of No IX Lancaster bomber squadron as a Wing Commander with less than six months experience in the role. He played a key part in Operation Overlord, the invasion of Europe. He commanded his squadron on the remarkable very long-range raids on the German battleship *Tirpitz*, 'the beast' as Winston Churchill described it, which culminated in it sinking on 12 November 1944, using the remarkable Tallboy 12,000lb bomb. IX squadron became adept at using this special weapon on a variety of targets including Berchtesgaden. He led his squadron with such drive and verve that it became on a par with the only other squadron to use the Tallboy operationally, the elite 617. For his leadership, he was awarded a DSO. To earn a DFC on fighter aircraft and a DSO on bombers is rare indeed. After the war he again returned to his beloved 607 Squadron as a fighter pilot, taking command of the squadron into the 1950s.

As is so often the case, Jim Bazin rarely spoke with his family of his wartime exploits and was never one to 'shoot a line', indeed he detested such a thing. Thus, much family and other research has had to be undertaken in order to write this book. There are some remarkable new insights, particularly of special bomber operations towards the end of the war. The result is an absorbing story and a valuable addition to the history of the Royal Air Force.

Ian Macfadyen February 2022
South Gloucestershire

Acknowledgements

Our warmest thanks go to all the members of the Bazin family, who were generous in supplying material and photographs, and reading early drafts: James and Sarah Bazin, Anthea (née Bazin) and Peter Cowley, Tom Bazin, Kate Bazin, James White, Elizabeth Main and Georgina Walton. Particular mention must be made of Miranda White (Jim's younger daughter), who sadly died on 18 February 2021 after a very long illness. Her collection of memorabilia is now safely in the hands of her son James White.

We are grateful to the Blackadder family, particularly Francis's daughter Libby Smyth for the gift of photographs from her father's collection, and Rob Blackadder, for his interest and advice.

In the early stages of the project we were indebted to Richard Forder, whose telephone conversations and correspondence covered a wide range of topics, particularly some of the technical aspects. Aldon Ferguson gave us much useful advice and encouragement, particularly in the early days when the book was beginning to be a real possibility.

607 SQUADRON

Our thanks go to David Charles, Official Historian of 607 Squadron, for his help in providing information and for putting us in contact with others connected to the period when Jim served with 607 Squadron, and to Mike Shuttleworth, CO of the squadron since February 2019. Others to whom we are grateful for help on this period are Edward McManus of the Battle of Britain Monument, who sent some combat reports that we had not been able to track down, and Geoff Simpson of the Battle of Britain Memorial Trust for pointing us in useful directions for our research. Tim Willbond's information and contacts for 607 Squadron as well as the chapter on Controllers were particularly helpful. Rosemary Gaskell's proof-reading of the early versions of the chapters on 607 Squadron was really useful. We are also grateful to Nicholas and Victoria Craig, who added to our knowledge of Nicholas's father Dudley Craig. Thanks, too, to Peter Gallagher, for additional research, particularly relating to the Preface.

HQ 14 GROUP AND HQ 13 GROUP

Sebastian Cox, Head of Air Historical Branch (RAF), Northolt, and David Lowry (Museums Member, RAF, FCA) gave invaluable help with Jim's period as a Controller in Inverness. As we were unable to travel due to border restrictions during the Covid lockdowns, Kevin Asplin's patience in copying the undigitised records referring to HQ 14 and 13 Groups at the National Archives, Kew, helped us to understand both Jim's role and the possible reasons why he volunteered to retrain as a bomber pilot.

IX SQUADRON

We are hugely indebted to Richard (Dicky) James, IX Squadron's Official Historian, for his endless patience and scrupulous attention to detail. With his help and advice, the account of Jim's time with IX Squadron has been greatly enriched. His work in gathering together the sons and daughters of IX Squadron members who served during the period when Jim was CO has been an unexpected and invaluable bonus. It is a group that was to be christened the Bazineers, consisting, strictly in alphabetical order, Caryl Carr, Malcolm Grant, John Harris,

Phil Hartshorn, Keith Harvey, Alison Keen, Gillian Lidsey, Allyson Macintosh, Jono Prettejohns, Larry Riches, Steve Shutler, John Tweddle, Sharon Wheeler and Maria Wiley. Correspondence, emails and Zoom calls with them have helped to bring a deeper understanding of the events that their fathers experienced.

Particular thanks must go to Allyson MacIntosh, Caryl Carr, Malcolm Grant, Phil Hartshorn, Keith Harvey, Jono Prettejohns, Larry Riches and John Tweddle for their generosity in allowing us to use extracts and illustrations from their fathers' memoirs. They have greatly assisted in bringing the story to life.

We were delighted that Philip Moore granted permission to use his father's fine photograph of Jim on his return to 607 Squadron after the war.

We are grateful to Andrew Berry, Frances Bury and Steve Colvin for reading drafts of the manuscript from the point-of-view of general readers unconnected with any of the squadrons or organisations concerned.

And finally, we would like to thank the National Archives, Kew, for making so much information available online during the periods of isolation during the COVID-19 pandemic, Ken Patterson, John Grehan and colleagues at Pen and Sword, and all our friends and family for their continuing interest in the development of the book and their patience when we became rather over-enthusiastic!

Finally, errors and mistakes are ours alone.

Preface

On a cold, snowy day in January 1985, the family and friends of James 'Jim' Michael Bazin gathered for his funeral service. The vicar gave the eulogy. We think Jim had probably opened up to him in a way that he never had to his own family: maybe our generation did not know how to broach the subject or, indeed, know what questions to ask. After he had remarried in the 1950s, opportunities for such conversations were few. Elizabeth, his first wife, knew little of his wartime career, yet another example of the tight security and secrecy typical of that generation and something that for many stayed with them until the end of their lives.

As the eulogy unfolded we learned about some of his wartime experiences, turning to each other, whispering, 'We didn't know that!' We were already aware that he had been a Battle of Britain fighter pilot and, as a bomber pilot, had taken part in the *Tirpitz* and other special raids. Since then, we have discovered how unusual it was for fighter pilots to convert to bombers. As with so many of Jim's contemporaries, we came to understand a little of just how much his experiences during the six years of the war had impacted on him and the people around him during the following years.

The findings of our research have been a revelation to those of us who knew him. Jim was not a self-publicist, and dismissive of those he described as line-shooters. His obituary in *The Times* was very minimal and we now know was not completely accurate.

Jim was involved in one way or another in aerial combat from the first day the Luftwaffe invaded British airspace in October 1939. He flew

Gladiators in France during the harsh winter of the Phoney War and Hurricanes in the Battle of France and the Battle of Britain. Later, he converted to bombers in time to take part in operations supporting the D-Day Landings. Then, in June 1944, he was appointed Commanding Officer of IX Squadron. Within a few weeks, IX and 617, the two squadrons using the 12,000lb Tallboy bombs developed by Barnes Wallis, were working together on special operations. Targets included the German battleship *Tirpitz*, synthetic oil refineries, U-boat pens, canals and viaducts. The more we learned, the more we felt that it was important to extend our research.

By the time the first COVID-19 lockdown was imposed in March 2020, we had already gathered together some useful material. We had also made contact with aviation historians who had given us valuable leads to follow up. Our initial thoughts were simply to put down on paper Jim's wartime story for the family. As the months went by, our contacts grew and details of his RAF career began to emerge. It was being suggested more and more frequently that the account could be of interest to readers beyond our immediate family circle.

Because information about his early life that does exist is not always accurate, we felt that it was important in this section to give a brief account of his youth and early adulthood. Although he was born in Kashmir, his was not a colonial childhood. His father, Walter Childs Bazin, a Canadian dentist and graduate of Harvard, was adamant that he was not part of the Raj. His mother May was born in Bombay in 1869. Her father, Michael Nedou, originally from Ragusa (now Dubrovnik), had become a naturalised British citizen in 1887 after he had lived in British India for twenty-five years. He was the founder of Nedous Hotel in Lahore, and later opened two more hotels in the mountains in Gulmarg and Srinagar, furlough retreats that were popular with British colonials. He had met his English wife Jessie Winders when she was on a visit to India to see her brother, a British naval officer.

Some time after her husband was killed in a train accident in 1919, May made the decision to take their five young children to their grandfather's home in Canada. She and her family, Jim, his sisters Barbara, twins Lucy and Dorothy, and younger brother Walter, sailed on the *City of York* to Boston, Massachusetts, where they were met by May's brother-in-law Dr Alfred T. Bazin. From there they went to stay with the children's grandmother in Ormstown, south-east of Montreal. Sadly, although May had intended settling in Canada, things did not work out and she finally made the decision to return to India, where she was initially able to get work as a school matron, later taking a teaching post at St Denys' School, 7,000ft up in the Murree Hills in the north of Punjab province, on the border of Kashmir. It was there that Jim probably acquired the highly accomplished use of a catapult. In later life, he took delight in using his catapult in order to speed the departure of dogs and cats that had dared to venture into his garden.

Although he never returned to the land of his birth, memories of his early youth remained with him all his life. He never forgot the glorious Himalayan sunsets, often commenting that English sunsets could never compare to those he had seen in his childhood in the mountains of Kashmir.

On 30 March 1928, the 14-year-old Jim and his younger brother Walter said farewell to their mother and the twins and sailed for England on the RMS *Kaisar-i-hind*, where they were reunited with their older sister Barbara, who was already at school there. Their address was given as Anerley in south-east London.

It was the beginning of a new and important phase in his life.

Michael and Fenella Bazin

Chapter 1

Pre-war

Jim Bazin's education in England, his early career, and his introduction to 607 (County of Durham) Squadron

Jim Bazin had force-landed behind enemy lines near Sedan after trying without success to bale out. He escaped into nearby woodland then, very cautiously, began to make his way back to fire his Hurricane. Just as he became aware of movement in the undergrowth, a hail of bullets rang out from the German line and he quickly abandoned the idea of destroying the grounded aircraft, moving away very quickly and very quietly.

This was 16 May 1940, the seventh day of the Battle of France. No. 607 (County of Durham) Squadron, part of the Auxiliary Air Force, had been posted to France the previous November. Flying Gloster Gladiators, biplanes that were already out-dated by the beginning of the war, they had already experienced combat over the northern skies of Britain during October 1939. Now, equipped with Hurricanes, they were charged with trying to slow the advance of German troops, which were forcing the British Expeditionary Force towards the coast at Dunkirk.

It was a tragic twist of fate that had led Jim Bazin's family to England. Jim was born and raised in Kashmir. After his father, a Canadian dentist, had died in a train accident, Jim's mother planned to settle with her children in Canada. It did not work out as she had hoped so the young family returned to Kashmir. When he was in his early teens, Jim and his younger brother Walter sailed to England for their education. His training as an engineer at Faraday House led to an appointment with Reyrolle, Hebburn, Tyneside, a company that manufactured switchgear for power stations and Electricity Distribution Networks worldwide. Initially he was in the T & R Department, later transferring to Central Planning.[1] This was a training that was to stand him in good stead during his time with the RAF and his later successful career in engineering.

It was through his colleagues at work that he became aware of 607 Squadron, which was based at Usworth near Sunderland, south of Newcastle. It was to play a major part in his life over the next nineteen years.

No. 607 (County of Durham) Squadron, 1935-1939

Now considered an extension of regular RAF squadrons, No. 607 Squadron (County of Durham) was one of twenty-one in the Auxiliary Air Force (AAF) founded by Lord Trenchard, first Marshal of the Royal Air Force. During their early years these part-time units were regarded as elite groups, different from the regular RAF. Trenchard himself likened the AAF to the Royal Yacht Squadron.[2] Sir Samuel Hoare commented that they were the successors to earlier heroes who 'would have been interested in horses but who now wished to serve their country in machines'. Because training and other events often took place on weekdays, candidates had to be able to have a private income or to be sponsored by their employer. Learning to fly at the expense of the government was certainly a very attractive proposition at a time when only the very wealthy could afford to take themselves to the air. For those who, like Jim, had no longstanding family contacts in

Britain, it was also an opportunity to build up a network of professional and social contacts.

There were four clear steps before being accepted as a member of the AAF. As there were always more candidates than vacancies, a serving officer of the squadron had to make the introduction. This was followed by an interview with the squadron adjutant, a regular officer with the RAF, perhaps an uncomfortable occasion as, according to Robert Dixon, the officer 'was not always a man from the candidate's own social standing.' After this interview, an air-experience flight took place, which would help to consider the applicant's suitability, particularly in terms of whether or not they might suffer from air sickness. In Jim's case this was a 35-minute flight in an Avro with Flight Lieutenant Singer on 26 May 1935. The final stage was an invitation to dinner at the Commander's home, bringing the Commander's wife into the equation. This could be the deciding factor, as social rank was an important element in the process. Inevitably, the system of recommendation meant that there was a strong sense of community, not only regionally but also in terms of occupations, among both officers and other ranks. Many of the officers of 607 Squadron came from the worlds of shipping, law, and engineering.

'Johnnie' Johnson, later to be a Wing Leader and recipient of the DSO and DFC, recounted his failure to meet these standards when, during his interview, he had to admit that he did not follow any of the famous Leicestershire foxhounds and the interview came to an abrupt end. A subsequent attempt also met with failure, until he was finally accepted by the Volunteer Reserves.[3]

Having been accepted, Jim had to wait until 21 September for his first dual flight. He passed his 'Action in the event of fire' and made his first solo flight on 16 November in the Avro, becoming a fully-fledged member of 607 Squadron when he was Gazetted as a pilot officer (Wapiti, Demon and Gladiator) on 9 December 1935. He was awarded his wings on 1 July the following year, two days before his first Annual Camp, which took place at Tangmere from the 3-17 July 1936, with gunnery practice at Lydd. By then he had already made his first cross-country solo flight, from Usworth to Turnhouse in low cloud with limited visibility. The squadron records note that there were sixteen officers and ninety-three men at the camp. Jim flew to a variety of airfields in the area, including Hendon and Rochester, as well as others that were to become familiar during the Battle of Britain. It was not until 26 September 1936, that the squadron was re-equipped with Hawker Demons, two-seater fighter aircraft, and re-named 607(F) Squadron, though staying as an AAF unit in Bomber Command. By the end of September, Jim had completed ninety-four solo hours and recorded his first aerobatics session.

Because of unfavourable weather at the beginning of 1937, there were no flights in February and few opportunities to be airborne until April, when Jim's logbook shows there was formation flying, camera practice, and exercises on R/T. There was considerably more activity in May, with formation flying and attacks. June proved busy too, with cross-country flights, including one to Hendon, and there was more instrument flying instruction. By the end of July, Jim had clocked up a total of 188 hours, including over 152 hours solo. His entries over the next few months reflect the increasingly uneasy international situation, with battle flight practice and solo night flying added to the growing list of skills.

Unlike the previous year, 1938 opened with an increasingly intensive programme of training, with greater emphasis on gunnery practice, including an air-gunner cross-country test in February. The Operations Record Book (ORB) notes that an invitation from the squadron's Honorary Air Commodore Lord Londonderry[4] to his estate in Northern Ireland for 15 May had to be abandoned because of adverse flying conditions.

Generally, Jim was now flying solo, though on 11 May Joe Kayll took him up for a 20-minute flight. Later that day, Jim noted that there was dive-bombing practice for Empire Air Day, with the celebration itself taking place on 25 May, when the squadron held an Open Day, attended by 3,700 people. Because of more bad weather, a feature that was to figure hugely in the squadron's experience in France eighteen months later, heavy rain, low cloud and poor visibility meant that the planned air display was curtailed, no doubt a disappointment for all concerned.

The atmosphere at the summer camp at Warmwell, Dorset, in July 1938, must have been very different from the previous year, as the threat of war was coming closer. Hitler had already absorbed Austria into Germany in March 1938 and was drawing up plans for the occupation of Czechoslovakia. There were still pacifists who supported Chamberlain's policy of 'peace in our time' but others were perhaps more aware of what was happening in Germany and urged the government to expand the armed forces. This is reflected in the continuing expansion of the squadron, which now consisted of the Commanding Officer Leslie Runciman, twenty-three Auxiliary officers, including the Honorary Air Commodore, three regular officers, and 150 Auxiliary airmen, including NCOs, an increase of roughly thirty per cent overall. Their complement of aircraft now included fourteen Demons.

It is interesting to note that by the end of the year, Jim's total flying time stood at 324 hours, including 270 solo. During each of the previous years, he had logged just ninety-four hours. The figure for 1938 represents an increase of almost fifty per cent over the total of the previous two years, suggesting that the squadron now had more resources, reflecting Parliament's decisions to increase the Defence Budget. At a Cabinet meeting in January 1937, the Secretary of State for Air had submitted a Memorandum covering a plan drawn up by the Air Staff for an increase in the Striking Force as soon as possible.[5] Among many other results, this had a direct impact on the amount spent on training.

Numbers of aircraft in the squadron had also increased. As well as the Demons, there were two Hart Trainers and three Avro Tutor aircraft, all single-engine biplanes. The Hart was particularly adaptable, as it could be converted from a two-seat bomber to a single-seat fighter.

On 27 September 1938, just six weeks after returning to Usworth at the end of the Summer Camp, and three days before Chamberlain's 'Peace in our time' speech, news came that, because of the deteriorating international situation, this auxiliary squadron was to be embodied into the RAF. Notices were immediately handed to the Post Office Authorities; the urgency of the matter can be judged by the fact that they were delivered by 8 o'clock in the morning of the same day. All but four personnel reported for duty: two were ill and two were abroad. The embodiment was completed in three days, subject to the arrival of some equipment that was not already in the store. There was no order to mobilise, but operations and general training continued. The situation lasted until 11 October, at which point the squadron was disembodied. At the same time, there was a two-month recruitment drive to bring numbers of NCOs and other ranks up to the full-time strength of 205. A similar campaign had been launched in the *Sunderland Echo* in August 1933 under the headline 'Recruits rush to new Bomber Squadron: Usworth 'Drome. Pilot numbers had already been met.'

Amidst all the activity, the excitement and the uncertainty, James Michael Bazin was married on 22 October 1938 to Elizabeth Anna, daughter of Edmund and Isabella Richardson. They had been introduced to each other by Francis Blackadder, a fellow member of 607 Squadron. The families remain in touch to this day. Elizabeth was born in July 1912 and came from a Quaker family that was well-established in the north-east. Her family owned and ran paper mills in County Durham. Her father was Managing Director of the Springwell Mills at Jarrow, 5 miles east of Newcastle (now Tyne and Wear) and in 1907 was appointed Managing Director of the Team Valley Mills.

A fortnight after the ceremony, the squadron was inspected by Air Vice-Marshal Leigh Mallory, but over the next few months there was little activity beyond the usual routine. Night flying training seems to have been the priority and was to become very important to the squadron when war broke out. Then, in December, came the news that they were to be equipped with Gloster Gladiators, a British-built biplane fighter developed privately. Although it was the first to feature an enclosed cockpit, it was the RAF's last biplane fighter and was already obsolete with the introduction of newer monoplane designs such as the Hawker Hurricane and the Supermarine Spitfire. The Gladiator had a top speed of about 257mph (413km/hr; 233kn) and had the qualities necessary for aerial combat in the early 1930s. However, they were now up against the German Luftwaffe, which was equipped with Messerschmitt 109s that had proved effective in the Spanish War. The German pilots had also gained battle experience in Spain. By the end of the month, the squadron had taken delivery of six Gladiators, although Jim had to wait until January 8 to have his first flight in one. Because these were single-seat aircraft, the air gunners who had flown in the twin-seaters were now redundant, so the strength of the squadron was slightly reduced and now included twenty officers. Two gunners were selected for training as pilots. Operations then ceased for Christmas, giving everyone a chance to share the festivities with their families. By the following Christmas and New Year, the situation would be very different.

The start of 1939 marked a period of waiting and change. The international situation became yet more serious with the expectation that war was imminent.

Lord Londonderry's five-year term of office as Honorary Air Commodore came to an end in July. Although there had been annual invitations to the officers of 607 Squadron to visit him at Newtownards, there had been no visits there since 1936, when fellow guests, German

Ambassador Joachim von Ribbentrop and his wife, had been among the party that had arrived in a Junkers 52. Leslie Runciman had been transferred to the general list and he now took over the role as Honorary Air Commodore. The occasion was marked by a squadron dinner in February. Flight Lieutenant Launce Smith was appointed Commanding Officer.

In March came the arrival of the remainder of the long-promised Gloster Gladiators and training continued during the first eight months of the year. There were regular operational exercises, including a joint event with the Tyneside anti-aircraft searchlight defence at the end of January. No aircraft were able to take part because of the unserviceable state of the aerodrome. Jim had been busy with training and exercises, including more night flying. Empire Day was again celebrated on 20 May. Germans had been invited as VIPs to another display taking place at Hendon that day, so there was probably a similar contingent carefully watching the proceedings at Usworth. Thankfully, unlike the previous year, flying conditions were good. Thirteen thousand visitors, including families of squadron members, enjoyed a full flying display and visits by a variety of aircraft.

With the looming threat of war, the annual summer camp took place as usual on 12 August, this time at Abbotsinch, now Glasgow Airport. Although the first Sunday was traditionally a day to attend church, there was a breakaway group, including Jim, who decided a more tempting option was to climb Ben Lomond. Jim and Alan Glover competed for the last 200ft to make it to the summit, though there is no record as to who reached the top first. The day continued with a swim in an ice-cold lochan, followed by a visit to the Buchanan Arms at Drymen to round off the excursion.

For once, the weather was good during the summer camp. General flying exercises took place, including gun-firing near Ailsa Craig. Visitors included Air Vice-Marshal Richard Saul, commander of

13 Group[6] and, on 22 August, Air Commodore Peake, Director of the Auxiliary Air Force. Everyone was following the developments of the impending war with keen interest.

The squadron was now up to full strength, with twenty-four AAF officers, three regular RAF officers, 206 AAF airmen and sixty-six regular airmen, including civilian equipment officers with *pro-forma* commissions.

When instructions came on 24 August that the AAF was called out for service, the squadron immediately returned on the same day to Usworth. Within a week came the news that Hitler had invaded Poland.

War was declared three days later, on 3 September.

Chapter 2

3 September 1939 to 20 May 1940

The 'Phoney War', 607 Squadron in France, and the Battle of France

The first few weeks of the war must have been somewhat of an anti-climax. There were no operations, although training and defence exercises were intensified. The early part of the war was confusing. Orders received on 2 October to move to Acklington were later countermanded, as they had been warned that 607 Squadron might be posted overseas. This immediately triggered the existing plans for the speedy relocation of ninety-five, then ninety-nine personnel, including sixteen officer pilots, one Warrant Officer engineer, seventy-six NCOs and airmen, and four aircraft hands.

By 5 October all preparations were completed. Forty-eight-hour embarkation leave was granted to those men who were being sent to France. As Usworth was rapidly becoming unserviceable and undergoing major repair work,[7] the squadron was successfully relocated to Acklington, although it was a day later than planned due to 'unsuitable' weather. They found that 609 (West Riding) Squadron was already established on the station; 152 Squadron was being re-formed and undergoing major repair work, and would not be operational until November. Because members of 609 Squadron were only qualified in day flying, 607 Squadron was immediately on training for day and night flying. Jim Bazin and Francis Blackadder were among those who were put on twenty-four-hour notice to proceed abroad.

On 16 October, the squadron was ordered to Drem, East Lothian, for operational work. Three patrols were airborne in the afternoon, including Jim who led the Green Section. Things did not go quite as planned. Ships in the Firth of Forth, including *HMS Mohawk*, had been attacked by aircraft from the Luftwaffe. A power cut had put Radio Direction Finding (RDF) out of action, so the Germans had been able to approach undetected at low level. As a result, the sections from 607 Squadron found themselves under fire from vessels of the Royal Navy, fortunately without any damage. There was a wartime RAF saying that as far as naval gunners were concerned, if an aircraft had one engine it was a Messerschmitt, if it had two it was a Heinkel, and if it had three, it was an unidentified enemy aircraft.[8] Jim's logbook entry simply notes 'Patrol of Firth of Forth (1st raid)'. In spite of flying four patrols, he did not see any enemy aircraft. The first enemy aircraft to be brought down that day were by 602 Squadron (City of Glasgow) and 603 Squadron (City of Edinburgh).[9] By 2300hrs, 607 Squadron was ordered to return to Acklington.

The next morning, 17 October, all sixteen Gladiators had left Drem by 0730. Just over five hours later, sections of 'B' Flight were ordered to intercept a Dornier 18, a German flying boat. This was to be the squadron's first experience of facing the enemy. Four 'double-engined' seaplanes were sighted just below cloud roughly twenty miles east of Blyth over the North Sea. Jim's Combat Report gives a detailed account of the action:

> 'Three seaplanes in Vic [Vee formation] with one other 1,000 feet above and behind and to the left. The fourth machine was different from the others in colour, i.e. (black with silver swastikas). When attacked they maintained Vee formation but dived through cloud. In only one case was fire returned from [indecipherable] in tail. Attacker returned home with ammunition exhausted.'

There was a more detailed description on the second page:

a) Enemy sighted 90° starboard and 6,000 feet about three miles away. Fighters at same target.
   Three fighters and four enemy aircraft.
   Fighters in search formation (vic) and enemy in wide vic with the fourth aircraft above and to the left.
b) Enemy approached directly from behind since they were flying away from fighter when first seen.
c) No standard attack. Enemy attacked in echelon right, i.e. No. 1 of fighters attacked No. 3 enemy formation. No. 2 fighter attacked No. 1 enemy and No. 3 fighter attacked No. 2 enemy.
d) Enemy made for clouds. These were about 2/10 at about 4,000 feet. Fighters followed through and continued attacking.
e) As the size of their seaplane was unknown at this time and, as this was underestimated, fire was opened at approximately 600 yards or more. Fighter leader continued firing until ammunition exhausted. Nos 2 and 3 fired in two or more bursts because enemy obscured by cloud at times.[10]

Later, they heard that a seaplane had ditched; the four crew members had been rescued by a trawler and taken prisoner. There were no further sightings of the enemy that day.

The rest of the month was quiet. However, one of the members of the squadron, Alan Glover, who had raced Jim to the top of Ben Lomond, was killed in a flying accident on 29 October, with the funeral held on 1 November.

During the first ten days of November there was little activity. Patrols kept a lookout for convoys moving north and south along the coast and there were preparations for quick reaction in the event of more sightings in the Firth of Forth. Operational duties were shared with

111 Squadron, which had arrived at Drem from Northolt with twelve Hawker Hurricanes, but there was little to be seen of enemy aircraft.

Suddenly, though, there was the first sign of their move to France. A civil Ensign aircraft landed at Acklington, with instructions to stand by to proceed once the bad weather had cleared. Bad weather was to be a recurring theme as the winter was to prove particularly harsh, with flights held up by heavy rain, high winds and, later in France, very low temperatures and snow. The next day – Remembrance Day – was again plagued by bad weather, and conditions had still not improved during the next twenty-four hours, although two more Ensigns were able to arrive in the evening, when the loading of equipment began. On 13 November, four de Havilland 86s left Acklington at 1415 to fly all 101 personnel to Croydon. The entire party consisted of sixteen Gladiators, two Ensigns, four de Havillands and an impressed Fokker. Refuelling at Digby, south-east of Lincoln, their convoy arrived at Croydon three hours later, where they met up with 615 Squadron, also equipped with Gladiators. They now received orders to proceed overseas. These two squadrons together formed No. 61 Wing for the period 1939-1945.

By 15 November the weather had cleared sufficiently to allow the move to Merville, close to the Belgian border. It was an area that was to play an important role in the invasion in June 1944. The convoy of forty-five aircraft travelling via Shoreham included Jim flying a Gladiator. The whole operation was free of problems and was described as a 'good trip over'.[11] There was some consternation at the state of the ground surface in Merville. Like all the airfields that had been allocated to the RAF, it had been sown with clover, making it totally unsuitable for the purpose. France had suffered weather that was just as bad as the squadron had experienced over the previous week or so, and everything was waterlogged. Because of problems caused by the clover, mud was frequently over a foot deep and machines were regularly bogged down. There was very little shelter: maintenance usually had to be carried out in the open on the aircraft dotted around the perimeter. Tents had been provided for the ground crew and storage space was in two Nissen huts, which like most Nissen huts, were subject to heavy condensation that must have presented huge problems for the maintenance teams. While officers were billeted in the town, the airmen found themselves having to cope with living quarters in a large silo that had been pressed into use. Preparations for the squadron's arrival that had been promised by the French had not been fulfilled, although they were able to supply the RAF squadrons with rations, wine and petrol.[12] However, there was another more serious problem. None of the designated airfields were in the area allotted to the British Army, which was supposed to supply the squadrons with 'rations, tents, fuel, pay, postal services, billets, etc.'

The day after their arrival was spent in settling in but the bad weather continued and the heavy autumn rain was still a problem. There was a bit of excitement on 20 November when a Heinkel managed to evade any action when pursued by 'A' Flight.

Otherwise, the patrols were of an operational nature and no enemy aircraft were spotted. A 'highlight' in the ORB entry of 2 December was the sighting of suspected enemy aircraft flying at a great height near the Belgian border, 'leaving smoke trails'. Along with fourteen unnamed other ranks, the CO and Flight Lieutenant John Sample travelled to Seclin on 5 December for a rehearsal for the King's visit the following day. Preparations were again in hand for yet another move on 13 December, this time to Vitry-en-Artois under 'extremely adverse weather'. There is a heartfelt entry in the ORB reporting that 'the squadron was operating under great difficulties owing to the waterlogged state of the aerodrome and the exceptionally bad weather conditions'.

It is hard to imagine what life must have been like during the month following their arrival in France. They would have been prepared for action but there was none. The weather was dreadful, the airfield often unusable and, as the weeks progressed and daylight hours grew shorter, it must have been difficult to keep up morale.

The move to Vitry must have come as a great relief as the ORB entry reported that the surface was 'both firm and dry'.

Jim at least had a change of scene when the Green Section of 'B' Flight was based at St Inglevert aerodrome from 20 December for special duties patrolling the English Channel.

Christmas Day, 1939 began with a trip into Calais, where Jim at last found a chemist shop, where his 'long enduring quest for liquid paraffin had its journey's end'.[13] It was an opportunity to relax and forget why they were in France. They went down to the beach for a couple of hours in the morning, messing about and generally letting off steam. They were back there again after lunch, with a slightly more organised game of four-a-side-football, playing with bare feet. Jim was one of the Mermaids team, Francis part of the Beach-lions. It quickly became shambolic, which, said Francis, made them all feel a great deal better. It was obviously a perfect way to relax and use up some of the nervous energy that must have built up over the previous weeks. After tea at the hotel, they made a gallant attempt at a jigsaw, though it seems unlikely that it was completed.

In spite of the circumstances, Christmas dinner turned out to be a splendid occasion. 'Two officers faced each other at various parts of each table, with airmen clustered around' and the party lasted from 7pm until midnight. Simple decorations included blue and white streamers, candles on each table, and a few Christmas cards. In pride of place on the mantelpiece was the card sent to the squadron by the King and Queen. A five-course meal featuring turkey and Crême Chantilly was washed down with low-alcohol French beer. There were toasts to sweethearts, wives and absent friends, music, and an 'A' flight song specially composed for the occasion and sung to the tune of 'Uncle Tom Cobley and all'.

Boxing Day turned out to be unsuitable for flying, so it was a day for gentle exercise. The evening saw the officers of 'A' and 'B' Flights entertaining a party of French officers, with music from both nations, followed by party games of the variety where it helps to have a regular supply of wine.

Two days after Christmas, Jim's Green Flight spotted a mine floating in the sea at Wissant. John Humpherson continued circling while Jim reported the presence of the mine and warned shipping by firing into the area so that they would avoid the danger zone. The discovery meant that 'B' Flight had to stay back a day to patrol the area until naval vessels were able to investigate the report. Its fate is unknown. Thankfully, due to that quick response, none of the ships was damaged.

The following day Jim began the flight to rejoin the squadron but had to turn back when he ran into heavy snow. However, by 28 December, both 'A' and 'B' Flights were back in Vitry. The end of the month ushered in a dramatic drop in temperature with weeks of heavy frost. On one occasion, the thermometer fell to show 26 degrees of frost (-32 degrees C), with layers of ice on the water pumps. Apart from the impact on the men themselves, the aircraft also suffered. It sometimes took hours of patient endeavour before the machines were ready to take off. Not only were the Gladiators covered with ice, but there would often be icicles hanging from the wings. Francis Blackadder summed it up with the comment, 'All in all decidedly unpleasant weather on the ground, but quite agreeable for flying'.

Because of the wintry conditions, there was often damage to the Gladiators on landing, with broken tailwheels a regularly recurring problem. More repairs were needed when there were problems caused by the ground crew manoeuvring aircraft. 'Our machines took more and more umbrage at being billeted in the open air,' noted Francis Blackadder. At one stage only four of the ten Gladiators were serviceable. The situation did not improve, and the winter was turning out to be the worst for forty-five years. Oil had to be drained from the aircraft overnight and heated every morning before being returned to the engine in time for the morning flight.[14] On one occasion, Jim, driven by utter frustration when the engine of his Gladiator was badly affected by the frost, took a blowlamp to it, causing the ground crew to retreat to a safe distance. Perhaps they were placing bets on the outcome.

There were, however, moments of light relief. Fine dining was still available and there are many entries in Francis Blackadder's diary describing mouth-watering hotel menus. In Lille a party dined on 'snails and oysters, sole, grilled kidneys, crepes suzette, Coupe Dame Blanche, accompanied by white wine recommended by the patron'.[15] A 'good pub' in Wissant produced a very good dinner and 'clean rooms with running water – cold'. There were numerous invitations to French messes, where members of the squadron 'fulfilled their duty' by getting very drunk.

On New Year's Eve, 114 other ranks including five NCOs arrived at Vitry by rail, after a slow and tedious three-day journey. The squadron was once again at full strength, though one can only imagine their feelings on learning that they were to be billeted in barns and stables, while the officers and senior NCOs were mainly in private houses.

New Year's Day saw a break from routine when the squadron had an official visit by the Under-Secretary of State, Captain Balfour, MP and Assistant Chief of Air Staff, Air Vice-Marshal W.S. Douglas. First Lord of the Admiralty Winston Churchill and Air Commodore Capel made a brief visit on 9 January, producing a wry, three-line entry in Francis Blackadder's diary that the visit lasted ten minutes and Churchill 'evinced no desire to see us, although we were all ready for him'. This conflicts with other reports stating that 'he delighted the men with his morale-lifting chat'.[16]

The ORB simply notes that there were regular patrols whenever possible. In the middle of the month all leave was stopped because of increasing tension in the Low Countries. More snow and heavy frosts made roads surrounding St Inglevert impassable. Drifts were five or six feet deep. On the afternoon of 16 January, a blizzard raged, reducing visibility to a few yards. Troops manhandling aircraft into the hangar were soon covered in snow.[17] Only two aircraft could be started on 19 January: there was 27 degrees of frost and the wind was bitter. As the month wore on, the airfield was pronounced unserviceable. Even so, a small party of officers and men would struggle dutifully through the snow to check that all was well, before returning to seek shelter from the desperate cold. To add to the general gloom, there was a lot of minor sickness, mainly sore throats. It was only small consolation to realise that the appalling weather was also keeping the Luftwaffe on the ground, a major factor that contributed to the Phoney War.

Light relief came in many forms. Dudley Craig reported that a German pilot brought down near the English coast was captured and asked if he was hurt. 'Not physically', he replied in perfect English, 'but morally. To be shot down by a bloody biplane piloted by a bloody barrister is more than I can bloody bear'.

A party, including Blackadder and Bazin, was the first of many to arrive at the scene to view a Dornier 215 that had been shot down. Fortunately, the French military had arrived in time to prevent the German captain from destroying the map that showed the sites that they were to have photographed. The small size of the Dornier surprised them, although they would have known that the wingspan was less than 60ft. They were interested to see that, although there was provision for a couple of cannons, there was no armament. What really impressed them, though, was the quality of the four cameras, the top-of-the-range instruments, and not one, but three compasses.

They lingered in the town, where some 'books of doubtful taste' were purchased.

The Dowding System was still to be implemented in time for the Battle of Britain but in France there was no Control Room to direct operations from the ground. Enemy aircraft had to be tracked down visually. Francis Blackadder described one such sighting when he spotted a trail of smoke high above them at 17,000ft. It was too far away to identify the machine, but it seemed to be moving at speed along the Belgian border towards Calais. As they all set off to investigate further, they spotted another couple of smaller trails mobbing the larger aircraft. By now they were low on petrol so reluctantly turned back for home while the two thinner trails were still intent on attacking the larger aircraft.

The deep snow led to days 'of extreme idleness'. The aerodrome had been pronounced unserviceable but, in spite of this, Francis Blackadder remembered that it was still considered a duty to put in an appearance.

A thaw at the beginning of February brought more problems with flooded roads that had begun to cut up badly. This led to a ban by the French authorities on the use of heavy vehicles. This effectively left the squadron marooned at St Inglevert. Operational exercises were possible, there was training in the use of Lewis guns, and a visit by the Honorary Air Commodore Leslie Runciman. For some unspecified reason, Jim missed an occasion when a group of fourteen officers 'dined well and long'. A small group met for lunch on 25 February, enjoying partridges 'poached' by Jim, whose exploits, according to Francis Blackadder, 'rivalled those of the celebrated Tartarin', a renowned French hunter.

Things began to look up in March. Jim's logbook shows that by 11 March there had been five days when flying was possible, with a mixture of exercises, tests, sector recces and operational patrols continuing for the rest of the month. At last, the weather began to improve and by the middle of the month the long-promised and long-awaited Hurricanes began to arrive.

Four Hurricanes had been flown to Boos (Rouen), the first two on 15 March and the others next day; Jim and a small party of men were sent to guard them. Unfortunately, Jim's logbook, which would have confirmed this, was lost during the chaos of the Battle of France. In the meantime, 'Bow-Wow' Bowen had ferried over a new Miles Master, a British two-seater monoplane with a retractable undercarriage, a feature new to many of the squadron members. Most of the pilots had managed to have at least half-an-hour's experience before a tricky landing by John Sample had put her out of action. Dudley Craig took over as guardian of 'the sacred four' and, on 6 April Jim, along with George Plinston, Peter Parrott and Trevor Jay, a young West Indian, returned to Rouen by road to fly them back:

> 'But were we allowed to use them? Not on your life. Group laid down that they were not to be touched until another four had arrived — and so we go on operating in these bloody little biplanes with small hope of opening our French count.'

There were tragic accidents and a run of bad luck. On 24 March, Nigel Graeme and Harry Radcliffe were killed when they collided. Two days later, Jim was one of the five officers who travelled to Douai for the burials in the British Cemetery.

Preparations were in hand as they had been warned that they might have to relocate at short notice, but in fact this was tediously slow in coming. It was not until 11-12 April that the move took place to Abbeville, ninety-four miles to the west.

Then, at last, a couple of days later, on 14 April, in the middle of all the preparations, ten long-awaited Hurricanes arrived at the airfield, piloted by men from 87 Squadron. This was the answer to all their prayers. Squadron Leader John Scatliff Dewar had brought three bottles of champagne with him, out of which, Francis recalled, he drank their health.

Conditions began to improve dramatically. Accommodation was along a narrow three-mile track from the aerodrome; officers were housed in a chateau, the men, in Nissen huts. Spring had arrived and the woodland was full of daffodils and violets. The food was better, too, and even the camp beds became tolerable after a day or two, which meant everyone was happier than they had been for a while. Morale was at a peak due, so the ORB records show, to Abbeville being a much healthier and cleaner district. There were patrols but, on the whole, the next fortnight was a welcome respite from the privations of the previous months.

Meanwhile, the war was hotting up. Neutral Denmark had been taken over by the Germans in a matter of hours and Norway, also neutral, was gradually occupied over the next two months. As a result, the Germans now controlled the waters of the Skagerrak, the only entrance to the Baltic Sea, as well as the coastline from the Netherlands to the Russian borders. Hitler's troops were now preparing to invade the Netherlands, Belgium and France.

At Abbeville, initial training began on a replacement Miles Master. One of the youngest members of the squadron was Peter Parrott, who had already flown Hurricanes, so was able to advise the older pilots. An off duty visit to Le Touquet started well but, when Jim, Francis and Milne Irving were inadvertently left behind at the end of the evening, they were very unhappy when they had to take a taxi back to Abbeville the next morning; Francis Blackadder noted that they were still 'very heated' when they finally arrived.

This comparative idyll was to be cut short when orders came to return to Vitry on 26 April. The ORB noted that no event of importance occurred until 10 May when, at 0415, the civilian alert was sounded, followed immediately by the firing of Bofors guns. By 0730, seven enemy aircraft had been accounted for by the squadron. Jim's flight had attacked an enemy aircraft north of Douai: a burst of fifteen seconds put the rear gunner out of action and one or both of the engines had stopped. As

Green Flight continued the attack the bomber lost height and Jim saw that, although one member of the crew had landed by parachute, the aircraft had crashed in flames, killing the rest of the crew.[18]

More interceptions followed and, by the end of the day, there had been eighteen enemy aircraft shot down, eleven damaged and five 'probables', at a cost to 607 Squadron of one shot down, two damaged and one pilot slightly injured.[19]

Later in the evening, news arrived that Prime Minister Neville Chamberlain had resigned.

The Phoney War was over.

The Battle of France

Virtually all the squadron's records for this period were lost, destroyed in bombing raids on Vitry, or during the chaos of the evacuation from France on and after 20 May. Under the section 'Place', the squadron's typewritten ORB summary simply gives the word 'France' and the date as '1940 during April and May'. There are four pages outlining events, with extra notes at the foot of page 3 running over to page 4 detailing personnel movements and casualties. The first page chronicles the move from Abbeville to Vitry-en-Artois, describing the first action halfway down page 2. There is only skeletal information about the air battles.

The turmoil of the next eleven days has to be judged mainly on accounts from sources other than the Operations Record Book, such as diaries written sometime after the event by squadron members, as well as more general reports. Consequently, it is often inevitable that there are some discrepancies, particularly in statistics relating to losses, kills and probables.

Although members of the squadron had been successfully involved in air combat from daybreak on 10 May, they were still unaware that the expected German invasion of the Netherlands, Belgium and Luxembourg had started. It appears that the news only came after the first sortie. British and French troops had moved into Belgium, where they had received an enthusiastic welcome. The Dutch had destroyed bridges over the Maas and Ijssel rivers to delay the German advance. By the early evening, Winston Churchill had accepted the King's invitation to form a government. He was now Prime Minister. Francis Blackadder recalled that while they were still unaware of the developments, they continued to respect the neutrality of Holland, Belgium and Luxembourg when they ran into hordes of enemy aircraft crossing what they still considered to be the borders between Germany and Allied territory.

There had been a dramatic start to the first day of the Battle of France. In the early hours of the morning of 10 May, they had been woken abruptly by the sound of German bombers and low-flying Me109s attacking the airfield. Francis Blackadder, Tony Dini, and Peter Parrott were already waiting for the lorry to take them the quarter of a mile to the airfield, so were the first to pursue the attackers not long after the raid had taken place.[20]

There were no fighter escorts to be seen. While still out of range of the German bombers, they realised that they were over the coalfields of northern France and very close to the Belgian border, so turned back. They were keenly aware of the warning that if they had to land in Belgium they would have violated Belgian neutrality and, if taken prisoner, would be interned for the rest of the war. It was only when they were back at Vitry that they learned that the Germans had invaded the Low Countries and that the Heinkels had been on their way home after bombing Arras. Most of the airmen completed five sorties that day. Peter Parrott shared a 'probable' with two French pilots, shooting down one and damaging another Heinkel on the fifth raid of the day.[21]

Over the next five days, many of the men of 607 were flying ten or more sorties every day. Because Jim's logbook was lost during the evacuation on 20 May, we can only guess that he was undertaking similarly intensive flying.

In the event, Jim was airborne not long after Francis and his flight landed. The sun was now above the horizon. Jim's Combat Report shows that at 0500 he led an attack on a lone He111 from 250yds at 8,000ft over Douai:

> 'No. 1 gave one burst of fifteen secs. Rear gunner put out of action and one or both engines stopped. Attack continued by No. 3. E.A. [Enemy Aircraft] observed to land on or near Belgian border. One of E.A. crew landed by parachute.'[22]

Alongside the section marked 'Enemy Casualties' it is noted 'Conclusive 1'. Sergeant Ken Townsend, Green 2, reported that Jim had attacked the enemy aircraft:

> '[Jim's] burst observed to converge on tail of E.A. and traverse longitudinally. I continued attack after leader broke away. E.A. observed to lose height. One of crew landed by parachute and E.A. landed close to Belgian border.'

A few seconds after Jim had started firing, Monty Thompson's windscreen was covered in oil, making it impossible to see anything, so he broke away. However, he was still trying to work out his position when he spotted an enemy aircraft about 3,000ft above him. In spite of limited vision, he climbed up and attacked from astern. There was no return fire, but he thought there was a thin trail of black smoke from the German aircraft. In *Twelve Days in May*, Cull and Lander suggest that the Heinkel was possibly piloted by Unteroffizier Gerhard Kasten, returning from an attack on Cambrai, who had been seen baling out. None of the rest of the crew survived.[23]

These were just the opening sorties of the day. Only a quarter of an hour later, Yellow Section of A Flight were in action attacking He111s. They were then intercepted by Will Whitty of B Flight, who had only just arrived at dispersal when his flight sergeant pointed out aircraft bombing Cambrai. He managed to catch two flying together, hitting one that crashed near Mons, but losing the other in cloud. Attacks continued during the day with little respite. In the early afternoon John Sample had to abandon his Hurricane when the engine was hit by several bullets and began pouring out oil, blinding him. His report concluded with the words 'I could not have seen well enough to land'. He sprained both ankles but continued flying on sorties in spite of having to wear carpet slippers all the time.

The final action came more than fourteen hours after the first attack on the German bombers, giving a total of eighteen confirmed, six probables and another dozen or so damaged, all He111s. There were still no more sightings of fighter escorts.

There was a slow start to the next day, 11 May. Taking off in 'filthy' weather, Francis was on an hour's patrol protecting the British Expeditionary Forces (BEF) as they moved west, recording that there was no interference. That afternoon there was an attack by the sections led by Jim and Francis in the area south-east of Brussels. They had just carried out one run when Jim spotted a single He111 flying east. He waggled his wings and the group set off in pursuit. The enemy aircraft was shot down, pouring smoke and bursting into flames as it hit the ground.[24]

This was probably the same attack described in one of Jim's Combat Reports of 11 May, which shows that he was credited with another 'conclusive' that afternoon over south-east Brussels:

> 'Blue section (two aircraft) patrolling with Red Section. Blue 1 attacked after one aircraft of Red Section. Starboard engine stopped after attack. Blue 1 attacked later (after several other

aircraft had attacked) with quarter attack. Flame seen coming from port wing root. E.A. crashed and burst into flames.'

After circling it, they set off further east, spotting another dozen bombers. Later, with oil streaming out of his left wing, Francis Blackadder landed, convinced Belgian soldiers he was 'on their side', and camouflaged his aircraft 'with branches and earth clods'. After five hours coping with the soldiers and streams of refugees, he managed to refuel 'with a sort of aviation fuel', returning to Vitry after yet more adventures, 'a badly-shaken pilot'.

It was not only the aircraft but also the airfield that came under attack. Charles Sims recalled such an event, possibly on 11 or 12 May. The attack began in mid-morning when the Hurricanes were dispersed around the airfield. Refuelling and rearming were in full flow when they were suddenly attacked by Me109s and Me110s, flying in at low-level with guns blazing. Although some of the precious Hurricanes were destroyed on the ground or while they were trying to take off, several managed to get airborne, taking part in what Sims described as 'one of the most vicious low-level dog-fights in the war up to that time'. The raid probably only lasted five minutes or so but left the airfield badly damaged. 'The air became a stage for twirling, turning and diving fighters', he wrote, remembering that the cacophony of machine guns and cannon even blotted out the sound of a nearby bombing raid. The next morning, flying home from a different airfield, they broke up a formation of bombers trying to carry out the same raiding tactics.[25]

From now on there were frequent daily patrols and everything was 'a jumble'.[26] For instance, it seems that there were very few maps of the area, many pilots having to rely on memorising a map pinned to the Nissen hut's door, or consulting one held by the CO, especially as many had to land at a different airfield almost every night. There was no place in the cockpit for a map but in any case, a pilot could be distracted and perhaps caught off guard if he was trying to check his position. One pilot officer commented on how wonderful the weather was, adding that they 'felt lively in the air but when we came down all we wanted to do was sleep'.

Events continued to be increasingly chaotic. Because there was no RDF or fighter control in France, patrols were ordered into the air on whatever military intelligence was available, or even at random. This meant that there were no 'scrambles', something that was to become all too familiar in the Battle of Britain. Any interception of enemy aircraft was purely down to chance, so it was impossible to predict numbers, height, or types of enemy aircraft they would encounter. To compensate for the loss of aircraft, there were occasional replacements of machines, reinforcements by flights or sections from other squadrons but no extra men to supplement the already-stretched ground crews. As the squadron was still flying straight and level in close formation, they were vulnerable to attack from behind. Rear-view mirrors were still a thing of the future. There were some very close shaves.

Without the records that failed to make it back to England, most of the detail of the next few days was lost. However, it is possible that Jim might have claimed one enemy aircraft shot down on 14 May. They were already receiving occasional reinforcements from other squadrons, but aircraft were becoming increasingly precious. So far, most of the aircraft destroyed in the skies above France were bombers, both German and British. For instance, on the raid on Sedan on 15 May, fifty-six per cent of British bombers were lost.

On the ground that had been so badly damaged in the 'war to end all wars' of 1914-1918, there was heavy fighting. Many of the 607 Squadron reports comment on the large number of refugees, people who had already survived the dreadful conditions endured by civilians in the earlier conflict. Jim was not the only one who was impressed by the streams of refugees moving westwards, travelling in cars, carts, bicycles, or trundling wheelbarrows. There were old men and women, children, young women with babies and even some pets. As far as they were able, squadron members gave them as much of their rations as they could spare, helped with repairs, but drew the line at giving them precious petrol.

During the Battle of France, the squadron lost several pilots including Flying Officer G.I. Cuthbert, Flying Officer Monty Thompson and Flying Officer A.E. le Breuilly on 14 May. Their CO from the pre-war unit, Launce Smith, was shot down and killed near Dinant on 15 May while escorting Blenheims that were to attack bridges over the Meuse. He had been leading five Hurricanes when his section, along with Joe Kayll's six Hurricanes from 615 Squadron, was bounced by Me109s and 110s.[27] W.E. Gore had been wounded but would rejoin the squadron later in the year once they were back in England. Peter Dixon returned from the same sortie, his oxygen supply having failed at 17,000ft, and with a bullet narrowly avoiding his foot. He landed at high speed without the use of flaps owing to battle damage. He commented that if he had had the same experience in peacetime, he would have radioed for the fire engine and ambulance to be in readiness.[28]

On 15 May, French Premier Paul Reynaud, in a telephone conversation with Winston Churchill, simply said, 'We have been defeated. We have lost the battle'. In spite of this, the British Expeditionary Force was ordered to fight on. The RAF's role was to keep the Germans back as far as possible to allow the Allied ground troops to move closer to the coast at Dunkirk, where there were plans to evacuate as many troops as possible. The loss of equipment was inevitable, but it was hoped that some men of the British Expeditionary Force could be saved.

Once back on English soil, Jim summarised the events of April and May. His report is so understated that, without other accounts, it would be impossible to gauge the drama of the events that were taking place:

1 April to 14 April	Self	Operational patrols. Cross-country and Sector Recce
15 April to 30 April	Self	Re-equipment with Hurricanes A/C at Abbeville
1 May to 9 May	Self	Operational patrols. Formation and Sector Recces from Vitry
10 May to 20 May	Self	Interceptions, offensive patrols, escorts, low-flying recces from Vitry and Norrent Fontes

There is no mention of the events of 16 May, when Jim had force-landed behind enemy lines near Sedan after trying without success to bale out. He began to make his way back to fire his Hurricane. As he became aware of movement in the undergrowth, a hail of bullets rang out from the German line. He quickly abandoned the idea of destroying the grounded aircraft and moved away at speed.

Francis Blackadder described how Jim eventually got a 'conveyance' and was missing for some time.[29] Jim's son Michael remembered his father telling him that he had been shot down behind, or close to, enemy lines, had walked over fields and found a jeep with petrol and keys, and was able to return to his squadron within twenty-four hours.

The road distance from Sedan to the squadron's airfield is 197km, or 123 miles. The jeep may have been 'the conveyance' mentioned but not elaborated on by Francis Blackadder.

Personnel then received orders to be ready to move immediately. They were to take only essential kit and stores. All the 'old crocks' were destroyed before they left at nightfall, which must have been after 2200, as sunset was at 2145. Francis Blackadder remembered that it was dusk when they landed at their new base of Norrent-Fontes and, thanks to two helpful members of the French Armée de L'Air, were found food and billets 'of a sort'. Those travelling overnight by road had a more difficult journey, subject to serious delays as they had to travel in the dark without lights, and because they encountered French Army Transport travelling in the opposite direction. At Béthune they had met Belgian Infantry and a few civilian refugees and it was not until the early hours of 19 May – sunrise would be just before six o'clock – that they completed their journey. Operations were in progress for the rest of the day.

The Germans had broken through the French defences north of the Maginot Line. On 16 May, Dowding had penned a powerfully worded letter to Captain the Rt Hon H.H. Balfour, Under Secretary of State at the Air Ministry.[30] It has been described as one of the most important documents of the early stages of the war. Although he still hoped and believed that victory was possible, he warned that defeat was not out of the question. The sentiment of the final three paragraphs of the letter could have left no doubt in Churchill's mind as to the course he should take. Hurricane squadrons in Britain were seriously depleted; to send more across to France would result in wastage. Dowding made an urgent plea to the Air Ministry that they 'consider and decide' what level of strength would be required for defence. In the penultimate paragraph, he requested assurance that 'when this level has been reached, not one fighter will be sent across the Channel however urgent and insistent the appeal for help may be'.

He concluded that, provided sufficient fighter force remained in Britain, and the Navy and the Home Forces remained strong and well-organised, 'we would be able to carry on the war single-handed for some time, if not indefinitely'. Conversely, if those forces were drained away in the defence of France, it would lead to the 'final, complete and irremediable defeat of this country'.

Churchill, under pressure from Dowding and Sir Cyril Newall, Chief of Air Staff, took the decision that no more fighters would leave Britain and that as many aircraft that could be spared should return as soon as possible. In a broadcast speech that same evening, the Prime Minister stated, 'a tremendous battle is raging in France and Flanders', the latter, a name that would have aroused strong emotions and memories for many of the struggles of the Great War only twenty years or so earlier. He referred to the strong columns of German armoured vehicles ravaging the open country and went on to pay tribute to those taking part in the air battles:

> 'In the air, often at serious odds, even at odds hitherto thought overwhelming, we have been clawing down three or four to one of our enemies, and the relative balance of the British and German air forces is now considerably more favourable to us than at the beginning of the battle.'[31]

Whether those involved in the air battles and the ground crews desperately struggling to keep aircraft serviceable would have agreed with Churchill is very doubtful. Although the squadron was still receiving a few reinforcements from other squadrons based in France, there were no additional ground crews to maintain them. It was not uncommon to encounter action several times a day; severe damage to aircraft meant that they were not airworthy, with the consequence that there were often more pilots than machines.

The Germans were now within thirty miles or so of Vitry. By 17 May, pilots from 607 Squadron were being sent back to England to join other squadrons patrolling northern France.

Jim was one of those who remained in France. The next days brought more action. On 17 May, Francis Blackadder describes the 'filthy job' of escorting a Blenheim carrying out low-level reconnaissance photography of the Albert Canal east of Brussels. Squadron Leader Joe Kayll, full of admiration for the skill of the Blenheim's pilot, also commented admiringly that at low level it was 'just about' as fast as a Hurricane, and that the pilot had turned sharply several times, even flying under the bridges 'where they were intact'. In spite of the skill of the pilot, the Blenheim failed to return and was presumed shot down by ground fire.

There is more information in the ORB about events on 18 May, described by Francis Blackadder as 'der Tag' ('the Day') when the third battle of Vitry took place. He had described an earlier encounter which had 'rendered the Heavens' with gunfire, when there was a tremendous battle. 'Mars' [the god of war], he stated, 'was indeed angry'. During the morning, Flying Officer R.F. Weatherill, who had been with the squadron since before the war, was shot down and killed near Cambrai. The aerodrome was bombed by aircraft in the late afternoon of 18 May by a highly organised formation of 'some nine' bombers first spotted at around 500 feet before approaching at fifty feet on a path parallel to the Arras-Douai road, dropping bombs with a short time delay. These continued to explode at intervals during the evening. Incendiary devices targeted the dispersed aircraft, tanks, and fuel dumps, whilst rear gunners opened fire on the dispersal huts. Fortunately, there were no casualties. This was to be typical of the raids on airfields over southern England. During combat earlier in the afternoon, several Me109s and Me110s had been shot down, and immediately before the raid there had been a dogfight over Arras. There were heavy losses to the squadron.

At 1740 on 18 May came the order to prepare to move immediately with the minimum of kit. The route to Norrent-Fontes took them via Douai, Lens and Béthune. It was a slow and frustrating journey.

Once again they were travelling without lights and encountering heavy French Army transport coming from the opposite direction.

On 19 May, Jim and Will Whitty ran head-on into a Ju88. They managed to get a burst in and chased the enemy aircraft in and out of cloud cover. They slipped in behind and continued firing while the German pilot made good use of the cloud. Although the Ju88 was hit, Will noted that there was nothing conclusive to report and the action was broken off when the two Hurricanes ran out of ammunition. That evening Jim Bazin and Francis Blackadder volunteered to make a reconnaissance flight over the German area east of Brussels, flying over Flanders Field. Although Francis was able to continue unscathed and make his report on the German mechanised column, Jim was forced to turn back as he had come under fire from Allied guns and received considerable damage.[32]

That night they were able to fall into an exhausted sleep in a deserted mining village a mile or two from the aerodrome.

There were operations on the morning of 20 May, then, early in the afternoon, orders came for the ground crews to abandon all kit and equipment and await transport, which, if it had indeed existed, was never to arrive, although it was supposedly forming up just beyond the aerodrome boundary on the north side:

> 'Having received instructions to proceed to Le Havre via Boulogne, transport proceeded independently in small groups. At Boulogne, congestion was so acute that instructions were given to return to the "rest camp". The greater part of the squadron arrived at Boulogne that evening. During the night 20/21 May several raids were made upon the town at intervals until approximately 0500 hours.'[33]

After ditching logbooks and any other remaining possessions in the waters of the English Channel, four officers, and 227 NCOs and airmen re-assembled and embarked on *TS Biarritz* (a vessel that would take part in the Dunkirk evacuation), arriving safely in Dover, before finally reaching Croydon at 2200 on 22 May. In the meantime, one corporal and twelve men who had remained at Norrent-Fontes were flown to Hendon.

For many of the ground crews, it was only by a combination of initiative, stamina and determination that they managed to make it back. 'M' Flight Warrant Officer Gomme and thirty-one NCOs and men managed to reach Cherbourg after a road journey of around 200 miles. One member of the party was Leading Aircraftman Bill Bowman. A trailer, packed with as many spares as it could carry, together with precious personal tool kits, was hitched to a lorry for the long drive to Le Havre:

> '... no ship was available, so we intended to go to Rouen, but heard that the Germans were travelling towards there as well, so we set off for Cherbourg and eventually arrived on the 21st and at night on the 22nd boarded a tramp steamer.'[34]

Even when they reached England their problems were still not over:

> 'We arrived at Southampton and were ordered down to the docks to unload the ship as the dockers refused to work overtime. We didn't feel too good about this and we were proposing to throw the aforementioned dockers in the harbour, but were persuaded by the foreman that perhaps this wasn't a good thing.'

They were astonished to see tanks being loaded for the return journey to France. 'It seemed a stupid thing to do', he commented. After this tortuous journey, the men eventually managed to rejoin the squadron on 25 May.

Meanwhile, Jim Bazin and Francis Blackadder were in the group of the 'war-weary pilots' who were flown from Merville to Hendon in a Douglas on 20 May. Nine Hurricanes from 615 Squadron and four from 607 Squadron escorted Sabena SM73P carrying twenty-three evacuees. Ken Buckley, Buck Courtney and Dave Blomeley piloted three of the four. All three men had been among the recent reinforcement pilots that had been sent to 607 Squadron to make good the losses. Few had air fighting experience. 'The four Hurricanes we flew back were immediately scrapped,' recalled Dave Blomeley. 'They counted eighty-seven bullet holes in one of them, which only had three engine bearers left.'

On their arrival, Jim and Francis were 'greatly incensed' on hearing that five members of the squadron had been posted elsewhere within forty-eight hours of reaching England.[35] Peter Parrott and Peter Dixon had already joined 145 Squadron at Tangmere and by 22 May they were already patrolling the area that they had left only a few days before. Peter Dixon was to go missing over the beaches of Dunkirk and Dini was killed in a flying accident.

Of the pilots that had arrived in France with 607 Squadron six months before, only six members remained. From 'A' flight, there was Francis Blackadder and Milne Irving, and from 'B' flight, Jim Bazin, Dudley Craig, 'Nit' Whitty and 'Chatty' Bowen. The following extract is reproduced exactly as it appears in the ORB:

During the frantic events of 10 to 20 May, the following casualties occurred:

S/L SMITH – Missing.
F/Lt FIDLER – Missing now believed Prisoner of War.
F/O BRULLE [sic] – Killed.
F/O WEATHERILL – Missing.
F/Lt TOWNSEND – Missing now believed Prisoner of War.
F/O M.H.B. Thompson – Killed.

F/O PUMPHREY – Missing now believed prisoner of War.
Casualties (continued).
P/O J.B. RUSSELL (reported missing on 15.5.40).
F/O G.I. CUTHBERT (90133) (reported missing on 14.5.40).
F/O (A/F/Lt) J.L. SULLIVAN (37643) Rptd missing on 14.5.40. – now believed killed.[36]

According to Cull and Lander, seventeen precious Hurricanes had been lost. This had been the cost of forty-one confirmed 'kills' and sixteen 'probables'.[37] However, these figures do not tie up with the ORB statistics, which is hardly surprising considering that the ORBs and most of the logbooks were lost during the chaos of battle and the evacuation from France. During the period 10-20 May 1940, the ORB confirmed that the squadron had destroyed seventy-two enemy aircraft, with damage to a further fifty-six, though this figure was unconfirmed.[38]

Because his logbook was destroyed during the evacuation, there is no record of the number of aircraft that Jim shot down during the Battle of France. Unlike some of the other men of the squadron, he did not make any notes once back in England, so his tally will probably never be known.

For those who had survived it had been a brief and bitter way to learn the techniques of aerial combat. They now had a wealth of experience. However, according to Roland Beamont, the authorities 'were slow to react to the facts and change came about the hard way'.[39]

'The road to France', wrote Robert Dixon in his book *607 Squadron: A Shade of Blue*, 'filled with hope and anticipation only a few months before, now bore the bitter pill of defeat'. The Battle of France was over.

The Germans now occupied the coastlines of mainland Europe from the Russian border to Brittany. It gave them control of the waters of the North Atlantic and the vital supply lines that linked the Allies and North America.

Chapter 3

June 1939 – December 1940

Rebuilding the squadron, June to mid-July 1940, and the Battle of Britain

It must have felt very strange when they returned from the chaos of the fighting in France to the comparative peace of England. With the Battle of Britain still six weeks away, the emphasis now was the rescue of as many men of the British Expeditionary Force as possible, as well as the survivors of the Belgian Forces and the three French field armies that had by 21 May become trapped by German forces. On 23 May, Hitler sanctioned a halt to the German advance on Dunkirk in order to consolidate their position and prevent an Allied breakout. This left Göring's Luftwaffe to attack the cornered Allied land forces. The order was rescinded three days later when Operation Dynamo, the evacuation from Dunkirk, began. The prospect of the German invasion of Britain looked very probable.

It is perfectly understandable that Jim and Francis Blackadder were, in Francis's words, 'incensed', with the news that so many of the surviving members of the squadron had been posted elsewhere. The men of the squadron must have become very close during the previous six months. Together, they had coped with the dreadful winter conditions and had then been hurled into action in a desperate attempt to delay the progress of the German ground forces. There had been no chance to bid farewell. Friends had been killed or captured. Many of those who had lost friends and colleagues vowed never to make a close friend again. This must have been a common response to the loss of colleagues.

However, the news was more positive when it was announced that Will Gore had been awarded the DFC and Joe Kayll, now Commanding Officer of 615, had received the DSO and DFC on the same day, an exceptional distinction. At the end of May, Francis learned that he, too, had been awarded the DSO and Johnnie Sample, the DFC. As Launce Smith had been lost in action, their new CO was now Squadron Leader J.A. (Jim) Vick.

From the beginning of June, the ORB lists a series of arrivals of personnel from far and wide. Jim was in the air again for an hour on 1 June. Typically, he gives no details but the next couple of days were devoted to Pip-Squeak, formation and RT, with a test on 3 June. The following day marked the return to Usworth, when nine officers and three sergeant pilots left Croydon by air with Jim flying P3668. They found the familiar airfield much enlarged, with two concrete runways and a perimeter track.[40] Francis, probably with a great sigh of relief, recorded that '607 had returned home'. As most of the squadron's equipment had been lost during the hectic evacuation, the Adjutant, Flying Officer Taylor, and 208 NCOs were able to travel by rail rather than by road. As the record shows that they reached Usworth on 5 June, it is possible that it was a long overnight journey.

There was no opportunity to relax and recover though. On 22 June, there was the welcome return to the squadron of Will Gore, back after a spell recovering from wounds when he was shot down in France. Francis Blackadder described him as having escaped from the 'lameless' and nurses of the RAF Hospital in Torquay.

Until the squadron became operational again on 22 July, the next weeks were spent in rebuilding the unit, absorbing the new personnel and retraining. In the early part of July, night flying training took place at Prestwick.

Between 4 and 30 June, Jim logged over thirty flying hours, including training flights with some of the new arrivals, as well as formation flying, interception, attacks, target practice, circuits and landings, quick getaways, and instrument and night flying. Many of the new pilots had come straight from flying school. Although the squadron was officially 'resting', it was vital to teach newcomers the hard-won techniques of aerial combat learned in France. This was not without danger; Sergeant Richard Glover was killed when he crashed after encountering a problem on a training exercise over Sedgefield. On two days, Jim made short twenty-five-minute flights between Usworth and Acklington, then, on 16 July, a longer flight to Prestwick where there was a night flying training programme. Although he was there for four days, there are no entries in his logbook.

Among the other new pilots were Canadian John Donald 'Scotty' Lenehan,[41] Robert George Lauder, and Patrick 'Paddy' Joseph Thomas Stephenson. However, Pilot Officer George Stuart Woodwark, who arrived on 19 June, was re-posted to HQ No. 10 Group by the end of the month. Two years later Paddy Stephenson would be appointed CO during the war in India and Burma, by which time the squadron was equipped with Hurri-Bombers. He served there from April 1943 until March 1944, survived the war, and was awarded the DFC.

There were more familiar faces too. Harry Welford returned on 18 June, Wilfred Oleson, who had been posted to the squadron in France in March, and Stuart Parnall, James Vick and 'Chatty' Bowen were also now at Usworth.[42]

A welcome return by their former CO, Honorary Air Commodore Leslie Runciman, on an official visit on 20-21 July, heralded another change. The squadron became operational on 22 July, though flying by day only.

The Battle of Britain

By now the Battle of Britain had already been raging for ten days in the south of England. In popular perception, it took place over the skies of southern England, with fighter aircraft operating from airfields such as Tangmere and Biggin Hill. Less familiar are the combats that took place in the north of Britain.

In the early part of August 1940, 607 was flying regular patrols to cover convoys off the east coast. By rotating flights between Usworth and RAF Catterick, flight times were significantly reduced to reach areas over Scarborough and Whitby. Apart from a few arrivals and departures of pilots, the first two weeks of the month were uneventful. Jim, along with eleven other pilots, had been on attachment to Catterick, flying back to Usworth on 3 August, while a senior NCO and twenty-three other ranks returned by road. On the same morning, 'A' Flight set off for Catterick, returning five days later.

The occupation of Norway and Denmark had been completed by June 1940 and the Germans had pursued an active programme of building and extending operational airfields, often using Norwegian prisoners of war as labourers. Sola, near Stavanger in south-western Norway, was strategically situated for the Germans to be able to mount bombing raids on Scotland and north-east England. It was an 800-mile round trip.

Early on the morning of 15 August, fighter and bomber stations along the German-occupied coast from Brittany to Norway were preparing for a decisive operation on British coasts. For the Luftwaffe, it was to be the day when the RAF would be destroyed and Germany would overrun Britain. The operation was to be a major attack on airfields and was intended to bring as many British fighters into the conflict as possible.[43] The Germans believed that Britain's northern defences had been weakened in an attempt to strengthen the south. They had also seriously underestimated the strength of Fighter Command, wrongly assuming that RAF squadrons were the same size as the German equivalents. Göring gave orders that targets were exclusively enemy airbases and factories producing aircraft.

Attacks began in the south-east of England at 1100, causing considerable damage to water and power supplies. By midday, northern radar began plotting formations of fighters and bombers approaching the Firth of Forth at a range of ninety miles. An hour's warning gave controllers the time to put into position squadrons of No. 13 Group, which was based at Kenton, Newcastle-upon-Tyne. About 150 aircraft were reported to have taken off from Denmark and Norway to attack the north-east of England, which the Germans believed was only lightly defended. In fact, squadrons that were 'resting' were manned by experienced pilotss well able to meet the force already over the North Sea. Eighty-eight bombers, minus their rear gunners to lighten the load for the 800-mile round trip, were escorted by thirty-five Me110s. It was the first raid by Luftflotte 5, based in Norway and Denmark. The first interception was by 72 Squadron off the Farne Islands. The squadron hurtled in through the gap between the bombers, producing such a dramatic impact that the formation split up with some of the raiders making for home. Pilot Officer Elliott (later Air Vice-Marshal Bobby Deacon-Elliott) later recalled that 'bombers quickly began jettisoning their loads. The sea below churned up white with bombs as if a colony of whales was spouting.'[44]

The scene quickly changed, though, when it was reported that enemy aircraft had turned south and were now flying towards Tynemouth. A vital merchant fleet was due to sail from Hull at noon and defences were on top line against attacks on these ships.[45] For all the squadrons in 13 Group, including 607, 15 August was to prove highly memorable. Apart from being the Group's first daylight raid, it was to be the most famous of the Group's actions and a vital element in the defeat of the Luftwaffe attack that day.

Aircraft from bases in Northumberland – principally 72 and 79 Squadrons and a flight from 605 Squadron – were busily harrying the enemy aircraft, which were again forced to break formation. Because of the warning of the approach, 607 Squadron and 41 Squadron (flying

Spitfires) had been on alert from 1230. After being in readiness for a frustrating thirty minutes or so, 607 Squadron was at last airborne but they were given no indication of where the enemy aircraft were. They were sent on what was described by some as a tour of most of County Durham but eventually had to return to Usworth. Orders then came to make for the mouth of the Tyne and five sections of 607 Squadron were scrambled at 1315 when it was reported that between forty and sixty He111s and Do17s were moving further south off the coast at Seaham Harbour. Once in the air, they climbed to 10-12,000ft. Francis Blackadder, heading two Sections of 'A' Flight, was the first to spot the enemy eight miles east of the coast over Whitley Bay. The action then moved south to the area off Seaham Harbour. Jim was leading the eight pilots of 'B' Flight. They were able to attack the enemy over the sea before the intended targets were reached.

The *Sunderland Daily Echo* described how a bomber flew over very low, ditching bombs into the sea where they exploded 'with a deafening crash'. It was then subject to two or three bursts of fire from three Hurricanes from the south and fell into the sea, where it floated for about five minutes before sinking. A lifeboat was launched but no survivors were seen.

The headline in the *Evening Chronicle* on the following day described it as 'a terrific battle', and the combination of air combat and 'a terrific barrage of anti-aircraft fire' must have been an added shock to the raiders, who, the journalist stated, 'had thought to surprise us'. An unidentified Hurricane pilot was reported as saying:

> 'It was a terrific battle. For a while the air was filled with diving and zooming aircraft. We caught the protecting Messerschmitt fighters about ten miles from the coast. Immediately we attacked they sheered off and they were never seen again. One of my pilots blew the tail off a German fighter. It was just like a balloon bursting. Pieces hit my Hurricane.'

In spite of the overall success of the action, some bombers managed to make it inland, bombing parts of Tyneside and a residential area of Sunderland,[46] but the report in the *Newcastle Journal* stated that 'no damage of any military importance was caused', though there were casualties, including civilian deaths. The boiler room of a hospital was put out of action and a train was also bombed and machine-gunned. Seaham Harbour was attacked, suffering much heavier casualties than neighbouring Sunderland. The few bombers that did manage to get through to Sunderland had little effect apart from wrecking houses. It was not only the towns that suffered. Village streets and rural areas were also hit. Airfields that were to have been targeted, including Usworth (mistakenly identified by German Intelligence as a major fighter base and a primary target), remained for the most part unscathed. Although many would not make it back to Norway, some of the raiders fled home, including one enemy aircraft that Dudley Craig had hotly pursued sixty miles out to sea before he was forced to turn back.

Although the ORB noted that fourteen Hurricanes were airborne for just thirty minutes, it is not clear how long the actual engagement lasted as they would have had to climb to 10-12,000ft to reach the invaders and then return to Usworth. During the squadron's head-on attack against a force of between forty and sixty He111s and Do17s in two Vic formations, they destroyed eight enemy aircraft, which were seen to plunge dramatically into the waters of the North Sea. A further six were logged as 'probables' and five were seen to be badly damaged, casting doubt on whether they would have been able to complete the return flight to their bases in Scandinavia. There were no losses to 607 Squadron. A year later, a Newcastle newspaper, reporting the birth of their first son to Jim and Elizabeth, described Jim as being one of the pilots who had helped 'smash the attack by German planes in the biggest daylight raid over the north-east coast.' It was an impressively co-ordinated response, highlighting the brilliance of the Dowding System.

The day that Hitler was to have made his triumphal march through London had now become 'Black Thursday' for the Germans. 'Hitler was to have dictated peace in London,' ran the editorial in the *Sunderland Echo* on 16 August. 'We in Sunderland, Seaham Harbour and other places on the North-East coast', it continued, 'know the kind of peace he brought and the reception he received'.

Although they had managed to break through the defence to bomb Montrose and Cullen on 15 August, Luftwaffe 5 made no more massed attacks on the north of Britain, though raids continued remorselessly. The following year was to prove 'the hardest year' for the Scots.[47]

A short time before Jim's death, Stan White asked him what the experience had been like:

> 'The memory of that day did bring a slight grin from him and he recalled for me the patchy cloud that for a time kept the enemy aircraft hidden (I think he said there were in places two layers of cloud, with the German aircraft flying between them). My question was directed at trying to get the "scene" for a painting, and while Jim established that the squadron did engage, he did not go on about any enemy aircraft [that] fell to the guns of the squadron. It sounded as though after the debacle in France, he was just pleased to be back on the winning side again! What success accompanied Jim's efforts on that day is not known. His logbook only shows that he had two operational sorties... His laconic style meant that he was never interested in cutting notches on his gun, much less recording the events more formally!'[48]

The ORB for the day, and the monthly summary, simply describe the one operation. However, Jim's logbook shows that he was in the air on two operations that day. The first flight in Hurricane P3117 lasted fifteen minutes and the second, in P2900, a full hour. Dixon's account perhaps gives some clue as to what was happening. Harry Welford, he notes, had stated that the squadron had been scrambled into action, but no one seemed to know where the enemy was. The aircraft had been sent on a tour of most of the county. Returning to Usworth, they were then sent to patrol an area simply described as east of the Tyne. It could have been at this point that Jim landed to change to another aircraft before taking off again to re-join the main group, staying airborne after the main combat was over.

While all this was going on in the north of Britain, the Germans had turned their attention back to the south of England, which continued to suffer heavy damage. Among the airfields that were attacked was Tangmere where, just a couple of weeks later, 607 Squadron would be based.

Not only had it been the biggest daylight raid, but it was to have a dramatic impact on the course of the next few weeks of the Battle of Britain. During the raids of 15 August there was a huge loss of German aircraft and, more importantly, pilots. Later that day, it prompted Göring to announce that in future only one officer was to fly in any single bomber crew. It had also shown that Stukas and Me110s were confirmed as 'unsuitable' for their tasks.

The Luftwaffe had switched from attacking ships and coastal objectives to new targets, paying particular attention to fighter aerodromes. On 19 August Air Vice-Marshal Keith Park issued new instructions to controllers in 11 Group. Fighters were only to engage large enemy formations over land or within gliding distance of the coast. 'During the next two or three weeks,' he emphasised, 'we cannot afford to lose pilots through forced landings in the sea'.

Jim logged a 50-minute operational flight again on 20 August, flying his trusty Hurricane P3668 but, as usual, there is no indication of what or where.

By the end of August, the RAF continued to lose aircraft faster than they could be replaced. The number of fighter pilots was also said to be insufficient to fill the gaps in the fighting ranks. Between 28 August and 6 September, 103 RAF pilots had been killed or reported missing, with 128 wounded, a high proportion of the total strength of 1,000. Experienced pilots were 'like gold-dust'. Dowding was also very aware of the emotional strain that young, inexperienced pilots were having to cope with. The Luftwaffe numbers had been hit too. With heavy losses, the German High Command believed they were no nearer to achieving superiority over Fighter Command. They had also been unable to assess the losses and damage to airfields after raids.

On 1 September, 607 Squadron was on the move again, this time to Tangmere, 330 miles/530km south of Usworth and three miles northeast of Chichester, an airfield that had suffered heavy damage a few days earlier during an attack. The squadron was now in Dowding's Category A, which meant that it was stationed within 11 Group, would bear the brunt of the fighting and only in the direst need would be pulled out of the firing line. They were met by forty-three walking wounded, some with crutches, others with arms in slings and some with bandaged heads.

By 7 September, the invasion was classified as imminent. However, the Luftwaffe now turned their attention away from the airfields that had been badly hit in the previous weeks, focussing on the bombing of London and other major cities. Much later, Dowding commented: 'It brought an intense feeling of relief to me – intense relief', adding, 'I could hardly believe that the Germans would have made such a mistake'.[49]

For the first few days, 607 Squadron was held in reserve, given time to explore the area and to memorise the position of balloons and gun-sites. Jim's promotion to Flight Lieutenant was effective from 3 September. The following week the squadron was back in action but a patrol over Shoreham during the evening of 8 September reported that they had seen no enemy aircraft.

The next day, 9 September, was to be very different. Attacks began during the afternoon and by 1655, a patrol led by Squadron Leader Jim Vick was in the Mayfield area at 17,000 feet. At 1730, sixty or more enemy aircraft, possibly Ju88s and Do17s, were spotted flying north. They were part of unsuccessful massed raids on targets in London, the Thames Estuary and factories at Brooklands. Fighter interceptions were so successful that many of the enemy aircraft turned back, but not before dropping their bombs over a wide area of East Kent, central London and Surrey. The resulting fires were markers for the raids that continued to take place over London during the darkness of the night of the 9-10 September. There were heavy casualties.

This was the first action for 607 from their Tangmere base; it proved to be disastrous. Almost half of their aircraft were lost.

Six out of twelve aircraft had been lost, among them Harry's best friends Stuart Parnall and 'Scotty' Lenehan. Nothing had been heard of George Drake. It was presumed that he had been killed but everyone continued to hope that he had been taken to hospital or had managed to land and was drowning his sorrows in a pub. There was no news, though, and Harry remembered that the only reference made to the losses were comments such as, 'You heard about Stuart and Scotty, rotten luck, wasn't it?' and someone would add, '...and young George Drake, bloody good blokes all of them'. Spyer and Burnell-Phillips, made forced landings and were injured. Harry Welford recalled that they had been 'well and truly bounced by Me109s that day'.

Jim's Hurricane P3668 was so extensively damaged that he had to make a forced landing, hitting his face on the gun sight in the process. Many years later, in conversation with Stan White, he commented that there was no time to panic. 'You just think,' he continued, 'how the hell can I get out of this'. The following day he flew P2617. He had already flown it at Usworth a couple of months earlier on a formation exercise on 10 June. This Hurricane is now on display at the RAF Museum at Hendon, with Jim's 90-minute flight described as being the only recorded participation of the machine in the whole of the Battle of Britain.

White suggested that the problem of finding the small settlement of Mayfield ten miles south of Tunbridge Wells might have been the cause of being 'bounced' by Me 109s 'while 607 were too preoccupied with identifying the Mayfield landscape'. Jim had commented that the controller had frequently ordered them to orbit Mayfield. 'God knows why', he said. 'But it always seemed we had to orbit Mayfield, and it would take us bloody ages to find this tiddly place. I must have spent hours looking at that part of the Sussex countryside – why they couldn't have given us some easier place to find, I'll never know.' Will Whitty partly blamed the debacle on the new controllers who were under training. It had been a hard day for the survivors.

Cloud and rain limited operations on 10 September, although Tangmere was machine gunned by a lone enemy aircraft after 1700.

On 11 September, the day originally designated by Hitler for Operation Sealion, the invasion of Britain, Jim was in the air from 1600-1650, though nothing was seen. The following day brought more bad weather, with cloud and rain, but on 13 and 14 September, some members of the squadron did see action, although Jim was not among them. Three new names now appear in the patrol lists: Polish Pilot Officers Surma and Wlaswonolski and Flying Officer Kustrzinski had joined from other squadrons for flying duties, although Pilot Officer Wlaswonolski was posted to 213 Squadron just four days after his arrival. Dowding had initially voiced misgivings about the wisdom of committing Polish pilots to combat. Apart from the language problem exemplified in the 1969 film *The Battle of Britain*, he had also wondered what the effect had been on them of their experiences in their own countries and France. His doubts were soon laid to rest. 'They were,' he said, 'inspired by a burning hatred for the Germans which made them very deadly opponents'. Although Polish airmen arriving in Britain were subject to interrogation, little notice seems to have been taken by the authorities of the invaluable comments they made about aerial combat based on this experience. They had practical advice about the best techniques for shooting down dive-bombers or methods that could be used to deal with formations of fifty or 100 bombers that had equally large fighter escorts and they were able to report that the Luftwaffe, with their experience in the Spanish war, were now using 'loose' pairs of fighters rather than the tight Vics still operated by the British, Belgian and French air forces.

It was on 15 September, later designated Battle of Britain Day, that the squadron was kept busy. Nothing was seen when on patrol for half an hour from 0800 and again from 1215 until 1330 but the third sortie was a different matter. Jim led action near Appledore at 1445 when approaching the Biggin Hill-Kenley area at about 18,000 feet. The account in the ORB records that:

> 'Hurricanes saw to the S.E. two formations, each consisting of between forty or fifty Do17s and Do215s flying two abreast towards the N.W. at about 15,000 feet. The squadron made a head-on attack on the left-hand formation, which broke up. Some pilots saw a number of Me109s and Me110s well behind the enemy bombers at about the same height. These enemy aircraft did not engage the Hurricanes. When head-on attacks were made individual pilots saw various enemy aircraft falling to pieces in the air, but owing to the head-on attacks, it was difficult to see whether damaged enemy aircraft other than those seen to break up in the air were destroyed or probable.'

Jim was leading the squadron as Blue 1. In his Combat Report he described the action as taking place at 17,000 feet over Tenterden.

> 'The squadron was given sections line astern and head-on attack ordered on the left-hand wave of bombers. I opened fire on three Do215s in my line of flight. The Do215s broke up in front of me and another appeared to be very heavily damaged in front. Attack broken off downwards and to right. Did not contact enemy again.'

Paddy Stephenson was slightly wounded and his Hurricane destroyed, but four Do215s were destroyed, another Do215 was recorded as a probable and a further five enemy aircraft were damaged.

Members of the ground crew were kept busy to make sure that the Hurricanes were ready for the next patrol, the fourth of the day for Jim and Sergeant Hewitt, which was to take place just two hours later, led this time by Francis Blackadder. The ORB reported that combat took place off the coast between Poole Harbour and the Needles:

> 'At about 1745, the squadron was vectored towards Southampton and climbed to 15,000ft when between thirty and forty Me109s and Me110s in line astern were seen to the south and above at 18,000 feet. Immediately afterwards Do17s were seen in small groups in Vic formation emerging from clouds below and to the south. These groups began forming into larger formations after having apparently completed their bombing. Made a stern attack on enemy bombers but the Me109s hampered the attack by diving down on Hurricanes.
>
> 'Own losses NIL.
>
> 'Enemy losses TWO Do17s destroyed in sea.'

Altogether, Jim had been airborne for 4 hours 40 minutes flying P3668, now restored after the forced landing four days before.

The next day was eerily quiet. There was only one patrol in the morning but nothing was seen. Operation Sealion, the German invasion of Britain, had depended on the Luftwaffe gaining superiority over the RAF. Even on 14 September, Hitler had been doubtful about whether the situation was such that success would be the outcome. By 17 September the invasion had been postponed, this time until the end of the month. There was still a window of opportunity until 8 October when the weather could be a barrier, but it was not until 12 October that the decision to postpone the invasion was finally settled. Interestingly, this was close to the date of another invasion, also mounted from France; the Battle of Hastings was fought on 14 October 1066, almost 900 years earlier, a date which at that time was considered outside of the normal season of fighting.

For the Germans, 15 September had been a date that was vital to the campaign. Losses, however, had been greater than any day since 'Black Thursday' on 15 August. German Intelligence reports seem to have been inaccurate: at the debriefings Luftwaffe bomber pilots complained that there had been 'incessant RAF attacks by squadrons that had long ceased to exist'.[50] Göring admitted that the German crews were tiring. The system of 'resting' a squadron by rotation in the RAF, a practice that was not followed by the Luftwaffe, no doubt gave the Allies an advantage. The combination of intense concentration and exhilaration during combat combined with the tension of waiting for the signal to take off inevitably led to tiredness and exhaustion in both the Allies and Germans. In later life, Jim commented that the worst part was sitting around waiting. 'Once the order to go was issued', he added, 'the mind was fully occupied'.

Morale was also an important issue. With only a core of the original pilots remaining, it was vital that their spirits remained high. Flying Officer Alan Deere of 54 Squadron commented that, provided that was the case, a squadron could continue to operate, but if a leader had reached the point of physical and mental tiredness, 'beyond which lies the realm of fear', this could pass down through the younger pilots like a disease affecting everyone including the ground crews. Their keenness and efficiency could be directly related to the morale of the pilots. To maintain a positive attitude, good leaders used devices including humour over the radio in the air.[51]

Although 15 September was an important milestone in the Battle of Britain, there was still more than six weeks until the official end date. Operation Sealion had been delayed, but there were more than 1,000 invasion craft ready to make the crossing of the English Channel. Bombing continued with daylight raids on targets from Plymouth to Wick. By the end of the month, the Luftwaffe's attention focused on the south-east of England, the airfields of East Anglia and, increasingly, the east coast as far north as Aberdeenshire. Usworth was targeted on 2 October. Merseyside, Manchester, North Wales, the Midlands, and cities such as Newcastle and Aberdeen were also subjected to night bombing raids.

In spite of this activity, 607's sorties saw very little of the enemy over the next two weeks, although, two days after 'Battle of Britain' day, Jim was in combat again, leading 'B' Flight on patrol over Biggin Hill and Gravesend. The first three patrols of the afternoon of 17 September returned with nothing to report but the fourth sortie, led by Jim, saw action over the Gravesend area at 1540. 'A' Flight was already on patrol so the Blue and Green Sections of 'B' Flight operated with 213 Squadron acting as rear guard. While patrolling at 17,000 feet, both squadrons were attacked almost simultaneously from above and behind by Me109s. Welford's Hurricane was hit by a shell, but he managed to bale out and was only slightly wounded. Sergeant Lansdell, who had joined the squadron on 19 June, was not so lucky. Pilot Officer Surma had seen him attacked by an Me109 and it was later reported that he had been killed. Red Section of 'A' Flight landed at 1503, the aircraft were quickly refuelled and took off at once but were unable to locate 'B' Flight, so teamed up with another Hurricane squadron as their rear section. There had been no enemy losses.

The next day, 18 September, Jim was in the air by 0705 for an hour, landing briefly before getting airborne again at 0820 for another ninety minutes, reporting 'Nothing seen'. This was to be the general pattern for the next few days, although anything up to eight or ten sorties a day was not uncommon. He made a landing at Rochester, not far from Gravesend, on 22 September, but no reason was given in his logbook or in the ORB.

Mid-afternoon on 26 September saw the squadron in action over Selsey Bill and Beachy Head. The ORB informs us that combat took place over the Isle of Wight, Portsmouth and at sea, south of the Needles. Fifty or sixty enemy aircraft had assembled over Brittany and were flying in mass formation at 12,000-15,000 feet, diving down onto 'the various targets' in and around Southampton. The particular target was the Supermarine factory, the home of the Spitfire. Ninety tons of bombs had wrought destruction, completely stopping production for a short time. The Hurricanes initially made a head-on attack. They later carried out a number of individual sorties on two separate enemy formations, one of which went out to sea, the other flying inland. Jim was airborne for an hour from 1600.

There was to be no respite. Although no enemy were seen when out on patrol over the next few days, being constantly on the alert must have been a drain on both mental and physical energy. The intensity of the sustained demands made on them led to exhaustion, in spite of the system of 'resting' squadrons.

Jim was again leading the squadron on 30 September, this time off Chesil Beach and Portland, when Me110s, circling at 18,000ft, were spotted offshore. A large formation of Do17s and Ju88s were spotted below the Hurricanes and individual attacks were made on the bombers. The enemy fighters then broke away out to sea, where they formed defensive circles, later joining with enemy bombers about twenty miles off the coast. Comparing his handwriting for the combat reports of 15 September and 30 September, it is not difficult to see the effect that tiredness was having on Jim. Never easy to read, by the end of the report, it is almost indecipherable.

It seems probable that Elizabeth drove the 350+ miles from Newcastle-upon-Tyne to Tangmere on 28 or 29 September. Nowadays the journey is estimated at just over six hours. During the war, driving with dimmed headlights on roads that were not only narrow – a remnant of the original A1 at Newark-on-Trent is only wide enough for two narrow lanes – but also without any direction posts, the drive would have been spread over at least two days. Family memories vary slightly, but all agree that they remember Elizabeth telling them that she had the company of three other wives. There is some doubt as to whether one already knew her husband had been killed or two had the news broken to them on their arrival. The ORB entry for 28/29 September notes that Bill Gore and Milne Irving were both reported missing. In any case, their arrival at Tangmere must have been a relief for Elizabeth but tragic for two of her companions.

The next morning, 1 October, the ORB reported that the squadron was again on patrol from 0900, although Jim's first sortie was not until 1040. There was to be no let-up. Before 'B' Flight was able to join Yellow Section, the squadron was ordered to patrol Swanage at 20,000ft when enemy aircraft were reported approaching from the south-east. In actual fact, a large number of enemy aircraft in three formations of twenty was sighted west-north-west on the starboard side of the squadron, probably consisting of a lower formation of bombers followed by Me110s above and behind, and a further formation of Me109s. The squadron in sections line astern turned east to meet the bombers head-on and from slightly above. The first group turned out to be Me110s. They broke their formation and returned the Hurricane attacks. A dogfight ensued while the general enemy formation turned out to sea. Flying Officer 'Chatty' Bowen, who had fought in the Battle of France, and Sergeant Brumby were reported missing.

In conversation with White, Jim mentioned the problems of aircraft recognition. Referring to this attack, he recalled: 'I was leading and turned in to attack what I had thought to be Dorniers, only to find out, too bloody late, that they were Me110s'. White has suggested that these could have been the Horst Wessel Geschwader, who painted their aircraft noses, which could have led Jim into thinking he was attacking twin-engined aircraft with glazed noses.[52]

In trying to read between the lines of these factual reports, it is impossible to imagine what such combat would have been like. Although three pilots were airborne for seventy-five minutes, the others, including Jim, were only forty minutes in the air, including climbing to 20,000 feet and returning to Tangmere. The intensity of the dogfight must have taken place over just a few minutes.

What they were probably unaware of until much later was that the Luftwaffe, targeting Southampton and Portsmouth, were employing new tactics, reserving bombers for night raids, by converting a third or so of the German force, some 250 Me109s and Me110s, to fighter-bomber duties. As this freed the heavy bombers for night raids, it gave Fighter Command new and difficult problems, imposing many fruitless hours of climb and chase upon the British pilots.

The pressure continued. There were patrols on the next three days, 2, 3 and 4 October, with occasional sightings but no interceptions. Rain, drizzle and poor visibility reduced the number of raids, although they continued on the south-east and east coasts as well as night bombing on London, northern England and Scotland. They would have been relieved to know that the Italian Foreign Minister had been present at the meeting of Mussolini and Hitler on 4 October. There he had learned that 'there is no longer any talk about a landing on the British Isles'.

Things were to change on 5 October when the squadron was ordered to patrol Swanage in the early afternoon. Within ten minutes of taking off, Jim had to make a forced landing, after a single bullet hit his oil tank. He seems to have been airborne very soon afterwards, re-joining the squadron and flying P3937. Francis Blackadder reported that he had seen an indeterminate number of enemy aircraft at 23,000 feet. For whatever reason, Jim, who was leading, did not hear the report. Pilot Officer Sulman, acting as rear-guard, reported that Me109s were diving on to the tail of the squadron from behind and above. In spite of breaking the formation immediately, several aircraft were hit and some pilots had to make forced landings.

By the end of the day, Fighter Command had flown 1,175 sorties.

Many years later, referring to his third forced landing, Jim was to comment laconically to Stan White that 'there was nothing wrong with the aircraft except it had no engine'.[53] It is an interesting comment on the forgiving qualities of the Hurricane. Roland Beamont was quoted as saying he would not have changed it for any other mount, describing it as rugged and stable, able to absorb enemy fire, cope with a pilot's ineptitude, keep airborne in bad weather and still outfly the enemy. Flight Lieutenant Freddy Lister was another who, in spite of severe damage to his Hurricane during combat, did not even think about baling out but, after a dramatic landing, stepped out of the cockpit, 'stunned by his good fortune' that he was unhurt.[54]

The next few days saw more patrols, but the sky was empty of enemy aircraft on 7 October when Jim was again airborne. By the time of Jim's second sortie at 1540, he was once again reunited with P3668.

Patrols continued with only sightings of friendly fighters. It must have been a huge relief to find out that the squadron was to head north to Turnhouse (now Edinburgh Airport) on 10 October. Jim flew to Usworth, stopping at Catterick, before joining the rest of the squadron the next day. By the official end of the Battle of Britain, Shores and Williams note that Jim was credited with ten enemy aircraft destroyed, although White suggested that this was an underestimate.[55]

On 25 October, it had been announced that Jim had been awarded the DFC. He received the award at Buckingham Palace. The citation reads:

> 'This officer has shot down some ten enemy aircraft. He himself was shot down on one occasion over enemy territory but, with amazing initiative and determination, he re-joined his unit within twenty-four hours. In August 1940 he destroyed two enemy aircraft on the north-east coast and in September 1940 he led two squadrons in a head-on attack against 100 to 200 enemy aircraft. The enemy were completely non-plussed and fled. As a leader, Flight Lieutenant Bazin has shown marked ability and initiative.'[56]

The move to Turnhouse marked the beginning of considerable change for the squadron. They were now joined by twenty new officers, eight of them British, the others, Polish. The squadron remained operational, although the few sorties logged by Jim in October and November produced no sightings of enemy aircraft. Although Scotland was the target of numerous raids by the Luftwaffe, Edinburgh suffered fewer attacks than other areas. While Jim was at Turnhouse, there was only one occasion that Edinburgh and Dunfermline were under fire. Although 607 Squadron was still operational, there is nothing in Jim's logbook to indicate that he was in the air on that occasion. By the end of November, he was at Drem.

Big changes were eventually to result in the squadron becoming the first to fly the Hurri-bomber, which was to see 607 Squadron in action in Burma. Their CO, Jim Vick, had failed an eye test, which meant the end of his career as a pilot; he was to be replaced by Squadron Leader A.W. Vincent. New pilots arrived for training, whilst some of the long-established members were moving on. At the beginning of the second week in November, Francis Blackadder became a sector controller at Turnhouse, marking his wartime break with the squadron. Will Whitty became an instructor to 56 OTU Sutton Bridge. In 1944, he, like Jim, was one of the very few pilots to transfer from fighters to bombers.

With all these changes, the atmosphere of the squadron must have been very different and probably very unsettling for those few remaining original members. For Jim it had been a major part of his life for over five years. It was the focal point of his social life in the pre-war days, training and flying alongside colleagues from Armstrong Whitworth and Reyrolle. With the outbreak of war, an even closer comradeship must have developed during the ensuing months. Aircrew and ground crew alike had coped with that desperately difficult winter in France, the subsequent fighting in the Battle of France, the evacuation in May, the re-forming of the squadron, and then the intensive and demanding weeks of the Battle of Britain. On top of all that, they had all had to cope with the loss of many friends, both in combat and air accidents.

Looking back at the group photograph taken at the last pre-war summer camp in Abbotsinch, and including those who were not in the picture, twelve had been killed either in combat or air accidents, and three were now prisoners of war. One of those was Dudley Craig, a pioneer of Hurri-Bombers, who was to receive an OBE in 1945 recognising his activities whilst a PoW. When he was captured and interrogated, he had been surprised how much the Germans knew about his life. They told him that they had read about him in the *Sunderland Echo*. Of the original 607 Squadron, only Jim, Francis Blackadder, Whitty, Welford and Forster were still taking an active part in the RAF by the end of the war.

Jim's elder son Michael remembered his mother telling him that she had a revolver and would have used it on their two boys then on herself if the Germans had marched up the Great North Road to Newcastle. Jim had shot down at least ten German aircraft and the Germans would have undoubtedly made sure that the families of Battle of Britain pilots would have been treated even more severely than the general population. Jim and Elizabeth may also have been aware of the speech made by SS Obergruppenführer Richard Darre in 1940, when he described in spine-chilling detail the plans to obliterate the British nation through a variety of means: enslavement, sterilisation and the farming of Nordic infants.[57]

Jim was now twenty-seven, considerably older than most of the newcomers. He was one of the few original pre-war number still with the squadron. What was Jim's role in the two months between the move north and his next posting? His logbook entries are sparse as flights were few, although personnel movements were frequent. There are entries in the ORB of arrivals and departures every two or three days. Whitty had left on 3 November, and Forster and Welford were posted on the same day that Jim had news of his next move. He was now a Squadron Leader. Beginning on 15 December, he was transferred to Ops Room Duties, first at RAF Station, Catterick and then the following June, at Ouston. Not only was this a farewell to the squadron that had been at the heart of much of his life since 1935, but on 11 December he made his final flight on his trusty Hurricane P3668, the aircraft that had seen him through so much action since the return from France seven months before.

Chapter 4

December 1940 to November 1943

'Resting': Training Controllers in GCI, Controller in HQ 14 and HQ 13 Groups in Inverness

Jim's life now took a very different direction. He was being 'rested' from operations as he had been effectively fighting on the frontline since 16 October the previous year. Unlike the Luftwaffe, the RAF had the policy of giving personnel time away from the action, helping them to recover, and preventing them from burning out. In spite of that, the cumulative strain of the previous fourteen months must have been intense. Now that the focus was on bombing it meant that fighter pilots like Jim could be given a break from operations. Experienced fighter pilots were perhaps also being held in reserve.

By 15 December 1940, Jim was on Operations Room duties at Catterick, where he had made a stopover on 10 October on the flight from Tangmere to Usworth. Just a few days before Christmas he was promoted to Squadron Leader. Men with first-hand experience of how Luftwaffe pilots operated in combat were invaluable both in the training of new pilots and working as controllers in operations rooms. They knew about the performance of both the Allied and enemy fighter pilots and machines, how long it took them to reach a certain height, and the best place to position the defending fighters to give them as much advantage as possible when meeting the enemy. Their knowledge and understanding was at the heart of the Dowding system.

Jim was still at Catterick in May 1941, when Elizabeth gave birth to their son Michael at her mother's home in Tankerville Terrace,

Newcastle-on-Tyne. Michael was born under his aunt's Ibach grand piano in case there was a raid. Fortunately, the Luftwaffe did not make an appearance that day.

By the end of June 1941, Jim was back at Ouston, again on Ops Room duties, but within two months he was posted to HQ Fighter Command as an Instructor at the Fighter Control School where he was training controllers in Ground Control Interception (GCI). The earlier system used at the start of the war had depended on visual sightings when tracking enemy aircraft once they had crossed the coast and were making their way to the targets. It had been difficult, if not impossible, to track enemy aircraft at night or in poor visibility once they had crossed the coast and were flying to inland targets. The development of GCI meant that it was now possible to plot them accurately after they had crossed the coast so that fighters could intercept them at an early stage.

On promotion to Wing Commander at the end of February 1942, Jim was posted north to Inverness as a controller at HQ 14 Group, the section of Fighter Command responsible for Scotland. Jim was familiar with the southern part of the country from his days with 607 Squadron during the first months of the war.

Scotland had been an early target in Hitler's sights, particularly following the occupation of Norway between April and June 1940. Important dockyards at Rosyth, Greenock and Clydebank were subject to major bombing raids though, in the case of Clydebank, there was greater damage to the surrounding urban areas. As a result of the bombing raids there on 13 and 14 March 1941, only one in 1,000 homes had been left undamaged, 4,300 houses had to be demolished and 55,000 people were made homeless. Estimates suggested that 1,300 people had been killed, though the number could not be confirmed.[58]

Royal Naval bases in Scotland played a vital role in the North Atlantic. The sheltered waters of the Scapa Flow gave protection to the Navy's ships as it had done in the Great War, providing easy access to both the North Atlantic and the North Sea. However, it proved to be vulnerable. The Churchill Barriers were quickly constructed after a German submarine had managed to slip unseen into the bay on 14 October 1939, sinking the battleship HMS *Royal Oak* with the loss of over 835 lives. Bombing raids followed. Once the Germans had invaded Russia in June 1941, massed raids on Scotland gradually diminished as Luftwaffe squadrons in Norway and Denmark were looking east to the Russian front.

By the end of October, Jim was listed as Operations (Day). He was flying again, covering the whole region of 14 Group. There were only occasional opportunities to take to the air, mainly flying Oxfords, a monoplane based on an early passenger design. His logbook also lists occasional flights in Spitfires whenever he was able to get his hands on one. It is said that it was easier to scrounge an aircraft in those days! Peterhead was visited more often than any of the other airfields, with Turnhouse and Dyce following close behind. Skeabrae also featured on a fairly regular basis.

In 1942, Jim received the Air Efficiency Award. He must have been one of the earliest to qualify for this new award which recognised ten years meritorious service. It was notable as it was open to men and women of the Auxiliary and Volunteer Air Forces, whatever their rank. By this time Jim had been with the RAF for only seven years, but there was a special weighting system in place to take pre-war experience into account. Jim's service with 607 Squadron from 1935-1939 was calculated as six years (4 years × 1.5), and the period of sixteen months from the outbreak of war was multiplied by three. It meant that he became eligible for the award in the early spring of 1941. More recognition was to come on New Year's Day 1943, when he was Mentioned in Dispatches though, as was the norm, no reason was published.

On 14 February 1943, Jim, along with other senior officers from HQ 14 Group, including Group Captain Somerville and Wing Commander McLennan, travelled south to take part in Exercise Spartan. This was one of the initial stages of the intricate planning essential for the D-Day landings. The exercise, held across parts of southern England, combined resources from the RAF and the Army, as well as ancillary support units necessary if the invasion was to meet with success.

Two of the main purposes were to practise an advance from a bridgehead established on an enemy coastline to see how the joint forces of the Army and the RAF would work 'to prevent dissipation of air strength'. The exercise was umpired by corps of Army and RAF men, many of them wearing decorations from North Africa and the Battle of Britain. There were three areas: Southlands represented a coastal area occupied by Allied troops, Northlands was in German hands, and Eastlands was neutral and prepared to defend her neutrality. The large-scale manoeuvres by 'tens of thousands of British and Canadian soldiers and airmen', was the biggest military exercise ever held on British soil. Forces lived and acted exactly as they would in battle, existing solely on military supplies. Hotels, pubs and shops had strict instructions not to serve them.

Journalists and broadcasters were also involved, including Richard Dimbleby, who submitted a detailed report to the BBC authorities with solutions to some of the issues he had encountered.[59] 'From the military point of view,' he wrote, 'it was only a qualified success', going on to explain that General McNaughton had failed to get to grips with the enemy within the time limit. It might have been only partially successful, but failure is always an important pathway to recognising where mistakes can be rectified and improvements introduced.

On 21 April 1943, the last of the major bombing raids on Scotland took place over the area of north-east Scotland that had been nicknamed Hellfire Corner. Described in the 14 Group's ORB as 'a sharp raid', between fifteen and twenty enemy aircraft dropped 171 bombs on the Bridge of Don, Fraserburgh and the nurses' hostel in Aberdeen, killing 113 and injuring 235. By May 1943, the airspace in Scotland was much quieter: the ORB simply reads, 'From the operational point of view, the feature of the month was the lack of activity.' The reduction in the number of attacks on Scotland from 1942 meant that the twenty-one months he spent with HQ 14 Group and later with HQ 13 Group were relatively quiet, although enemy reconnaissance aircraft and Zenits were plotted, often on a daily basis, though rarely over land, undoubtedly searching for vulnerable shipping to attack.

As the months went by, enemy aircraft were flying well away from mainland Scotland, though they were often plotted over the seas surrounding Shetland and Orkney, some making landfall. There were occasional interceptions. On 25 August a Ju88 was shot down over Fair Isle after it was hit by twenty-seven bursts from ack-acks. A month later some bombs were dropped north of Aberdeen; two fell near inhabited areas, but fortunately there were no injuries or damage to property. Air/sea rescues were largely successful. A message of congratulations was sent to 13 Group HQ, praising them on their constant diligence in rescue operations, which had saved many Allied lives. A particular mention was made of the rescue of American airmen.

When HQ 14 and HQ 13 Groups were amalgamated in July 1943, Jim remained in Inverness. Between April and October 1943, he made just ten solo flights as well as thirty with passengers, usually unidentified. On 6 August 1943, during a five-day visit by the Air Officer Commanding, Jim flew Air Vice-Marshal Malcolm Henderson and three passengers to Turnhouse and Peterhead. Most of the flights made by Jim during his time in Inverness were within Scotland, ranging from Ayr in the south-west to the exposed and windswept airfield at RAF Sumburgh on the southern tip of Shetland, nearly 200 miles north of Inverness. There were, however, occasional flights south of the border. On 9 July, his flight took him to Northolt via Newcastle, giving him the opportunity to meet his second son James, who had been born a week earlier. From the end of August, Jim's flights were becoming more frequent, focusing mainly on RAF Stations Peterhead, Turnhouse and Dyce. With the exception of a single flight on 10 October, he was accompanied by two or three passengers, with visits often entailing overnight stays.

It was clear that an Allied invasion of mainland Europe was becoming a distinct possibility. From late summer of 1943, notices issued by 13 Group HQ called for airmen to volunteer as aircrew and applications were invited for personnel to train as wireless operators, cypher clerks and photographers, even if they had no relevant experience. An interesting request was for anyone to come forward who had information about localities in enemy-occupied territory, particularly relating to the slopes of beaches, the condition of sea walls, jetties and wharves, and, significantly, knowledge of exits from beaches. Another sign that an invasion was being planned was the transfer of the Beach Unit[60] to Tangmere. The congratulatory message received by 13 Group HQ in August had also referred to 'the growing Allied air offensive'.

These indications, along with the growing awareness that the Luftwaffe was a weakened force, and that the thrust of the war now had to be bombing raids against Germany, must have had a strong effect on Jim. He would also have been conscious that his experience in aerial combat both as a fighter pilot and then as a Controller would be invaluable to a bomber squadron. As a man with a strong sense of service and duty, he would not have been content to stay as a Controller in the north of Scotland. He volunteered to be transferred to bombers. How Elizabeth felt on receiving the news, is not on record. There were now two boys in their family: Michael, now two years, and young James, still a babe in arms.

On 8 November 1943, he was posted to RAF College SFTS for a refresher course with an onward posting to Bomber Operational

Training Unit (OTU). Although it was an unusual move, it was not unique. Will Whitty, a friend from 607 Squadron, was to join 76 Squadron in July 1944, flying Halifaxes, moving on to 640 Squadron in February 1945, again on Halifaxes. Tony Iveson, another Battle of Britain veteran, converted to bombers and joined 617 Squadron about the same time that Jim took command of IX Squadron in June 1944.

Was it purely coincidental, or was it the result of careful planning that, by the time of the run up to the D-Day landings, Jim had already qualified as a Bomber Pilot and was ready to fly on operations over France?

The DFC citation of 1940 had referred to his qualities of leadership in the Battles of France and Britain. These would certainly be tested during the final two years of the war.

Chapter 5

Mid-November 1943 – 31 August 1944

Conversion to bombers, 49 Squadron and CO of IX Squadron

Jim now embarked on a series of courses over the next six months. In mid-November 1943, he began a four-week refresher course on twin-engine aircraft at 21 Group flying two or three days each week, usually a couple of times each day. His assessment reads, 'Pilot and navigation both above average'. By mid-December he was at 16 OTU on Beam Approach, usually known as Blind Approach. It relied on two audible signals, A and N in Morse code, which originated in different quadrants of the airfield. It meant that a pilot could judge the approach he was making. Once they were of equal strength, and there was a continuous sound, he knew he was on the right line. Ancillary signals meant that aircraft could be landed in very poor conditions. In theory it was straightforward, but it took a lot of practice to be able to operate it successfully. From 19 January he was flying Wellingtons.

It was during this time that he would have teamed up with some of the men who would be his crew for the next fifteen months. Pilot Bob Knights remembered the experience as a very haphazard affair, adding, 'I didn't really get the crew, they got me'.[61] His Rear-Gunner was 'an old sweat', who had already identified a Navigator, a Bomb-Aimer, and a Wireless Operator. He chose Knights with the comment, 'There's a

Pilot over there who's had a crash, so he'll be more bloody careful next time'. Wireless Operator Bob Woolf conjured up the scene:

> 'Heavy bomber crews were neither allotted nor selected by any scientific method because there was none. Instead, inside a large room, part-trained aircrew stood and sat about in their groups. The bomb aimers were together, navigators together, wireless operators together and the pilots starting drifting between them. It was like a quiet party with no drinks, one of those occasions where the idea is to circulate, not to have a good time.'[62]

Bomb aimer Jim Brookbank described the strong bonds that developed between crew members. It was based on the knowledge that, whatever the dangers and challenges, each man could be relied on completely. It would only be at the Lancaster conversion unit that they would be joined by a flight engineer.

Flying was supervised by ex-bomber crews and because the aircraft used were not always in good condition, there were accidents during the training period, so aircrews were often relieved to get back to operations.

In February, there were simulation tests, followed in early March with 'Bullseye', a long-range navigation exercise testing the reactions of pilots and crews to being fired on. Jim recorded a flight of six hours ten minutes but there is no indication of the route flown. It was here that Jim would almost certainly have completed conversion to the Lancaster. By the beginning of April he was signed off as a heavy bomber pilot, again as 'above average', an assessment unusual during training when 'proficient' was more normal. However, he was an ex-fighter pilot, obviously rated highly by the instructors. By this time, he was at 51 Base, Scampton, with three weeks on supernumerary training. This was followed by a move to Swinderby to 1660 Conversion Unit, flying

Stirlings and completing day and night high level bombing practice. As the Stirling was a four-engine bomber, he would have been joined at this stage by a flight engineer.

The final stage was to be at 5 Lancaster Finishing School at Syerston, near Newark.

49 Squadron

Back in active service as a pilot, and reverting temporarily to the rank of Squadron Leader, Jim was, by 23 May 1944, a Flight Commander at RAF Fiskerton with 49 Squadron, flying Lancasters. It was just a week before the date scheduled for the D-Day landings on the Normandy beaches. The RAF was to take an important role, though at the time, this was not fully acknowledged in media reports. Wartime Chief of Bomber Command Sir Arthur Harris was initially reluctant, voicing reservations about Operation Overlord as he felt it would be a distraction from the raids on German industrial and other strategic sites, which he saw as a priority for the heavy bombers.[63] In mid-January 1944, he had described the involvement with the operation as 'an inescapable commitment', and that the RAF's involvement was only possible by night and in suitable weather conditions. In spite of his misgivings and once the Normandy campaign was well underway, he was to state that 'it had been obvious to him that the heavy bomber offered the only conceivable means of breaching the Atlantic Wall.'

Jim's crew consisted of Sergeant H. McDonnell, Flight Sergeant K.L. Lewis, Sergeant R. Collins, Sergeant C. Cameron, Canadian Sergeant J.R. Gran, and Sergeant S. Evans, a team that was to remain essentially the same for many of the next fifteen months.[64] Unusually, most of his crew moved with him to IX Squadron. Richard James has suggested that there could have been several reasons. As a crew they had worked well together, he wanted to keep them, and they wanted to stay with him although, as CO, he would be leading raids, which would be more dangerous. They clearly regarded him as very good. Their loyalty was rewarded as within a few months several had been commissioned.

Their first raid was on the night of 27-28 May, taking off at 2200 for the naval guns at Morsalines, one of 272 aircraft aiming to take out the five coastal batteries in the Manche department of Normandy. Although the bombs dropped by his crew were reported to have overshot the red marker by some 200-300 yards, the ORB noted that the sortie was considered successful. The attacks on the French coast continued without a break. They were part of the preparations for the D-Day landings, which were originally scheduled for 1 June 1944 but delayed because of consistently bad weather, confirming the reservations that Harris had made months before. Although it was not until 6 June that the landings were able to go ahead, bombing raids continued. The destination on the last night of May was the gun battery at Maisy, but the attack was abandoned as the weather forecast was said to be 'completely erroneous.' On the morning of 1 June, seventeen of the squadron's aircraft were detailed for operations, but once again this was cancelled at 1800. The target for the night of 2-3 June was Wimereux, not far from Boulogne. Jim's aircraft had reached the target and visibility was good at lower levels in spite of 10/10ths cloud, which presented one of the greatest dangers as it carried the risk of mid-air collisions. The Target Indicator (TI) went out just as a bombing run began, so the attack was aborted.

At this stage most of these attacks were on the Atlantic Wall, a massive and hugely expensive line of defences along the coasts of northern Norway to the Atlantic. These fortifications, built between 1942 and 1944, included colossal coastal guns, batteries, mortars, artillery, radar installations and barracks. Designed to defend German-occupied countries, they were largely constructed by forced and slave labour. In fact, those along the French coast were the prime targets in the run up to the Normandy landings and would be shattered within days, effectively removing fixed German radar coverage for large parts of the Channel. The Germans did, however, have Ansbach mobile units with a normal range of 25-35km (15-22 miles).

Jim's next sortie was part of a 1,000-bomber raid on the eve of the Normandy landings. The target was the coastal battery at La Pernelle on the Contentin Peninsula of north-western France, an area that was to be particularly vital for the US troops landing on Omaha beach. Conditions were good and the markers well concentrated, but the ORB noted that the attack appeared to have been rather scattered. Jim's aircraft had taken off at 0133 and he and his crew were back at Fiskerton just before 0600. It was probably on the return flight that Jim had seen and been greatly impressed by what has been described as the greatest invasion fleet ever to cross the Channel. Perhaps he was thinking of Exercise Spartan the previous year, hoping the lessons that had been learned then would have a more successful outcome now the invasion was under way.

The squadron was airborne again on D-Day evening, with just eighteen hours between raids, as part of another 1,000-bomber operation, but this time bound for the city of Caen. In spite of 10/10ths cloud, visibility below the cloud cover was good and several crews reported light but accurate flak. The target was well marked and bombing generally carried out satisfactorily. However, there was a narrow escape when flak hit Jim's aircraft and a shell exploded inside the cockpit. A fragment hit Jim just above his nose and he had to spend the remainder of the flight with blood running down his face into his eyes, seriously impairing his vision. Members of the squadron reported that the bombing seemed to be concentrated.

Constant stress, nervous exhaustion, sheer weariness and night flying would have combined to disturb sleep patterns. Any of these issues would prevent healing sleep, with the danger of being overtaken by exhaustion at a time when it was vital to be alert. To keep them awake and focused, white tablets – 'wakie-wakie' pills – and flasks of coffee were distributed to crews before raids.

There was a forty-eight-hour break before the next two raids, giving Jim and his crew much-needed rest, and allowing the hard-working ground crew the opportunity to repair the damage sustained by the Lancaster. The first of the two raids that took place on successive nights was to Pontaubault, close to the border with Brittany, on 8-9 June. This region included the naval bases at Lorient, St. Nazaire and Brest, ports that were vital to the German campaign as they were strategically important for both the surface fleet and the U-boats. For the same reason, it was equally critical that they should be captured by the Allies so that trans-Atlantic supplies could reach the forces on the west coast of mainland Europe. Jim and his crew arrived at the target at 0057. His summary reads: '4,600 ft. 1st wave. On run up to target received "Standby" and orbited starboard. On second run saw red spot fire but owing to smoke at this end of run up went round again and at the same time received "cease bombing". On final run up saw red spot fire backed up by green TI and this was bombed.'

The next night, 9-10 June, saw Jim flying one of the 100 No. 5 Group Lancasters targeting the railway junction at Étampes south of Paris. He was in the first wave of the attack and on his safe return was able to report that bombing was concentrated on the markers. Six Lancasters went missing that night; two from Fiskerton had crashed in France, one with complete loss of life. One crew member from the second aircraft had survived the crash, only to die later as a PoW.

This was Jim's final raid with 49 Squadron before being posted to IX Squadron as Commanding Officer on 15 June 1944. If the weather had been better, they could well have been on further sorties, but operations were cancelled for the next few days, again probably due to bad weather, the proximity of Allied troops, or saturation of the target.[65] He and his crew had completed seven operations in fourteen days, six of them over nine nights. They had had a lucky escape on the evening of D-Day when the shell had exploded in the cockpit. Air Gunner Norman Wells mused about the qualities of a brilliant pilot. 'Possibly they all were, or most of them, but most of them weren't lucky'.[66] Leonard Cheshire appreciated that luck played as strong a role in survival as skill. 'An ace pilot,' he commented, 'should know where every enemy shell will burst'. He knew that was not always possible. 'It was only luck,' he wrote, 'that meant that a pilot, ace or otherwise, avoided a shell that exploded neither where he anticipated its explosion nor when the enemy gun crew intended it'. He went on to describe some of the unknown factors. 'The weather affects the fuse or charge of a shell; a conscript Czech in the Skoda works deliberately makes an inefficient projectile; a gunner lays inaccurately, then the shell explodes where no one can have known it would explode', again emphasising that only luck could determine the outcome.[67] However skilful the pilot, it was the experience and teamwork of the whole crew that was vital if they were to be able to have any chance at all of avoiding trouble.

On 10 June, Jim's logbook entry records a flight home in an Oxford to RAF Woolsington, now Newcastle International Airport, for a short leave and some breathing space before taking up his new command.

IX Squadron

Wing Commander E.L. Porter, Jim's predecessor at Bardney, moved to No. 54 Base on the day that Jim arrived. Under the seven months of his command, the squadron had taken part in successful attacks over Germany. During the early summer of 1944, bombing had been increasingly accurate and this trend was to continue during Jim's period as Commanding Officer. Once again, his experience of combat as a fighter pilot was to prove invaluable. Early that morning, Lancasters, part of a large-scale raid, had returned from a devastating attack on German troops at Aubay-sur-Odon, in the Calvados Department of Normandy. The report made by General Leutnant Bayerlein, Commander of Panzer Lehr Division, gives a chilling account of the damage that 6,500 tons of bombs had wrought in an area less than one square kilometre. 'Equipment [destroyed], seventy per cent troops killed, wounded, crazed or numbed by concentration of bombs, all forward tanks knocked out.'[68]

On the evening of Jim's arrival, seventeen Lancasters joined a night raid on Chatellerault, a town with a long tradition of armaments manufacture, helping to clear the area ahead of the Allied invasion troops. It was reported that visibility was good, bombing was concentrated, and several large explosions and fires were also seen. In his account in the ORB, Flying Officer Doug Melrose noted that two neighbouring fires close to the target were of a deeper red than normal.

The next three days were uneventful. On 18 June the squadron was called upon, but orders came later to cancel the operation and two days later crews were recalled after an hour. The Nordstern synthetic-oil plant in Gelsenkirchen, the target of numerous raids, was the next operation on 21 June. It was Jim's first experience of leading IX Squadron. Jim and his crew (who had been practising high-level bombing the previous day) took off soon after 2300 for the Ruhr, reaching their target around two hours later, bombing at 17,000 feet. Although bombing was concentrated, no fires were seen. Once again, there was 10/10ths cloud cover and it was reported that marking was scattered. Jim and his crew were home at 0323. Interestingly, this was his first raid over Germany. Both with 607 Squadron and 49 Squadron, he had flown over France, Belgium and the Low Countries, but never over Germany.

It was to be a month before Jim saw action again, but the squadron was kept busy, taking part in raids on successive nights. Flying Officer Don MacIntosh recalled that while waiting to take off on a raid:

> 'I watched as the hands of the clock came closer to start-up time and in case the yellow recall flare was fired from the control tower. Jim Bazin drew up, as he did to all the aircraft, in his little Hillman car, and gave the thumbs up, which I returned, not so much to indicate that everything was fine or V for Victory, as that nothing was wrong that might prevent our going. More than ten minutes late on take-off would find you straggling behind the stream and easy meat for the fighters.'[69]

The Gnome et Rhône aero-engine factory at Limoges was the target on 23-24 June. Bombing was concentrated and explosions were seen as they left the target. One large fire just north of the marshalling yard kept flaring up and explosions were still seen for twenty minutes after leaving the target. Fires were visible from eighty miles away.

The 24-25 June saw nineteen of the squadron's Lancasters joining 720 other aircraft on a clear, moonlit night to attack the V1 Flying Bomb site at Prouville and others in the Pas-de-Calais region. The V1 'Doodlebug' attacks had begun ten days earlier and more than 8,000 were launched against London over the next nine months. Unsurprisingly, the sites were heavily defended, and three aircraft failed to return to Bardney. Harry Rae's Lancaster was seen to explode and crash in the Pas-de-Calais area, whether from an attack by an enemy aircraft or flak was not clear. The marking was said to be poor and all the crews reported that there were no conclusive results. Accounts in the ORB indicate that the organisation was chaotic, with crews reporting that no instructions were received as to which markers were to be bombed. Orders to cease bombing were received leading to ten or more highly dangerous minutes of orbiting the target. One crew reported that, as no orders had been received, they jettisoned their bombs, adding that it would not have been too late if instructions to stand by had been given instead of the order to cease bombing. Jim's frustration at the inefficiency of the raid on Prouville was marked by his terse entry in the ORB: 'Marking late so unable to attack. Jettisoned at 2325 hours.'

Rear Gunner Sergeant Fred Whitfield commented that the attack was considered an 'easy' trip as it was such a short distance. 'Coned continuously from time of crossing enemy coast,' reads the ORB. After several dummy runs had been made, an Me109 was the first of three enemy aircraft to attack within five minutes. Gunfire from a Ju88 hit the port outer engine which caught fire. The Lancaster continued without bombing the target but jettisoned the bomb load in the target area. No order was given to bale out. 'The Skipper (Flying Officer R.F. 'Lucky' Adams)', wrote Fred, 'was coolly working out the best method for escape for when we got back to base.' Six feet of the port wing as well as the starboard fin had been shot away. Even then, they were not out of danger. They were fired on by 'friendly' ack-ack after they had crossed the Channel. Fred realised it was a V1 that was the subject of the attack, which was successfully shot down by the gunners. 'How [the Lancaster] remained airborne,' he continued, 'seemed to be a miracle, but it was really due to our Skipper's skilful flying.' Unsurprisingly, the aircraft never flew again, ending up as a training frame.[70]

Awards of eleven DFCs, two DFMs and twenty 'Mentioned in Dispatches' were made to members of the squadron at the end of the month.

Over the next weeks between Jim's arrival and the end of July, raids were ordered, only to be cancelled. Flight Sergeant Bob Riches summed it up:

'Bombed up. Keyed up and then fed up. Sortie cancelled as we sat in aircraft five minutes before take-off. Was then chastised by supersticks [not identified!] crew for not revealing it was my twentieth birthday. Played cards all night as we had taken "wakie-wakie" pills.'[71]

Flying Officer Doug Tweddle, who joined the squadron on 24 July, remembered it as 'a very, very busy period, in fact we were in danger of completing our tour in about three weeks.'[72] Eighteen operations were completed in the six weeks up to the end of July, ten were cancelled and one, on 30 July, was aborted. Fifteen of those raids had taken place after 8 July, with Jim on three of them, including a daylight attack on the V1 site at Creil, where there was a network of caves and underground tunnels. The intention was to block the entrances and surrounding roads to prevent access by German troops. Generally, V1 sites were poorly defended against the hundreds of sorties as Hitler's promised ack-ack guns and fighters were still to arrive. The destination on 18 July was a daylight raid on Caen, with Jim leading the squadron. Doug Tweddle recalled 'a very, very stiff briefing' when 5 Group were allocated to bomb the steelworks at Cordeil as there were Allied troops on the opposite side of the canal to the target. Other targets included the shipyards at Kiel, Thiverny, marshalling yards at Givors, south of Lyon, on 26 July and Joigny-la-Roche on the last day of the month.

Following the Normandy landings, attempts to stop the movement of German troops meant that marshalling yards across France were the targets of intense raids. Jim led the attack on Givors south of Lyon on 26 July. The operation was plagued by atrocious weather conditions, rare in July, and so extreme that they were still vivid decades later in the memories of many who took part.

One Lancaster crew member, Warrant Officer Clayton Moore, recalled that they took off at 2100 on what he described as one of the most tiring and exacting flights he had ever experienced. The weather conditions were extreme. Flying in thick cloud for most of the way, they began to ice up really badly when they were only thirty minutes away from the target. Flight Lieutenant Bill Siddle made the difficult decision to abort the mission and returned to base.

Navigator Flight Lieutenant Noble Frankland spoke of a violent thunderstorm breaking out as the time for take-off approached, going on to say, 'We sat in our aircraft watching the control tower fully expecting to see a red Very fired which would have told us that the operation had been cancelled. It was not and so we took off.'

In spite of aircraft wings icing up, compasses that were unreliable because of the electrical storm, engines cutting out, and shortage of fuel, two of the nine Mosquitoes managed to drop their markers, enabling some of the squadron's Lancasters to follow up with concentrated bombing. Jim noted that it was not up to the usual concentration and it was obviously a frustrating raid for him. His comments are again brief: 'Target was not attacked owing to late take-off. All bombs brought back to base.' Before his next raid, aircraft from the squadron attacked Donges and Stuttgart on 24 July, and two days later took off to attack Cahagnes but the attack itself was never made.

Although the first two weeks of Jim's command had been relatively incident-free, July had gradually turned into a nightmare. The month had seen heavy losses: eight crews had failed to return from France in July, resulting in the deaths of forty-five men. These letters to the next of kin were the first of many that Jim would have to send over the next months. A further fifty-eight were now in prisoner-of-war camps. Doug Tweddle recalled that:

> 'When checking the intelligence lists of crews lost, practically all the people who had been to OTU with me and later to Conversion Unit, were taken out on that sortie, so the bulk of them must have gone out with no more than four or five trips to their credit, some probably less.'

Throughout all this activity, there had been intensive practice every day in high-level bombing and cross-country flying, regardless of whatever was happening in the air. School French was also part of the schedule. There was no respite for the crews, however. 'Wingco Bazin', according to Thorburn, 'was living up to his reputation as a slave-driver'.[73] Jim had been hit hard by the losses and was very well aware that the more practice they could put in the better the chances of dealing with emergency situations.

Don MacIntosh's wireless operator was Sergeant Phil Tetlow, whose accounts give factual descriptions and, more unusually, vivid and rare insights into some of the emotions experienced during flights.[74] His first raid with IX Squadron was to St Cyr-l'École in the daytime, on 25 July, attacking the Military College and nearby radio equipment not far from Versailles. 'For God's sake, don't bomb the Tuileries', Jim Bazin had warned us before we left. 'They're next door to your target – the German communications at St Cyr.'[75]

Escorted by Spitfires, about 200 aircraft, each carrying one 4,000lb and eight 1,000lb high-explosive bombs, flew at between 6,000-8,000ft on the route in and out, though Tetlow adds that the bombs were dropped from 9,000ft. 'Bombing', he noted, 'was carried out extremely quickly, only four minutes elapsing between the first and last bombs falling.' Later photographs showed that they had achieved excellent results. 'The sky', he added, 'was seemingly black with Lancs.' Passing through heavy flak, the blacked-out interior of the fuselage was lit up by flashes, the aircraft was hit several times, and it was shaken by nearby blasts.'

Phil Tetlow was in the air again three days later on a night operation to bomb the large railway junction and factories producing essential supplies in Stuttgart. Jim had begun the briefing by apologising for the late arrival of the tea and cake ('the usual cock-up with admin.'). 'The target for tonight is Stuttgart,' he added. 'Women and babies again, I suppose', he continued, leaving an unspoken 'regrettably' hanging in the air, perhaps thinking of his mother, now living in London, and Elizabeth and the two boys at home in Newcastle-upon-Tyne. The thought of bombing civilians was perhaps one of the driving forces behind his insistence on the bombing accuracy that was to become a characteristic of his time as CO. He clearly believed that the accurate bombing of one factory or synthetic oil refinery would have a far more effective impact on the German economy than the random destruction of cities.

Again, flying at 6,000ft across France, they climbed to 18,000ft for bombing. In spite of heavy flak, photographs proved that the bombing was very accurate. Phil Tetlow recalled that it was the crew's first night operation:

> 'From the time of crossing the enemy coast, there were very few minutes when fear was absent, and relaxation was out of the question. Enemy fighters met us near the French border and we seemed to be taking evasive action continuously for about two hours. As we levelled up for the bombing run a fighter was sighted following us, but we carried on, bombed and then managed to lose our unwelcome shadow. Whilst at 6,000ft we spent most of our time looking for cloud which we were briefed to fly in, but which never materialised in any great quantity.'

He went on to comment that it was a really hard six hours over well-defended enemy territory in bad visibility, best described as nerve-wracking.

The next night the target was Cahagnes. Phil Tetlow described how the British troops were desperately striving to hold their hard-won bridgehead in Normandy, while the Americans who had landed on Utah beach were pushing further west to seal off the Contentin Peninsula. Thick cloud meant that they were unable to locate the target, so they ditched their bombs over the North Sea on their return flight. The bomb fuses were designed to burn in mid-air. As the aircraft was flying at only 600ft and 'in spite of all precautions possible', they exploded, damaging the aircraft and severely affecting the nerves of the crew. Flying the famous WS-J 'Johnny Walker', which was close to its 100th operation, they did at least get the aircraft back to Bardney. 'Its regular captain, Doug Melrose and his crew were furious that we might have damaged *their* aircraft, as they had been promised two crates of Johnny Walker whisky when that landmark was reached.' He added, with a sigh of relief, 'Eventually, it was!' One can only imagine Jim's reaction.

The marshalling yards at Joigny-la-Roche were the focus of the next raid on 31 July. The ORB simply records that ten aircraft carried out accurate bombing, with a further four, including Jim, detailed to attack Rilly-la-Montagne. Of these, one failed to return. Jim's logbook is even more terse than usual: 'Primary attacked'. One hundred and three aircraft focused on the target at Rilly, which was a V1 flying bomb storage site. The bombing had been so accurate that both ends of the tunnel collapsed. Phil Tetlow was in the group attacking Joigny-la-Roche, again bombing marshalling yards that were used to supply food and arms to German troops in Normandy. It was, he notes, completely successful, and resulted in 'almost complete obliteration of the target'. It had been an uneventful flight out but, once they reached the target, the situation quickly changed. 'All hell broke loose,' he recalled, 'and the sky was filled with those little black puffs which appear so harmless until you hear the shrapnel rattling against the fuselage.' Wryly, he compared the appearance of the Lancaster to a colander.

The target on 1 August was Mont Candon, a V1 site near Dieppe. The fourteen aircraft were ordered to return without dropping the bombs as the site was covered in cloud, but Tetlow reported that, not only was there no opposition, but that his crew dropped their bombs in the sea 'rather than risk the lives of our French allies'.

The next day they were aiming for Bois de Casson, sixteen miles from Paris. The bombing seems to have been scattered. The Lancasters were tightly packed in layers and there were few fighters. There was another massed raid on 3 August, this time on Pontoise, with 'about 200 [Lancasters] sailing majestically through the flak-filled skies' above Paris. Once again, the target was a storage depot for flying bombs. Flak was met on the way over, particularly round Rouen but there were no German fighters to break through the Spitfire screen. Phil Tetlow noted:

> 'During this trip a new menace showed itself – a dual menace that was more nerve-wracking than the extremely accurate flak. As a protective measure the aircraft closed up tightly and then commenced to weave independently. At times it seemed impossible to avert collision. Each time Pete took over and started his run up, an aircraft immediately above us would open his bomb doors and we would find bombs whistling down all around us.'

In spite of this, all the squadron's aircraft made it home.

There were soon to be dramatic changes to the squadron's role. Until now, raids had been carried out in the company of hundreds of other aircraft. Now the squadron was to be deployed on what Phil Tetlow described as 'specialist raids', working with just one other squadron. The disadvantage is obvious: fewer aircraft would be more susceptible to flak. No reference to this is made in the ORB, but on 4 August Jim led IX Squadron's thirteen Lancasters in a group of only thirty aircraft on a daylight mission to destroy an important bridge at Étaples, a vital link in the supply lines of the German Army in Northern France. Smoke obscured the view of the target after the attack so it was not possible to see if it had been successful. Armed with 14 × 1,000lb bombs, 'the other squadron' (617 Squadron) carried the new 12,000lb bombs. Although

Tetlow had considered that this was 'the best bombing carried out yet' and because it was not clear whether the bridge had been sufficiently damaged, fourteen aircraft attacked the target again the next night. This time there was no doubt that it had been damaged but there was no conclusive evidence that it had been destroyed.

Over the previous seventeen days the squadron had been on fifteen operations. A telling comment by Bob Woolf noted that 'Some of the chaps, armourers and so on, hadn't been to bed for three days,' continuing that the ground crew never received the recognition they deserved.[76]

The next destination was Lorient, a port in Brittany that had been under constant attack in the previous months because of the submarine pens there. Four thousand tons of bombs had failed to achieve any lasting damage. On 7 August, when the squadron had reached the target, the order came to return home without releasing their bombs. It was the day that the Americans had reached Brest, so the order to cancel might have indicated that the location of the US troops was not clear. While this port, together with Brest and St Nazaire were still occupied by German troops, there was now a considerable part of north-west France under the control of Allied forces. From now on aircraft would be largely flying over friendly territory when attacking ports on the Atlantic coast. It must have been about this time that Fred Whitfield noticed 'V for Victory' fires that had been lit by members of the French Resistance. 'They were very risky,' he commented, 'but very heartening'.

Jim's wife Elizabeth often had little idea of the operations he was involved with. She would sometimes receive a phone call in the middle of the night when a voice simply stated, 'Bazin's done it again!' and the line would go dead. Although there was no indication of the source, she believed the calls may have been made from someone at the *Newcastle Journal*. Perhaps this was one of those occasions. Conscious of the strain on families, many decided to draw a veil of secrecy over the dangers they were encountering on a daily basis. Fred Whitfield decided not to tell his mother that he was flying on operations. 'When I took leave,' he recalled, 'I would remove my Air Gunner's Brevet to hide the fact I was flying'.

The La Pallice U-boat base at the deep water Atlantic port of La Rochelle on 9 August was the target for another daylight raid led by Jim. The Allied siege of La Rochelle would begin in September 1944, but the port continued to be held by German troops until the end of the war. Although 617 Squadron was bombing the U-boat pens with Tallboys, IX Squadron was still armed with conventional bombs to attack the oil storage depots. In spite of the bombsight on his aircraft being 'partially u/s', Jim recorded that one stick was seen to burst on the target although the others were slightly scattered, another example of the high standards he set for himself and the squadron.

Jim was leading two more daylight operations on 13 and 14 August. The target for IX Squadron was a tanker in Brest Harbour. The Battle of Brest had begun on 7 August 1944 when US VIII Corps reached the port, but the Germans were to hold out for a further six weeks. On his first raid Jim reported that the bombing was 'very concentrated', going on to say that one bomb was seen to hit the tanker, which was left on fire and listing by the stern. 'It was,' noted Fred Whitfield, 'one of the most frightening trips ever.' Doug Tweddle commented that he thought 'this was an attempt by the Navy to get two of the best squadrons wiped out in two days', adding:

> '617 was allocated the battleship and we were allocated the tanker, but what we didn't know at the time but were to find out the hard way, was that the gunnery defence at Brest were German naval gunners who had every small portion of the sky completely plotted. Till we were committed to our bombing

run they didn't fire… Normally after you drop your bombs, you keep on the same steady course until you get the photograph which is really synchronised to go with the bomb burst, so you are still committed to fly straight after the bombs have gone down… I'm talking about "target of accuracy" rather than a bulk area target so that on these ones that we were particular about, the ship at about 16,000 feet was very small.'

There were many qualms when the same target was announced for the next day, as Brest was said to have 'the doubtful honour' of housing the most accurate anti-aircraft guns. Jim was not happy. He was heard to say that 'Group tell me I can take the rest of the squadron tomorrow *just* as support', implying that he felt 617 Squadron should have gone on their own.[77] When Doug Tweddle went to see Corporal Bert Savage, his Ground Crew Chief, he said Bert looked very down in the mouth:

'He said, "Same place, Doug, same bomb load, same petrol load." These lads became very expert at forecasting targets by bomb load and petrol. They knew the ranges, they knew everything. I must say the idea of going back there, really, probably was our all-time low. Because it worked out we had sunk our tanker, and 617 had not visibly disabled the Cavour class, they were briefed to go back on that one and we were to go for another ship, which they had pulled out into the middle of the water, one assumes to take the place of the tanker. What really upset us was, it was a safe bet there were thirty vessels there, all suitable for sinking across the bowl which, let's face it, they could have sunk any time they liked in any one of the twenty-four hours that we were there and achieve the purpose; yet the Navy were wanting us two to go out and sink two, just to sink two.'

Jim was back over Brest at 1057. This time the intention of the attack was to destroy a hulk that was being prepared to block the entrance to the harbour. 'We all had holes in our aircraft', noted Bob Woolf, adding that the German gunners could plot the bombing run accurately and were able to put up a box barrage that the Lancasters had to fly through.[78] Bombing from 16,000 feet, the ORB record states: 'The first stick of bombs either hit or was a 10-yard overshoot.' In spite of this degree of accuracy Woolf felt that it was not as good as the previous day adding, 'I think Group is pitting 617 against IX to see who is best'. There was, he notes, a rhyme often quoted at Bardney that went: 'Six one seven shoot the line, Got their gen from Number Nine'.

On 15 August, the squadron's attention was turned towards Gilze Rijen, a German-held airfield not far from Rotterdam. This was a mass raid with 200 Lancasters on a German night fighter force, which by this time was the only part of the Luftwaffe that had any success and, consequently, their morale was high. Phil Tetlow remembered that this was the only target he ever got a good look at, both before the attack and afterwards when, 'through a pall of smoke, mushrooming high into the air', he was able to make out runways pitted with bomb craters and buildings either flattened or engulfed in flames, concluding that it was 'a very successful sortie'. A daylight raid was described by Don MacIntosh as 'one of the nicest things' that he had done. 'We plastered it with holes all over the place', he continued, adding, with a note of irony, that they had hit their Mess, which he was sure would cheer them up.[79] He also commented in the same interview that bombing runways sounds good, but he felt that it was not very effective, as the airfield could be operational within twenty-four hours. 'We dropped 500 tons of bombs inside the peri track on the runways in two minutes', mused Doug Tweddle. 'When you remember that the Germans dropped nearly 500 bombs on Coventry spread over about seven hours, you get some idea of the progress of heavy bombing in the concentration and in the timing'. He also recalled seeing photographs taken by Dutch people 'from a fairly short distance', confirming the accuracy of the bombing.

The last fifteen days of August saw only three raids, to La Pallice, Ijmuiden and Brest, giving Jim the opportunity to ramp up the number of practice bombing exercises that had been logged in the first part of the month. The emphasis now was on honing skills needed for extremely accurate attacks on difficult targets; particular emphasis was given to exercises on bombing, fighter affiliation, cross-country flights, and air firing. Speculation among air and ground crews must have been rife.

La Pallice was the target again on 16 and 18 August. Phil Tetlow vividly described what happened when his crew was chosen to calculate an accurate wind speed for the rest of the squadron. They found themselves behind everyone else and having to go through the defences on their own. 'Unpleasant. Every gun trained on us as we weaved towards target going flat out. We only straightened for a few seconds in order to bomb accurately,' he continued, describing how they 'squirmed' their way out again with the aircraft 'shuddering under the blast of the near misses.' He put their success at evading the fire down to excellent crew cooperation, telling Mac where the flak was bursting so he could manoeuvre the Lancaster to avoid trouble.

Ijmuiden, 16kms west of Amsterdam, is a deep water harbour. During the war it was the site of two well protected and heavily fortified pens housing fast torpedo boats (E-boats) and midget submarines. Because they made their attacks in darkness, they were a serious threat to shipping carrying essential supplies to the Allied forces. This made them particularly important targets around the time of Operation Overlord. The attack was described as most successful with most bombs falling in the target area.

Phil Tetlow's entry for a further raid on Brest on 27 August gives a real insight into how the crews responded when they were told they would be returning to Brest:

> 'After our previous experiences over this target every crew was keyed up to a high pitch during the short time before take-off. The most inane jokes would result in shrieks of hysterical laughter. Aircraft were checked and double-checked to ensure they were on the top-line... Our target was a large merchant ship anchored alongside the wharf. Every man knew that this entailed running the gauntlet of the entire harbour defences.'

It must have been an extraordinary sensation, and perhaps something of an anti-climax, to realise that the guns were 'strangely silent', adding that it could only mean one thing – there would be fighters in the vicinity. Even after they had dropped the bombs, there was still no sign of activity from the enemy. It was 'the easiest operation the squadron [617] had had to date': more than one crewman had noted in his logbook – 'No flak'.[80]

'I was just as scared by Brest's uncanny inactivity', Phil Tetlow noted, 'as I had been previously by the normal warm welcome.' Even after returning to Bardney, he was still unable to believe what they had seen, adding, 'The Army and Navy both had a hand in this victory'.

Chapter 6

September 1944

Operation Paravane, the first *Tirpitz* raid

The first ten days of September were packed with bombing practice at the Wainfleet and Epperstone ranges, wind-finding exercises, and cross-country flights at night. Between Jim's arrival in mid-June and the end of September, there had been more practice bombing by IX Squadron than any other, a record that built on the achievements of Jim's predecessor Wing Commander Porter. Jim's programme of intensive practice was producing results, leading to the selection of IX Squadron to provide half the force for the attack on *Tirpitz*. There was no let-up. Jim told them that they were going to be the best on the job. 'The enemy', he stated, 'was just a nuisance getting in the way'. Jim Brookbank clearly remembered that the combination of hard work and the sudden cancellation of afternoons off certainly paid dividends. When IX Squadron snatched the Camrose trophy from 617, he realised that not only was the squadron the best in 5 Group, but also that his crew was top of the squadron's ladder, which made him, 'a mere sergeant', the best bomb aimer in 5 Group.[81]

The squadron had been taken off operations and it had become increasingly obvious that something spectacular was about to happen. There had been practice bombing every day for a month. Rumours were rife: Phil Tetlow noted that many of them were ridiculously impractical:

> 'From time to time we were given particles of information. For instance, engineers were told that petrol consumption would have to be cut down to the absolute minimum on the

forthcoming trip, then navigators were told that their only aid would be the stars, yet they would be expected to navigate over a vast area. Gunners were told they would be able to do shifts in the rear turrets as mid-upper turrets would not be available. Pilots were told they would have to get a Lanc off the ground carrying a greater weight than had ever been attempted before.'[82]

Doug Tweddle had been given a hint that something big was being planned when he experienced problems with his Lancaster, 'U'. He got hold of the Chief who was the rigger, who told him, 'I'll sort that out for you, Doug. I'll come down with you and we'll get that right because we're trying to get these aircraft in top nick for this trip abroad.'

It was on the same day, 6 September, that Air Marshal Sir Ralph Cochrane arrived at IX Squadron, ostensibly for bombing practice, something he insisted all pilots should continue, whatever their rank, arguing that, 'if they could not drop bombs, how could they control people whose job it was to do exactly that.' Before Cochrane joined Doug's crew for a bombing run, Jim had offered some advice. 'Tell your crew,' he whispered, 'that they must call you Captain. He won't have all of these nicknames and other things that you do.' After the flight, Cochrane invited Doug to join him for a meal:

'"Now I'll tell you about your crew." He started at the turret at the back end. I don't even recall that he saw Ken, but he came forward through the aircraft Mid-Upper, Wireless Op, Navigator, Engineer, Bomb Aimer and he gave me a character and ability assessment of my own crew, and he was absolutely right. It had taken me, what eighteen months, getting on a bit, to find out all these things and this man had been airborne with me for about three quarters of an hour, which had got to be some measure of his ability and why he became the boss of 5 Group. Wonderful man Cochrane, completely ruthless.'

OPERATION PARAVANE: The first attack on *Tirpitz*

Finally, conjecture was replaced by fact. The importance of the briefing became even more apparent when they were ushered into the main hall of Woodhall Spa. Phil Tetlow had vivid memories of the occasion:

> 'Then at last the crews selected were told to report for a briefing destined to last forty-eight hours. Covering about half the floor of the briefing room was a large-scale model of towering mountains almost completely encircling an inlet, but our attention was fixed on an object sheltering under the lee of those towering cliffs right in the corner of the inlet. The *Tirpitz*!'

There was absolutely no doubt that this was to be a demanding operation with 617 Squadron. Don MacIntosh also vividly described the scene:

> 'At the door of the room stood an RAF Sergeant with a .32 Webley strapped to his blancoed belt. On one side of the table, apart from the be-ribboned pilots and navigators, stood the Air Marshal (Cochrane), conspicuous by the thick blue rings and gold laurel leaves, and round him, his senior officers. The Marshal nodded to the Intelligence Officer and the WAAFs whisked the dust sheet off.'[83]

The Intelligence Officer emphasised that ships of the Royal Navy that were desperately needed elsewhere had to be stationed off the Norwegian coast in case the *Tirpitz* sailed into the open sea:

> 'You all know what happened when the *Bismark* got out and sank merchant ships like turkeys at a shoot. As the season of mists and darkness approaches, she can come out with a few destroyers, and with her big guns and radar, pick off a dozen

of our merchant ships like herons in a goldfish pond, and slip back to her lair in Norway.'

Phil Tetlow went on to record that they were told by Wing Commander Willie Tait of 617 Squadron, who was to lead them, that the ship was considered unsinkable, protected by a powerful smoke screen that could completely fill the fjord in under eight minutes.[84] There was only one direction for the approach, an approach that the Fleet Air Arm had named Flak Alley. The battleship was almost 1,200 miles away and it was highly likely that they would meet with some intense opposition during the run-up. 'This', Phil noted, 'would be a tough nut to crack'. The situation then became even more serious. They were told that they should allow for up to a month away from home as the operation would be conducted from a Russian base. Three suitably loaded Lancasters had already flown around the coast of the British Isles, proving that the return flight to the *Tirpitz* was just out of range, so the airfield that was chosen as the Russian base was Yagodnik, close to the port of Archangel. All that was needed was a clear blue sky, which they learned was rare at that time of year in the part of Norway where the battleship was based.

Tirpitz, Hitler's apparently indestructible battleship, had been the subject of numerous unsuccessful raids by the Navy, the RAF, the Fleet Air Arm and groups from the Norwegian Resistance, events that had granted the *Tirpitz* an almost mythical status. It was indeed a tough nut to crack!

By the summer of 1944, the battleship was moored alongside a steep hillside in Kaafjord, a tiny, well-sheltered inlet of Altenfjord, bordered on the west by a 3,780ft (1,149m) mountain. The mooring gave easy access to the Norwegian Sea. It was also protected by heavy artillery at Harstad, a port 160 miles (255km) to the south-west which controlled both the western entrance to the shipping lane from the sea and the approach over the stretch of open water south of the Lofoten Islands. Without even leaving her anchorage the vessel's very presence in the area was enough to terrify the Atlantic convoys on their way to the ports of Murmansk and Archangel. Churchill famously referred to the battleship as 'the Beast'. Probably the most tragic example of the reaction the *Tirpitz* could trigger took place in July 1942, when the battleship was erroneously thought by some to be moving out into the open sea. Admiral of the Fleet Sir Alfred Dudley Pound ordered the Royal Navy escort to abandon the North Atlantic convoy PQ17, telling the thirty-five merchant vessels to scatter. There were heavy losses; only eleven of the thirty-five ships reached their destination in Russia.

With the thought of 'something out of the ordinary and landing in an unknown country', Don MacIntosh recalled that everyone was in high spirits at the final briefing. Although he admitted to not paying much attention to the Met advice, he felt that there would not be too many problems as they would be arriving in daylight. He did have a vague memory of hearing that the cloud cover would lift and was happy that all the preparations had been meticulous, even thoroughly cleaning the 'greenhouse' windows, ensuring there were no spots on it that could be mistaken for fighters.

The original idea to attack *Tirpitz* on the outward journey had been abandoned in the early hours of 11 September. Instead, they were now to fly to Yagodnik before making the attack from there. An added advantage was that there was no German radar on the approach from the east. A Mosquito reconnaissance plane would then check that weather conditions were suitable for the operation.[85] Crews would also have a chance to recover from the demands of the long flight to Russia and would be fresh for the attack.

The Senior Engineering Officer Squadron Leader Eric McCabe's Official Report confirms that this was indeed the case:

> 'On 11 September 1944, it was decided to alter the general plan for the operation by delivering the attack from a Russian base. This decision was taken because of the prevailing weather conditions,

because of the comparative closeness of Russian bases to the target and because an attack routed from the east gave the best chance of achieving surprise. Events proved that this alteration was sound and wise from a tactical point of view, but it did produce many difficulties which were unforeseen and which almost prejudiced all possibility of a successful operation.'[86]

Twelve Lancasters from IX Squadron armed with Tallboys and Johnny Walkers and accompanied by a camera-laden Lancaster from 463 Squadron Film Unit, took off from Bardney between 1659 and 1726. The revised plan now directed them into Norwegian, Swedish and Finnish airspace before crossing into Russia. When conditions allowed they would then make the attack.

Don MacIntosh recalled that there was still some light in the sky as they left Scotland but within an hour they were enveloped in the welcome darkness:

'I attended to the small autopilot wheel on my left constantly, keeping our height between 800 and 1200 feet, my fingers touching the release lever. In the event of engine failure, only ten or twenty seconds in which to take corrective action separated us from the sea.

'We flew on into the pitch-black night, hour after hour, the Merlins purring steadily. The world became the disembodied instruments glowing luminously in front of me. Each of us was wrapped in his own thoughts, the quiet hum broken occasionally when I called the gunners. For the moment, we were safe from attack.'[87]

It was a demanding journey, initially flying low over the North Sea to avoid detection by enemy radio location. Their first landfall was

German-occupied Norway, then across Sweden which, unlike its neighbours, had managed to remain neutral. Most crews were impressed by the sight of towns fully illuminated. The Swedes, however, were clearly intent on preserving their neutrality as the crews were to find out when they were targeted by flak, reportedly fired in a sufficiently half-hearted way to avoid any major damage.

Phil Tetlow described one or two close encounters on their journey:

> 'The first lap of our journey lay across the North Sea to Norway, and we kept fairly low so that Jerry's radio location on the Norwegian coast wouldn't detect us. There was some shipping just off the coast and as we flew over it an object loomed up right in our path. Mac heaved back on the stick and a barrage balloon was clearly visible a few feet beneath our port wing. We crossed Norway without mishap, but the Swedes decided to put on a show for us. They fired tracer shells off in all directions and some of it came uncomfortably close. One or two crews said afterwards that they were firing to form V's in the sky, but I didn't think so. At 2,000ft, tracer shells do not make you feel exactly at home. The Finns didn't bother us at all and we crossed the Russian front line quite uneventfully.'

Finland still had a considerable number of German troops on the ground, in spite of the truce that had been signed between Finland and Russia in early September. A deadline of 15 September had been set for the departure of the Germans, but this agreement had not yet been honoured.

Once the aircraft reached the Finnish-Russian border with still two or three hundred miles to go, there should have been few problems. However, this was not to be. Worsening weather conditions with a low cloud base meant that altitude had to be reduced to 1,500ft and once they were close to their destination heavy rain reduced visibility to between two miles and half a mile.

Don MacIntosh was not happy, expressing his opinion in his usual highly-colourful language. It appeared that the Russians had sent a signal to 5 Group HQ shortly after the Lancasters had taken off from Scotland, telling them not to set off. They were to learn on arrival that the weather was 10/10ths cloud at 100ft, visibility 800 yards with fog patches. 'You wouldn't send a dog in there', Mac commented. 'Command did sod all.' He came to the conclusion that 'some clown' at Met HQ had bent the isobars on his chart and said it would clear for their arrival. 'Bloody idiot, contradicting the local boys from 2,000 miles away,' he concluded. 'I can guess the hand that twisted his arm. All these merchants at HQ flying their mahogany bombers'.

Navigation became increasingly problematic, presenting even more of a challenge after what had already been a demanding, cold and tiring flight. Low cloud blanketing an unknown landscape was the first problem they had to contend with. The area has few outstanding landmarks; there are no great rivers, the coastline is unremarkable, and there are numerous areas of small lakes and wetlands so, given the tiredness of the crews, the lack of radio communication and the worsening conditions, it was inevitable that there would be problems. Added to this, there were further complications trying to make contact with Yagodnik. The code which the crews had been briefed with had confused the Cyrillic letter B (sounded as 'V') with the Roman one. In any case, although the Russians had their beacons turned on, the systems were also incompatible.

As they approached the area, Don MacIntosh's Navigator Sergeant Nigel Hawkins commented on the inadequate large-scale maps of the tundra that the Russians had supplied. 'They're pretty ropey,' Nigel reported, 'with dotted lines of the rivers wandering all over the place. I don't expect the Russians would give us any recent maps.' He expressed his opinion that they 'dated back to the Czar'. After crossing the White Sea, Don MacIntosh was flying his aircraft at roof-top height. Although the aerodrome was only three or four minutes flying time from the town, it took an hour to locate it and petrol was 'perilously low'.

Flight Lieutenant Tom Bennett of 617 Squadron described the scene as being like something from a Hollywood horror film, with 'tips of pines sticking up through a sea of mist'.[88] As Doug Tweddle emerged from the cloud over Archangel, he saw the tops of the masts of ships looming up out of the morning fog. He ordered the wireless to be turned off, as there was a lot of distracting chatter from other aircraft desperately trying to locate somewhere they could touch down. With scarcely any fuel left, he eventually managed to land at an aerodrome that he had spotted on an island:

> 'When I got nearer I saw one or two of them were pranged, standing up on their noses and it was a grass field and I didn't know the length of it but I got in, taxied over to a group where I could then see a Liberator there. We had two Liberators accompanying us. They were supposed to go there ahead of us and set up some aids, in fact they came there no sooner than we did so they were no good.'

Other crews were not so lucky. A horse had raced across the landing strip just as Squadron Leader 'Duke' Wyness was coming in to land. He avoided the horse, but the Lancaster was written off after the undercarriage collapsed.[89] Ray Harris had been piloting one of the Lancasters that Doug Tweddle had spotted with its tail pointing skywards. He had been preparing to land and was distracted by all the confusion, finishing up in a potato patch. Fortunately, all the crew managed to scramble to safety, but the aircraft was damaged beyond repair. Several others had made forced landings and some even had treks of several hours before crews reached the relative haven of the Russian base.

Two aircraft landed safely at an airfield near Yagodnik, but in total four Lancasters were so badly damaged that it proved impossible to repair them. There were some minor injuries but thankfully no casualties. 'The Russians', mused Stan White, 'were probably delighted to acquire the bomb sights and the latest radar equipment of these aircraft!'[90] Doug Melrose admitted that he had smoked forty cigarettes during his Navigator's efforts to successfully locate Yagodnik.[91] With fuel at a dangerously low level, Flight Lieutenant George Camsell was fortunate to make it to a landing strip at Belomorsk. Flying Officer Laws had also run into problems, but eventually touched down heavily at Vascova. The undercarriages on both aircraft collapsed.

After it had managed to refuel at a nearby airfield, another Lancaster arrived at Yagodnik after darkness had fallen. It was a good landing, guided in by the headlights of a Russian lorry.

Along with the Lancaster from 463 Squadron, only seven of IX Squadron's aircraft had reached Yagodnik safely, meeting up with those from 617 Squadron that had also managed to land there. The remainder of Jim's squadron was scattered over neighbouring airfields. According to the ORB for 463 Squadron, it was skill that was the only reason for most of the safe landings at Yagodnik. Jim's Navigator, Flight Lieutenant Edgar Jones, was awarded the DFC for his work in helping to plan the operation and for his meticulous briefing of his fellow Navigators. There were no concrete runways, just hard-packed sand and landing conditions were just about as bad as they could be. Of the thirty-nine Lancasters, two Liberators and one Mosquito that had left Scotland, only half had landed successfully at their destination.

The flight from Bardney to Yagodnik had taken Jim ten and a half hours. Much of the credit for reaching their destination had rested with his Navigator Edgar Jones. Everyone would have been suffering from the bitter cold and restricted space. Fred Whitfield remembered it as his 'longest ever flight.' The rear turret was the coldest and most cramped section of the aircraft. It must have been a huge relief to have arrived in one piece. Don MacIntosh, who had been flying for some time at just 50ft, exactly the same height as the length of a Lancaster wing, eventually made it safely to Yagodnik. His reaction was understandably euphoric:

> 'Relief, surge of spirit and reaction set in… Alice in Wonderland! A grass island on the River Dvina, no radio contact, impossible weather and a bloody brass band. In aviation, expect the unexpected.'[92]

After Doug Tweddle had landed, he found he was not at Yagodnik, but was at an airfield a few miles along the estuary. Trying to get just enough fuel to allow them to continue seemed an unsurmountable problem, until Doug realised that the overload tanks from the Mosquitoes that were in the pranged Lancasters could be the answer. Once the Russians saw what they were doing, the bowser was produced and his Lancaster refuelled. Doug commented that, if the Russians were worried about losing out on the deal, 'What he gives us out of the tanker, he can take back out of those overload tanks.'

As Squadron Leader Bill Williams was landing at Yagodnik, Gerald Prettejohns was suddenly aware of the engines revving hard. He looked up from his Flight Engineer's log to see that halfway along the runway was a red flag in the middle of a pond. 'The skipper,' he wrote, 'had to hop over it before we came to a halt'. Once safely on the ground, he was also amazed to see up to 300 aircraft dispersed across the field.

Flight Lieutenant Roy Harvey commented that the Russians had been rather caught on the hop by the sudden change to the initial arrangement, expecting aircraft to land after the attack, requiring only repairs and refuelling before returning to the UK. However, this was not the whole story. Instead, at very short notice, thirty-six aircraft had arrived at Yagodnik and in the surrounding area. There were now 325 RAF personnel at the base, seventy-five more than the Russians had expected.[93] In spite of the new arrangements, there was a warm welcome at Yagodnik, with the Commander, Colonel Loginov, making a speech emphasising the Russian-British co-operation. There was a band, and a huge banner praising 'The Glorious Flyers of the Royal Air Force'. Lunch was followed by movies celebrating the solidarity between the capitalistic Great Britain and communist Soviet Union against the common Nazi enemy. Jim, though, would have been kept occupied, debriefing air and ground crews, checking that his Adjutant was making a thorough inventory of the locations and conditions of men and aircraft, talking to Willie Tait about the situation and facilities, making contact with 5 Group HQ and dealing with queries until he was finally able to go to bed for a much-needed rest.

Accommodation was found for them all, however, and the meals, initially at any rate, served on china, with cutlery and napery borrowed from Moscow, were said to be good, helped down with generous quantities of vodka. Now that the stay would be much longer, everyone was aware that it put pressure on Russian food rations that were already in short supply. Every effort had been made to provide the visitors with what to the Russians were 'extras', and there was always a large bowl of hard-boiled eggs on the breakfast table. 'There were no milk or dairy products,' recalled Roy Harvey. 'The bread was black, the tea, slightly sweetened, was in a large samovar (and rather nice!), and tinned meats that had been brought by convoys around the Norwegian coast and under threat by the battleship we were to attack.' Gerald Prettejohns remembered yak meat and cream cheese, butter and brown bread. 'It was a change,' he reminisced fondly, 'from home cooking.'

Accommodation for officers was on a paddle steamer, though some of the latecomers found themselves housed in underground huts. Some aircrew even considered sleeping in their aircraft but quickly changed their minds when they learned that the guards were armed, trigger-happy naval ratings. In any case, wherever they bedded down for a well-earned sleep, there was also an enthusiastic welcome from the numerous bedbugs, who, no doubt, welcomed a change of diet. The RAF doctor who had travelled with them had anticipated this and in spite of vigorous dusting with Keatings powder, several men suffered severe bites.

The ground crews were now concentrating on maintenance and repair. Work on the two aircraft that needed replacement engines had to wait while the other ten, eight armed with Tallboys and two with Johnnie Walkers, were made ready for the attack. There is an interesting note in the squadron report that it was most regrettable that Flying Officer Ron 'Lucky' Adams' Lancaster 'W' could not be made ready for the operation, adding that in spite of great difficulties, all the crew members had made every effort to take part. Their attempts were considered worthy of mention. In spite of having had to feather an engine because of a coolant leak when approaching the Norwegian coast on the outward journey, and not yet at the point of no return, Adams had made the decision to continue, making a safe landing at Yagodnik with their bomb load.

It had clearly been a wise decision to change the original plan to cancel the attack on the outward flight. By the time they landed, not a single Lancaster was fit to fly. Two needed engine changes, another had suffered considerable flak damage, a burned-out exhaust valve had to be replaced and there were also broken ailerons, cowlings and fuel tanks.

There was yet another problem to be overcome. The bowsers that had been promised turned out to have capacity of only 350 gallons instead of the 3,500-gallon equipment that had been indicated, so on 13 September it took eighteen hours to refuel the twenty-nine Lancasters that were to make the flight to Kaafjord. Weather conditions were still unfavourable. Fortunately, there are still about fourteen hours of daylight in that part of Russia during the middle of September, although of course it is darker earlier if skies are overcast.

At last, Russian personnel under the supervision of flight engineers, had refuelled all the aircraft, and checked the oil and air coolant. However, when double-checked by the RAF ground crew, they found that some tank caps had been left off, and petrol loads varied by as much as 200 gallons either way. The petrol load was finally changed to 1,750 gallons. As soon as it became possible to travel to the crashed aircraft, fittings essential for repairs were stripped to replace damaged items on serviceable Lancasters. The ground crews from Bardney and Woodhall Spa worked tirelessly and efficiently for forty-eight hours, often under extremely trying conditions, but had managed to get some sleep. Eric McCabe reported that they were 'in every way satisfactory', the meaning of the word carrying much more weight in 1944 than it does today. The men had settled down quickly and needed just a little supervision for the first two days as the work they were carrying out was far from the usual everyday routine. Several were mentioned by name, among them Flight Sergeant Hopgood. Sergeants King and Cooper had cured a large number of magneto drops, which had resulted in all possible serviceable aircraft being able to take part in the raid. He also gave credit to Sergeant Little, who had overseen the replacement of the nose cone damaged on landing at Kegostrov.

Phil Tetlow recalled that those not involved in the preparations were 'successfully entertained with concerts, dances, film shows and even arranged a football match which the Russians won easily', summed up as 'A diplomatic defeat that was fruitful'.[94] He remembered that the days passed quickly, though, adding that the atmosphere was friendly and congenial.

The Attack

At last, the weather cleared. By Friday, 15 September, the aircraft were ready. Shortly before 0900 the Mosquito that had taken off in the early hours of the morning returned to Yagodnik, firing a green Very cartridge to signal that the skies over Kaafjord were clear and the attack was on. No time was lost in preparing for take-off. Phil Tetlow remembered that 'wildly enthusiastic Russian troops' turned out to cheer them on their way. As their aircraft was still not serviceable, Gerald Prettejohns and his fellow crew members watched as the Lancasters, drawn up in three rows, took off, then flew over the airfield in low-level formation, 'a wonderful sight'.

Once the last aircraft had taken off, the Lancasters continued in loose formation, flying at low level through passes and gullies until they split up into two forces. It had been decided that the squadrons should combine once they approached the target. This was an unusual tactic. Those equipped with Tallboys were designated Force 'A' and those with Johnnie Walkers as Force 'B'. The description in the ORB gives details of the plan in the usual dispassionate way, without any indication of the difficulties and challenges the crews would encounter. The scale of preparations for an attack that would only last minutes is phenomenal. Don MacIntosh summed it up in his account of their flight from Yagodnik to Kaafjord:

> 'Apart from a nagging worry over the Focke Wulfs that might be lying in wait, I felt extremely cheerful. By a bit of luck we had got to Russia in one piece with a serviceable aircraft. We had no fuel worries and at least we knew what the airfield was like for our return. Above all, it was clear underneath, and if our luck held for an hour or two, we would get the ship at

anchor in our bombsight for half a minute and justify all the time and effort we had spent.'[95]

As soon as they were 140 miles from the target the wind-finders, who were three minutes ahead of the main body, were to find a wind eighty miles further on, then were to fall in behind Force 'A'. At this point Force 'B' was to take a different route to put them ten miles to starboard. All aircraft were to fly below 1,000ft as far as the Finnish border, then to climb to their bombing height plus 2,000-6,000ft, so that the final approach could be made in a glide as fast as possible.[96] When they were over Sweden, nineteen of the Lancasters were fired upon by anti-aircraft guns. Then, crossing into Norway, German soldiers at an observation post alerted the Luftwaffe at Alta, estimating a force of forty bombers.

The Commander of the *Tirpitz* had his first warning of the attack at 1046 and within ten minutes the ship was largely covered by a smoke screen. Unsuccessful earlier raids and the heavy defences in Kaafjord ensured that the RAF bombers would receive a warm welcome.[97] By the time the first bombers arrived a few minutes before 1100, the ship was just visible but within minutes could only be located by German gunfire. Phil Tetlow recalled seeing the 'formidable' smoke screen start up while they were still six minutes away, but by the time they reached Kaafjord they could only locate the battleship by the constant flashes from her guns. He also reported that flak from support vessels in the fjord was intensive but not as effective as that from the batteries on the *Tirpitz*. Doug Melrose was the first of IX Squadron to attack at 1055, followed within the next two or three minutes by Tweddle, Taylor, Pooley, Jones, MacIntosh and Stowell. Lancasters carrying Tallboys approached three miles or so above the battleship's stern, described by some of the bomb aimers as 'looking about the size of a Swan Vesta'. They had to release their bombs a mile and a half in advance. By the time they arrived over the target twenty-five seconds or so later, they could see if the bomb had hit the target. Jim's aircraft with its Tallboy was the last to go at 1104 before Force B moved in with the Johnny Walkers. His account in the ORB reads:

> '[The target] was identified by intense light flak from position of ship. Smokescreen started at 1055. On first run ship believed visible but made second run to make sure: smokescreen however prevented accurate observation and no results of bombing seen.'

There seems to have been some confusion about the timing of the first bomb. Doug Melrose said that, 'regardless of the official timings', he saw Tait bomb a few seconds before him.[98] Whatever the order of bombing, no one from 617 Squadron reported a hit, with only some near misses. Intelligence later reported that a bomb that had smashed into the foredeck and exited near the ship's waterline had created a huge hole in the bow of the *Tirpitz*. This was identified as the bomb dropped at 1055 by Doug Melrose, whose bomb aimer was Flying Officer Sammy Morris. The battleship would never again go out into the open sea and was now limited to sailing within three miles of land. Thorburn comments that the fact that anybody came anywhere near the target was a marvellous tribute to the determination and sheer flying abilities of these crews. In spite of the long, taxing flight a few days earlier, little rest in the flea-ridden bunks, and the generous liquid hospitality of their Russian hosts, they had succeeded in inflicting crippling damage on the apparently impregnable *Tirpitz*.

Not all the Tallboys had been released; two failed to release and, because of the formidable smoke screen, others were taken back to Yagodnik. There was a general mood of disappointment, not helped by a very cool Russian reception when they touched down at the airfield:

'After we landed, the Russians went off us pretty rapidly. They too felt that they had gone to tremendous trouble and effort for a non-event which they didn't believe in, in the first place. They looked on us as a bunch of amateurs whose behaviour confirmed their low opinion of our flying abilities. We all wanted to get back to base. The feeling was mutual. Our plane was ready to go and I offered to be amongst the first off. Some of the rest stayed to talk and lick their wounds.'[99]

Meanwhile, the Lancaster from 463 Squadron Film Unit, piloted by Flight Lieutenant Bruce Buckham had flown on to Lossiemouth, arriving with fuel tanks that were almost dry. He and his crew had been airborne for a long and lonely flight of fifteen and a half hours, establishing a Bomber Command record.[100] Once the film footage had been processed, it showed that *Tirpitz* was still afloat, though sufficiently damaged to need considerable repairs before she was even able to leave Kaafjord. It was not until a week later that news reached the squadron that a 120ft hole had been carved in the battleship's bow. She was now effectively unseaworthy. Ships of the Royal Navy that had been patrolling the area could now be deployed to other duties, principally to the war in the Pacific.

Although most of the squadron's aircraft were to leave Yagodnik between 17 and 20 September, Jim's logbook shows he was back at Bardney on 16 September after a nine-hour flight. The route would have taken him across Finland, the Gulf of Bothnia, Sweden, and over the Skagerrak between Denmark and Norway.

Those who were unable to fly back on 16 September were looked after by the Russians. Their hosts seemed to have revised their original verdict on the lack of total success, entertaining those who were waiting for their aircraft to be ready to make the long return journey. Mac was only an hour into the return flight when engine trouble developed, forcing him to return to Yagodnik, much to Phil Tetlow's delight. There were certainly high spirits. A river cruise to a hotel in Archangel, when there was much wining and dining, and a Russian opera ended with an incident that was the result of the continuing rivalry between the two squadrons. It culminated in one crew member from IX Squadron being tossed into the icy waters of the river during the return journey. There was a more serious incident, though. After they had taken off, a couple of pilots from 617 Squadron decided it would be fun to beat up Yagodnik airfield. It proved effective and they no doubt enjoyed it, but it did mean that none of the IX Squadron Lancasters, with engines running and using valuable fuel, were able to leave until they were sure they had finished the exercise. Wing Commander Tait ordered one of the pilots to find his own way to Bardney on his return to make a personal apology to Commanding Officer Jim for such 'rank bad manners'. The second pilot, Bill Carey, had lost two engines from flak damage, making a forced landing in Sweden, arriving at Woodhall Spa three weeks later.[101]

Crews whose aircraft had been abandoned in Russia were allocated places among the surviving Lancasters.

Although records show that all aircraft returned safely, the journeys were not always easy, as Phil Tetlow recalled. Bad weather meant that navigation was extremely difficult. At one point they found themselves over German-occupied Denmark to the south of Skagerrak. After about eight hours flying, when they were over the North Sea, Mac handed the controls over to a pilot whose Lancaster had crashed on landing on the fraught flight to Yagodnik. When they were only an hour's flying or so from the Scottish coast, their rear gunner sighted an unidentified aircraft. As it continued to close in, he instructed their temporary pilot to corkscrew. This he did with such enthusiasm that everything in the aircraft, including the crew, became glued to the roof for a matter of seconds. Anyway, they saw no more of their 'shadower' and around about four in the morning touched down safely.

Gerald Prettejohns flew home as a passenger on 17 September as Bill Williams was in hospital with dysentery. Roy Harvey's journey home with Flying Officer Stowell was far from uneventful. Soon after take-off, it was realised that the GEE set was u/s, so the Canadian pilot returned to Yagodnik, circling the airfield for some time but failing to attract attention:

> 'The pilot asked for any ideas what to do next and, as he and his flight engineer had made sure the fuel tanks were full, I suggested we set course for home. This was agreed by all... Bearing in mind the navigator had no way of checking his position and, except for recording the times we crossed coastlines, he had no means of checking our position when we crossed the English coast.
>
> 'To assist aircraft in this dilemma, a "Mayday" procedure had been devised. A network of red beacons was installed the full length of the coast. The procedure was for any aircraft in trouble to circle a beacon and fire off "the colours of the day." This referred to the colours of the cartridges carried in the aircraft and the wireless operator had no knowledge of what these were. So the pilot told him to fire off whatever colours he had and at the same time called "Mayday" over the R/T.'

Once the aircraft was recognised as friendly, the ground station procedure was to inform the nearest airfield and searchlight battery and a searchlight would shine vertically and then swing downwards in the direction of the airfield.

The runway lights were then switched on and the aircraft was in contact with the control tower. They touched down at RAF Ouston fifteen minutes later. After a meal and a rest, and repairs to GEE, they refuelled and returned to Bardney.

After such a tough few days, it seems grossly unfair that those who had not actually taken part in the attack on the *Tirpitz* were not credited with 'this epic' as an operation. Roy Harvey added resignedly, 'At least we were given two days leave'. Tragically, one crew from 617 Squadron had gone off course on the return trip, hitting a mountain in Sweden. There were no survivors. Doug Tweddle's rear gunner reported that, as they were heading out into the North Sea, they were pursued by what appeared to be an FW88. Fortunately, he 'got chicken' and never pressed his case any further.

Before they had left Bardney, Bill Campbell, the bar officer, had promised Doug that on their return to Base, he would open up the bar:

> 'Well, it turned out to be 5 o'clock on a Sunday morning which didn't mean much really and we did exactly as Bill said. We opened up the bar and got stuck in... We were in a pretty merry pickle by about 9 o'clock... Benny [Flying Officer Taylor] and I decided to go back to our billet, we were pushing our bicycles, and for our Russian trip we had a rucksack and also for the first time we were carrying our .38 Smith and Weston revolvers on a lanyard around our necks. These were issued to us normally, but most pilots, I think, adopted my opinion that if we were liable to bale out over Germany you didn't want anything like a revolver hanging around your neck...'

As they rounded a corner and encountered the Church parade, the pair of them collapsed in a big heap and Benny got up, pulled out his revolver and threatened to shoot [the Adjutant], only to be rescued by their Batman. 'I believe there was quite a lot of tittering going on,' he said afterwards. 'It was quite an interlude'.

For the others, there were no doubt plenty of other colourful stories, probably highly embellished, to be told when the remainder of squadron members eventually returned to Bardney. It had been a memorable operation, though one pilot described it as 'a damned interesting trip, but I wouldn't want to do it again.'[102]

Early in October, Jim was interviewed about his experiences by Joseph McLeod, a BBC announcer. The interview was transcribed and printed in the Reyrolle *Monthly Letter* of October-December 1944. The article began: 'We have all been very proud to read in the papers recently of the exploits of Wing Commander Bazin, who up to the outbreak of war was a member of our staff', continuing that they thought that a permanent record of his latest exploits would be of interest to all workers in the factory:

> 'My Lancaster, O for Oboe, was one of the first aircraft to make the bombing run, and we met a considerable amount of inaccurate flak from the heavy guns which are situated around the fjord. As we were about to bomb, my bomb-aimer reported that he was unable to see the ship; she was obscured by a small amount of cloud. So we went round to make another run. Fortunately, other aircraft, flying from slightly different directions, were able to get the *Tirpitz* in their sights, and several 12,000-pounders were observed to be falling on or near the ship. Huge mushrooms of smoke and water rose up through the smoke screen, which was slowly filling the fjord up to about 500 feet.
>
> 'We were now in a position for a second run, but the smoke screen had thickened, and though the cloud had drifted my bomb-aimer was again unable to get the ship in his sight. But at that moment the *Tirpitz* started to fire her own light ack-ack guns, so we bombed the centre of the flashes.
>
> 'When our bombing photographs were developed they confirmed the general opinion of the crews that at least one

direct hit by a 12,000-pound bomb had been obtained, and we were all very pleased to learn from subsequent reconnaissance photographs that the *Tirpitz* had received such a hit, and is now down at the bows.'

On his return to Bardney after giving the interview, Jim was heard to say, 'They made me shoot a horrible line!'[103] A favourite saying of his was 'Bullshit baffles brains!'

It is extraordinary that the operation had met with the success that it had. The battleship was now so damaged that she would be unable to go out into the open sea again. This had been an operation with many unknown factors to contend with. In spite of the detailed and meticulous planning it was inevitable that there had been unforeseen hitches. In particular, the misunderstandings between the RAF and the Russians over the call sign, as well as the failure to communicate the latest meteorological information from Yagodnik, had combined to make this first attack on the *Tirpitz* extraordinarily difficult. The change of plan less than twenty-four hours before take-off certainly didn't help, as this report shows:

> 'The change of plan meant hurried preparations by Nos. 9 and 617 Squadrons during the afternoon of 11 September 1944. The squadrons were ordered to take off from England at 1700 hours so as to arrive at Yagodnik airfield near Archangel soon after dawn on 12 September, and to be prepared to operate that afternoon if weather conditions at the target were favourable. The original plan provided for two Liberators of Transport Command conveying the ground staff to arrive at Yagodnik ahead of the Lancasters and to prepare for their arrival. The last-minute change made this impossible, a fact which is regretted because it is more than probable that the ground

staff could have done much to assist the Lancasters to find the airfield at Yagodnik.'[104]

Aware that such an attack would probably have to be attempted a second time, Eric McCabe made the following recommendations:

1. The ground staff should arrive at least twenty-four hours before the main force to enable them to unload transport aircraft and get all facilities organised.
2. Facilities at advanced bases should be fully understood before leaving UK, e.g. 'Hucks starters' were available but no starter trolleys. Tankers stated to hold 3,500 gallons only held 350 gallons, hence sixteen hours were required to refill all aircraft, and adequate petrol of correct octane plus may have eliminated excessive number of Magneto drops.
3. Some form of permanent transport is essential to engineer staff because aircraft were dispersed approximately one mile from end to end, also a full-time interpreter is necessary.
4. Flight engineers could easily acquire more knowledge of doping, daily inspections, refuelling, etc. at base stations. This would assist and save time when on detachment. Some engineers were an asset, while many a liability.
5. Spare engines should be 'built up' as completely as possible to save time. No arrangements were made for Mosquito. One corporal had to be fully employed on this aircraft to give priority serviceability.
6. A light-weight collapsible trestle would be a great asset; ladders are not sufficiently stable for changing engines, ailerons, etc.
7. At least ten engine sets of sparking plugs were required to cater for the number of Mag. drops, but it is considered that the 97-octane petrol (coupled with long cruising at low rpm) was the main cause of this trouble, otherwise the equipment brought was quite adequate.

May Nedou Bazin and family in 1925. Jim, aged 12, is standing centre back.
Photograph courtesy of Elizabeth Main

Elizabeth and Jim enjoy a pre-war riverside picnic. *Bazin Family Archive*

Usworth, July 1939. Left to right: Sqn Ldr Smith, Fg Off Craig, Sqn Ldr Gale, Plt Off Griffith, Fg 0ff Wardale, Fg Off Bazin. *Bazin Family Archive*

Abbotsinch Summer Camp, August 1939: the slopes of Ben Lomond. Left to right: Francis Blackadder, Jim Bazin and Alan Glover. *Bazin Family Archive*

Abbotsinch Summer Camp, August 1939, Skelmorlie Hotel: Left to right: Jim Bazin, Will Gore and Will Turner engrossed in the crisis news. *Bazin Family Archive*

Abbotsinch Summer Camp, August 1939: Jim lost in a moment of thought at the Skelmorlie Spa Hotel. *Bazin Family Archive*

December 1939: Jim Bazin at Wissant, Northern France, with a mine. *Bazin Family Archive*

YEAR	AIRCRAFT		PILOT, OR 1ST PILOT	2ND PILOT, PUPIL OR PASSENGER	DUTY (INCLUDING RESULTS AND REMARKS)	SINGLE-ENGINE AIRCRAFT			
						DAY		NIGHT	
	Type	No.				Dual	Pilot	Dual	Pilot
					TOTALS BROUGHT FORWARD	52.5	349.50	.15	18.00
April 1st to April 14th	Gladiator		self	—	Operational patrols, Cross country and Sector Recco.		7.00 approx.		
April 15th to April 30th	Hurricane		self	—	Re-equipment with Hurricane A/C at Abbeville		20.0 approx		
May 1st to May 9th	Hurricane		self	—	Operational patrols, Formation & Sector Reccos. from Vitry.		15.0 approx		
May 10th to May 20th	Hurricane		self	—	Interceptions, Offensive patrols, escorts, Low flying Reccos. from Vitry and Norrent Fontes. (Authorisation book lost during evacuation from France.)		45.0 approx		
				GRAND TOTAL [Cols. (1) to (10)] 543 Hrs. 50 Mins.	TOTALS CARRIED FORWARD	32.5	486.50	.15	18.00

Jim's logbook was lost during the chaos of the Battle of France. This extract summarises the events of April and May 1940. *Bazin Family Archive*

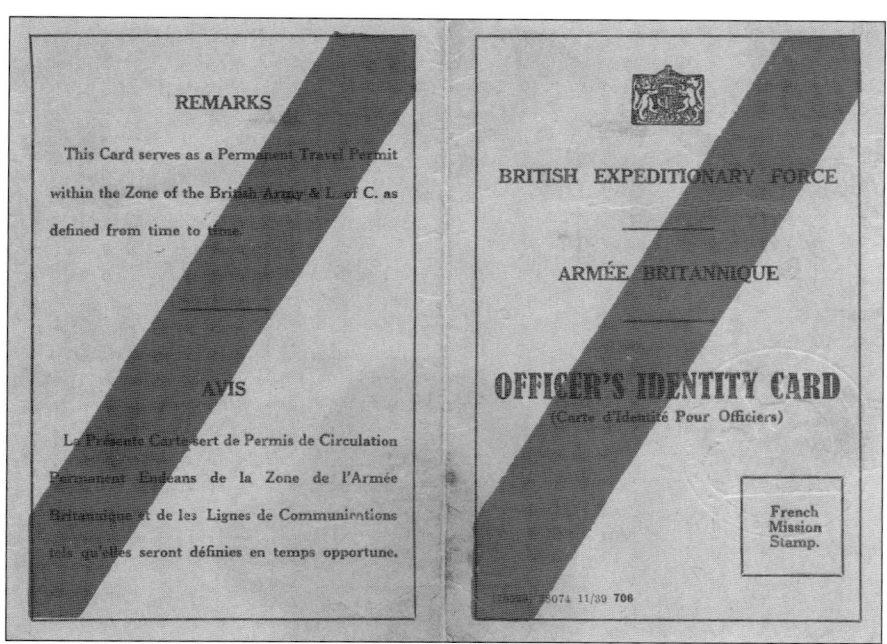

Above and below: January 1940: Jim's identity card issued for officers in the British Expeditionary Force. It also served as a travel permit within the British Army Zone. Note that the squadron number has been totally erased. *Bazin Family Archive*

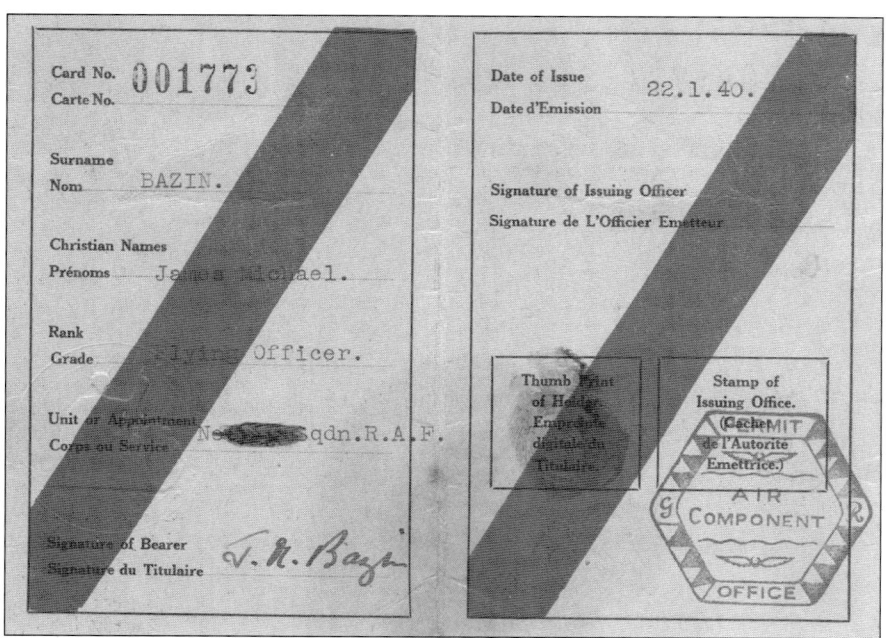

CENTRAL CHANCERY OF
THE ORDERS OF KNIGHTHOOD,
ST JAMES'S PALACE, S.W.1.

8th February, 1941.

Sir,

The King will hold an Investiture at Buckingham Palace on Tuesday the 25th February, at which your attendance is requested.

It is requested that you should be at the Palace not later than 10.15 o'clock a.m.

DRESS-Service Dress, Morning Dress or Civil Defence Uniform.

This letter should be produced on entering the Palace, as no further card of admission will be issued.

Two tickets for relations or friends to witness the Investiture may be obtained on application to this Office and it is urgently requested that the application should bear the same reference number as on the card enclosed.

Please send an immediate acknowledgment to the Secretary, Central Chancery of the Orders of Knighthood, St. James's Palace, London, S.W.1, on the enclosed card.

I am, Sir,

Your obedient Servant.

Flight Lieutenant James M. Bazin,
      D.F.C., R.A.F.

Secretary.

February 1941: The investiture letter issued on the occasion of Jim's DFC. *Bazin Family Archive*

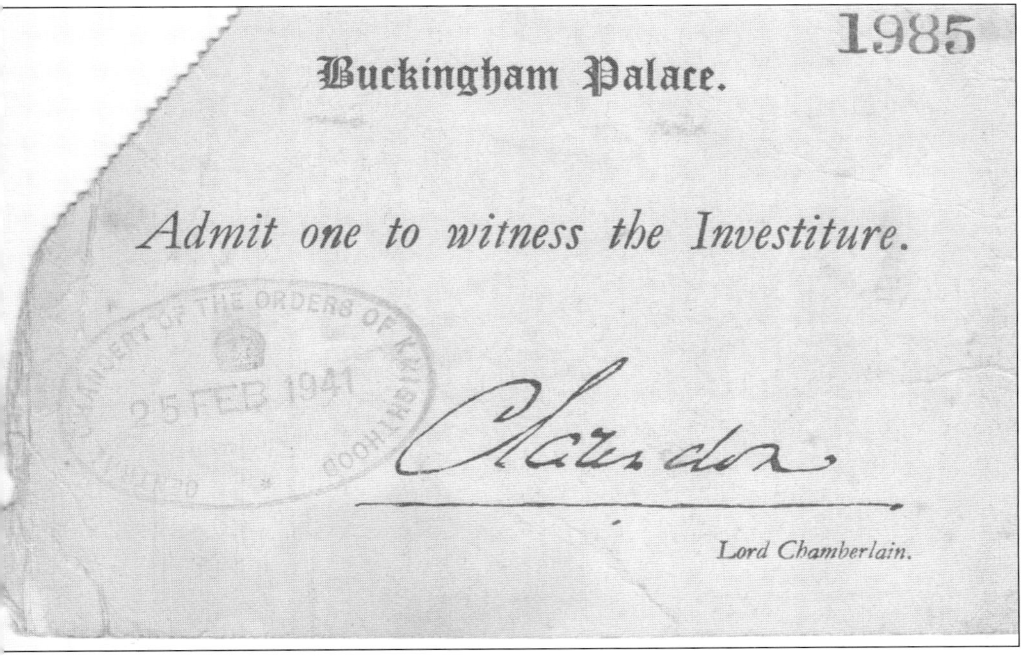

Buckingham Palace.

Admit one to witness the Investiture.

1985

Clarendon

Lord Chamberlain.

Above and below: February 1941: Admit one to witness the Investiture. This had been carefully kept as a souvenir of the event, although Elizabeth has written a shopping list on the reverse. *Bazin Family Archive*

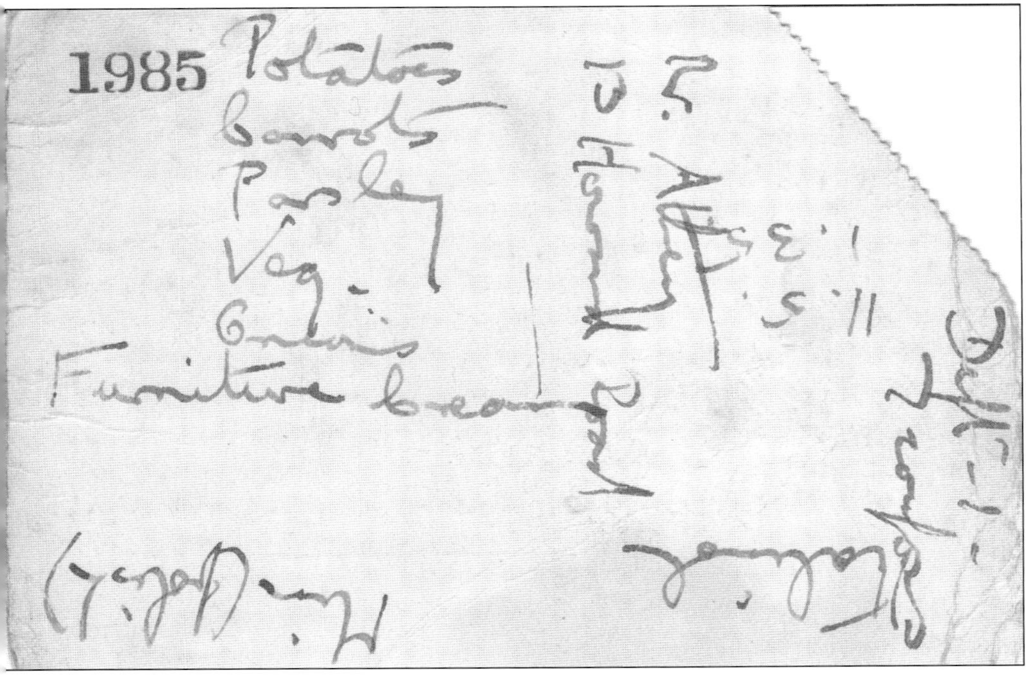

Above: August 1939: Abbotsinch: the last pre-war Summer Camp. By the end of 1940 twelve of the men in the photograph had lost their lives in combat or air accidents, and three were prisoners-of-war. *Bazin Family Archive*

Left: 1943: Jim's elder son Michael with his mother Elizabeth. *Courtesy of Elizabeth Main*

YEAR		AIRCRAFT		PILOT, OR	2ND PILOT, PUPIL	DUTY
		Type	No.	1ST PILOT	OR PASSENGER	(INCLUDING RESULTS AND REM...
MONTH	DATE	—	—	—	—	TOTALS BROUGHT FOR...

STIRLING HIGH LEVEL BOMBING
DAY 1. Close Group 111 yds 12000 feet (175 yds 20000 feet.)
NIGHT 2. Close Group 63 yds 12000 feet (80 yds 20000 feet.)
NIGHT 3. Close Group 187 yds 12500 feet (235 yds 20000 feet.)

Assessment as Bombing Pilot : ABOVE AVERAGE.

BOMBING LDR

April 1944: the next stage would be the move to No 5 Lancaster Finishing School in early May. *Private collection of James White*

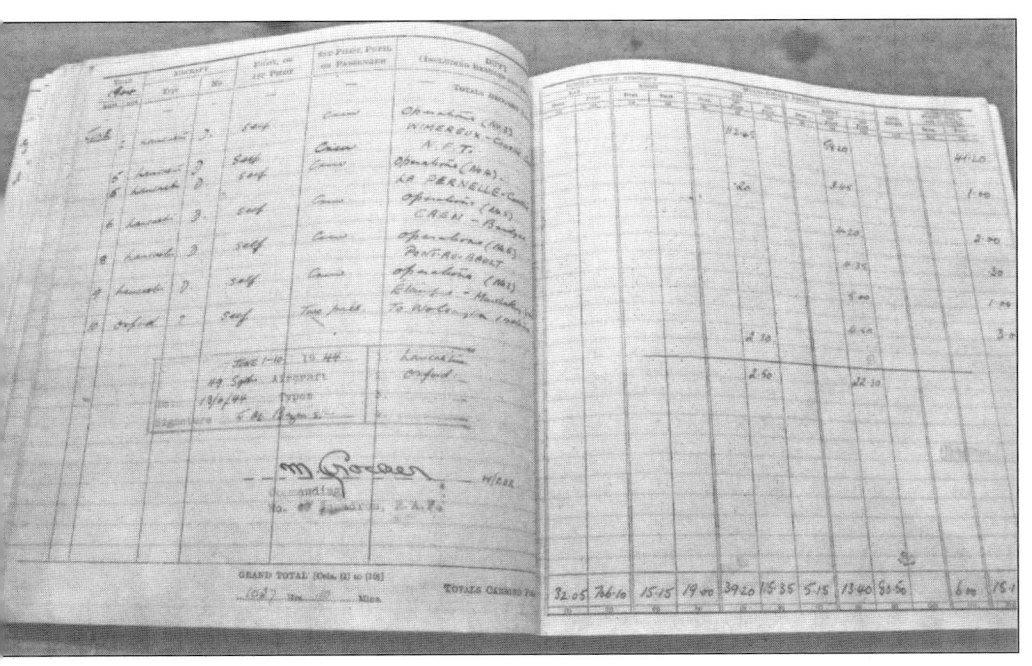

June 1944: Jim's logbook with entries for five operations over eight days during the early period of the D-Day landings. It was on 6 June that Jim was hit by a fragment from the shell that exploded inside the cockpit. There were no further entries after his flight to Woolsington until ten days later. *Private collection of James White*

The attack by Jim and his crew on Brest, 13 August 1944. Jim reported that bombing was very concentrated and that 'own stick seen to hit tanker which was left on fire and listing by the stern.' *Private Collection of James White*

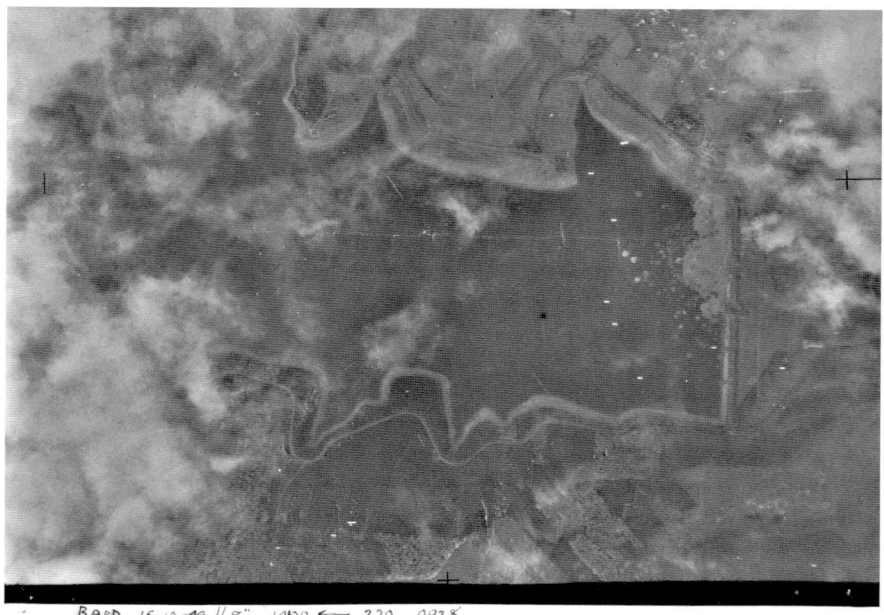

Sorpe Dam, 15 October 1944, Keeley's photograph taken two minutes after Don Macintosh's Tallboy had exploded in the centre of the concrete on top of the dam. He reported that his rear gunner had seen the breach in the dam. *Private collection of James White*

A Mess Party to celebrate the sinking of the *Tirpitz* showing bar (top) and 'eats' (below) and the artistry of both the painter of the picture and of the baker who made the Squadron Crest and model Lancaster. The squadron plaque is displayed and Tallboy Cocktail Bar sign is painted on the tail section of a Tallboy. *Photograph courtesy of Keith Harvey*

Above: Lübeck Summer Camp, 19 September 1947. Left to right: Flight Lieutenant Collingridge, Jim Bazin, Flying Officer Kennedy, Joe Kayll, Flying Officer Baxter, Flying Officer A.B. Dunford, Francis Blackadder, Pilot Officer H.O. Thompson and Flight Lieutenant M.C. Hope-Pool. Perched above the propeller was Flying Officer G. Raine. Flight Lieutenant McConnell had positioned himself on the wing. *Bazin Family Collection*

Left: Jim takes command of 607 Squadron in 1949. *Photograph by Garnet (John) Moore, courtesy of Richard Moore Collection*

Jim on 13 September 1984 with the painting by Stan White of Jim's Hurricane in action over Newcastle-upon-Tyne during the Battle of Britain on 15 August, 1940. *Private collection of James White*

Jim's memorial stone at Tangmere. Note that there is no reference to IX Squadron. *Bazin family archive*

Battle of Britain, 15 August 1940: Jim's Hurricane P3668 over the Tyne Bridge, Newcastle-upon Tyne. Painting by Stan White. *Private collection of James White*

Meanwhile, the German High Command took the decision to move the *Tirpitz* west to Tromsø, only 13 miles (22km) south of Alta, once the necessary essential repairs had been carried out, intending to use it as a static coastal defence. It was an interesting move. The site chosen was a sheltered stretch of water between the main island of Tromsø and Håkøya to the west. It was a risky journey for a ship that was vulnerable to heavy head winds or seas. Once the convoy had left the sheltered waters of Altenfjord, there was open sea to the west before reaching the more sheltered waters of Grøtsundet, a journey of almost 280 miles (450km). The new anchorage also put the battleship within reach of the British Isles. The slow progress was closely monitored by members of the Norwegian Resistance. Hammerfest, forty-nine miles (79km) to the north would have been a better option as the route there takes it along the comparatively sheltered waters of the Inner Passage. A nearby fjord surrounded by high mountains offers good shelter but deep water. Additionally, the extra distance would certainly have kept the ship well out of range of bombing raids flown direct from airbases in the British Isles. However, Hammerfest was no longer under German control. Tromsø was by now the most northerly city occupied by the Germans, although there were still troops in the north of Finnmark. *Tirpitz* was now only of use as a static coastal defence in the shallow waters off Tromsø.

There was to be no rest for the crews though, with a return to the intensive programme of continued high-level bombing, cross-country and fighter affiliation practice. There were three sorties into Germany before the end of the month, though Jim's next operational flight was to be the Sorpe Dam in mid-October. A raid on 23 September on the Dortmund-Ems shipping canal, again with 617 Squadron, was plagued by 10/10ths cloud with only five crews able to release their bombs. The attack led to the loss of two of the squadron's aircraft, including that of Glaswegian Jock Scott who was on the last trip of his tour. Conditions again meant that it was impossible to see what, if any, damage had been done.

The target on 26 September was Karlsberg, the final day of the Allies unsuccessful Operation Market Garden. The following day the destination was Kaiserslautern, in which sixty per cent of the city was ultimately destroyed.

Not knowing just how much damage had been inflicted on the *Tirpitz*, Churchill was still determined to sink 'the Beast', regardless of losses to men and machines. Tromsø was only just within range, the days were getting shorter and the Germans would no doubt be expecting another attack.

Chapter 7

1 October – 12 November 1944

The Walcheren Campaign, the Sorpe Dam and Operation Obviate: the second *Tirpitz* raid

After Jim had returned to Bardney on 16 September with his next raid a month away, he was far from idle. Just a week later, plans were already in place for another attack on the *Tirpitz*, now anchored in shallow water off the west coast of Tromsø. Her hideout in the fjord had been located and photographed by naval aircraft from HMS *Implacable*.

The squadron's next major target was the Sorpe Dam, which had been attacked by 617 Squadron the previous year using Barnes Wallis's bouncing bombs. This time it was to be a 'solo' raid by IX Squadron, employing very different techniques.

Meanwhile, there were more conventional raids over Germany. Twenty aircraft took part in a daylight attack on Wilhelmshaven on 5 October. Because of thick cloud and as there was no sign of any markers to locater the target, they were using H2S, a system evolved for Bomber Command to identify targets on a grid in the dark or under conditions of poor visibility. Cloud cover also meant that few results were seen though there was one sighting of a hit on a ship in the harbour. Pilot Officer P.W. Reaks commented that he had seen numerous crews randomly bombing areas before they reached the coast on the outward journey, though these were not believed to be from IX Squadron. Curly Read was on the run-up to the target when his mid-upper gunner suddenly warned, 'Oh my God, we've been hit!' A Lancaster that was overhead had dropped a J-type cluster on the starboard outer engine, starting a fire. Rear gunner Jack Linaker remembered that the flight engineer managed to extinguish the fire and feather the engine, so they continued straight in and dropped their bombs. It was only sea below them. Jack said, 'For Christ's sake don't ditch. We'll have to bale out over land'. In spite of the damage, they made it back to Bardney and made a safe landing.[105]

A night-time raid to Bremen twenty-four hours later was the last and most successful of more than thirty attacks on the city. It produced reports of well-placed Target Indicators (TIs), fires were clearly seen with streets burning on both sides of the river, and more than 5,000 houses and fifty factories were destroyed, including those of Focke Wulf and Siemens. The glow was still visible 100 miles away on the return flight.

Memorably it was the 107th and final flight of Lancaster 'J' Johnny. She had outlasted many of the men who had flown in her. It is a sobering statistic that 100 of the 220 different airmen who had crewed WS/J had died in other aircraft. Doug Melrose had piloted her on twenty-four raids, more than anyone else.

There was also the first of three daylight raids over Holland on 7 October, a series described as the Walcheren Campaign, designed to breach dykes near Flushing in order to flood large areas of the surroundings. Walcheren Island had been the main stumbling block in the British and Canadian advance along the Dutch coast. Doug Tweddle recalled that Montgomery had decided that ground troops should open up Antwerp, but Doug's thoughts were with the Dutch civilians:

> 'Unfortunately, the big island overlooking the entrance to the Scheldt was still in German hands and any [Allied] shipping, of course, that came down there was going to get into trouble. So it was decided, and I can't imagine the Dutch would be

pleased about it, that we would try with Tallboys to burst the sea dyke and let in the water and flood them out... But what I remember most vividly was the Westkapelle end, the top end, and the water did of course flood Holland and went right across as far as Middleburg, which I think is probably the largest city in that particular island. It took the Dutch a hell of a long time after the war to pump all that out and recover it from an agricultural point of view.'

Phil Tetlow was also on what was nicknamed the 'Milk Run', probably because of the short flying time and the lack of defences. The weather was good and they were in the spearhead of the attack on this target. It was only an hour and a half flying time from Bardney. The defences were meagre and gave them no trouble at all. He also noted that the majority of crews were certain that the dyke wall had been destroyed, leaving a gap about 200yds long.[106]

They were back again on 11 October attacking the heavy guns on the Milk Run, Phil Tetlow was in one of the two crews chosen for wind-finding:

'... this meant we took off about half an hour before the others. We then made our assessment of the strength and direction of the wind at bombing height and I relayed it back to Group HQ. Group would then take a mean of the two winds sent in and transmit it to the main force. This was repeated three times – once every fifteen minutes – after which we bombed with the last formation.'

He had a curious experience about ten miles from the target, which he only learned about afterwards as he had been absorbed in taking a message from Group while the incident was taking place. The bomb aimer had sighted a fighter curving round to get on their tail. He informed the gunners and they waited until it got within range and then let go at it. After enduring two or three bursts of their accurate fire, the fighter sheered off without firing a shot. Phil knew nothing about it until after they had landed!

Until now, IX Squadron had been part of a large force or had worked with 617 Squadron. Jim led the attack on the Sorpe Dam on 15 October. It was to be very different. Unusually, this top priority raid was planned and carried out by IX Squadron on its own. Phil Tetlow recalled it as particularly memorable. Pride in the squadron's achievement shines through every word of his account:

> 'It was a spectacular milestone in the magnificent record of our squadron. On this top priority job we were given a completely free hand to plan our own tactics and to test a method of precision daylight bombing which we had perfected.'

Accompanied by nine squadrons of Mustangs – five Mustangs to each Lancaster – eighteen Lancasters took off from Bardney between 0627 and 0653, meeting up with their escort about fifty miles from the German border just as the sun rose. A Polish Squadron, 315, was among them. Unlike the raids on the dams the previous year when 617 Squadron used bouncing bombs for the dangerous low-level release, for this attack IX Squadron was armed with Tallboys that had to be dropped from at least 14,000ft.

No flak was encountered during the entire operation and there was no sign of enemy aircraft during the run up to the target. 'There were only light defences at the dam,' reported Jim, adding that they were not worried by them at all. He went on to say that they were able to attack as planned. The squadron lined up in a gaggle consisting of two separate formations in single file. Jim had emphasised the importance of accuracy and Phil Tetlow commented that the squadron rose to the occasion. The attack lasted just three minutes. Jim led the raid. His bomb, released at 0925, was seen to burst on top of the dam on the starboard side. Don MacIntosh saw their Tallboy hit the target. His Rear Gunner reported that it was breached. Another crew also recorded seeing a crater there.

That the dam was not completely breached is not surprising. It was quite unlike any others in the region, with a reinforced central core 2,300ft long, 220ft high and 33ft thick. Both sides were heavily banked: by earth on the air side and by stone-faced hardcore on the water side. The bouncing bombs of 617 Squadron had made no impression at all the previous year but IX Squadron had inflicted some damage, bombing with Tallboys, a very different type of weapon. It had certainly been weakened as the Germans had to lower the water level. It had now been proved beyond doubt that the destruction of the Sorpe Dam was impossible from the air. Phil Tetlow quoted from the magazine *Flight*: 'An excellently-planned attack painstakingly conducted, which resulted in the most accurate piece of concentrated bombing ever accomplished.'

Coincidentally, it was the same day that the *Tirpitz* was making her slow, careful voyage from Kaafjord to Tromsø, hugging the coast as she rounded the islands of the Lopphavet.

The night after the Sorpe Dam operation, two aircraft took part in a night attack on the Westkapelle dyke, which was breached in two places. Explosions continued for twenty minutes after leaving the target and the fires were still visible from 140 miles away.

Nürnberg was the destination for nineteen Lancasters on 19 October. One failed to return and several reports contained criticism of the controller's instructions.

Just two aircraft took off from Bardney on 23 October, joining a large force that was once again bound for Flushing. Don MacIntosh and his crew were again selected for wind finding and the target was a batch of heavy guns that had only just been discovered as they had been so well camouflaged. Mac recalled that Jim had warned them that gunfire was likely to be intense as by this time the Wehrmacht was crowded into a small area. 'If you are in any doubt,' he advised, 'come back. There's always tomorrow.'[107] Phil Tetlow remembered that as they roared across Flushing at about 3,000ft, every type of gun imaginable was fired at them. Tracer shells 'climbed lazily' over their wing whilst light flak burst all around. They were forced to go round twice due to bad visibility and as they ran the gauntlet the second time they saw seven little parachutes floating down beneath. At last they were able to drop another precious 500ft and were able to identify their objective. Once they had bombed it, Mac manoeuvred them out of the inferno.

They were greatly relieved to learn the next day that there were to be no more raids on the 'Milk Run'.

Operation Obviate

The detailed plan code-named Operation Obviate was now coming into force. Word had got round that Air Vice-Marshal Sir Ralph Cochrane of 5 Group had been 'furious' that the *Tirpitz* had not been sunk in September but was determined that there should be another raid. Churchill had written to Admiral Cunningham of the Joint Planning Staff, emphasising that every effort had to be made to sink the *Tirpitz*, regardless of losses to men and aircraft. This time the battleship was just within range of airfields in Scotland but there would still have to be an incursion into Swedish airspace. After the first raid the Foreign Office had expressed sincere regrets 'for these regrettable incidents' following a formal complaint by the Swedish Government. The Swedes, however, did not follow it up.

By this time, it had become clear that the Germans were no longer the powerful force they had been at the beginning of the war. On

28 October, Hitler ordered the implementation of a scorched-earth policy in northern Norway. The last of the German troops were beginning to retreat south, destroying everything in their path, leaving Finnmark, a county the size of Denmark, devastated. Whole towns were destroyed. Some civilians were evacuated south in small fishing boats, negotiating the tricky waters of both the Inner Passage and the stretches of open sea during the increasingly dark days and nights of early winter above the Arctic Circle. On their arrival at the Lofoten Islands, there was little food or accommodation to spare. Many of the refugees were met with suspicion as no news of the devastation further north had reached the islanders. Babies were even born on the journey, labour brought on by rough seas and the harsh conditions. Although the west coast was heavily defended, the eastern border remained relatively free of controls, so a number of people were able to escape into Sweden with young children. Those Norwegians who had been unable to leave in time took shelter in coastal caves or dugouts, or in the iron mines in Kirkenes close to the Russian border. It was a particularly cruel Arctic winter. While desperately trying to avoid the retreating troops, people had to survive on what they could hunt or catch, returning to a style of life that had been abandoned centuries before. The enemy for everyone, troops and civilians alike, was now the climate. 'It is told that friend and foe sought shelter with each other in an attempt to survive' reads one of the captions in the Borderland Museum in Kirkenes, Finnmark.[108]

Tromsø had been spared as there were generous mooring facilities and billets were needed on the island for those sailors from the *Tirpitz* who were not required on the ship. The battleship was over 1,000 miles away from Britain but by using bases in Scotland it was just within range. A scoping document of 22 October set out the detailed procedures and requirements for the Scottish-based raids on the *Tirpitz*. It was followed the next day by a signal requesting forward-base facilities for Lancasters operating on or after 27 October. The airfields chosen were

Kinloss, Lossiemouth and Milltown; Scatsca in Shetland was also to be made available should any of the returning aircraft need emergency landing facilities. All these airfields were already familiar to Jim from his time as controller at Inverness.

Accommodation was needed for around 350 personnel including aircrew and accompanying ground crew. Essential supplies included 15,000 gallons of 100-octane, 500 gallons of oil, four starter trolleys and what was described as 'limited Messing'. Moving all personnel from Bardney and Woodhall Spa was in itself an exercise that required detailed planning. Both COs were to ensure an even distribution of engineers, signals, photographic and armament staff to each station. As soon as the operation was ordered, a total of about thirty HQ staff and essential maintenance personnel were to be flown to Lossiemouth in transport aircraft. Although a 617 Squadron Admin Order stated that 'Lancaster aircraft are each to carry two maintenance personnel,' none of the logbook entries refer to any additional ground crew being ferried to Scotland from Woodhall Spa. The need for Dakotas to ferry ground staff to Lossiemouth was also mentioned in the admin order and station commanders were also requested to give any extra help that was required to be supplied from station resources.

For the engineers at Bardney and Woodhall Spa there was still the problem of the fuel consumption for the round trip of over 2,000 miles; this was solved by fitting in the rear fuselage of the Lancasters standard ferry/overload tanks from Wellingtons, plus a 252-gallon Mosquito tank. The mid-upper turrets had already been removed for the long run to Yagodnik, so it raises the question of whether these had been restored for raids that had taken place between the two *Tirpitz* operations. Dr Robert Owen, Official Historian of 617 Squadron, suggests that this was not the case with the Lancasters at Woodhall Spa because of the serious amount of engineering work for a large number of aircraft that would have had to have been carried out at relatively short notice.

Even with these modifications, crews were advised that if they had fewer than 900 gallons left after the raid, they were to head for Russia.

Because of this additional weight the Lancasters would still be too heavy to take off so everything that could be spared was stripped. Dorsal gun turrets were removed, ammunition was dramatically reduced and even part of the armour plating behind the pilot's seat was taken out. The more powerful Merlin 24 engines were installed and paddle-blade propellers were fitted. Sourcing these was a huge job: around 120 engines were needed. Everything was removed that could be reasonably safely dispensed with. As they would be flying most of the time below 10,000 feet, even the number of oxygen bottles was pared down to the minimum. Doug Tweddle remembered that they were trying to do what was a 2,100-mile trip with 2,100 gallons. 'If you were getting a mile-a-gallon out of a Lanc you weren't doing too badly,' he wrote. 'This left us with no margin whatsoever. Even with the overload that risk was still there.'

Finally, in the early hours of 29 October, aircraft of IX and 617 Squadrons, armed with Tallboys, took off for RAF Lossiemouth and Kinloss in Scotland, with only enough fuel for the journey to keep the aircraft weight safe to land with the Tallboy on board. Fourteen Lancasters from IX Squadron landed at Kinloss: the squadron's remaining six were joined by eight aircraft from 617 Squadron at Lossiemouth. The other twelve from 617 Squadron touched down at Milltown. At the three airfields they refuelled, final checks were made, and the crews attended a briefing where they were given the most up-to-date Met information, before setting off in the evening for the flight to Tromsø.

Phil Tetlow felt that, especially after the problems encountered on the previous attack, it must have been a terrific strain on the meteorological experts who were trying to predict weather eight hours ahead for a region over 1,000 miles away in the Arctic Circle. At last they were given the go-ahead and at two o'clock on a mild morning on

29 October they were flying at 1,000ft over the Scottish coast. 'We only vaguely realised,' he remembered, 'that it would be twelve hours before we saw it again.' They settled down to the boring, four-hour flight across the North Sea, with no attempt at formation, as each aircraft was ordered to proceed independently to the rendezvous point. Roy Harvey remembered that it was not only to avoid German radar but also to save oxygen, which they knew was in limited supply.

Meeting up at a rendezvous in Swedish airspace, over a distinctively shaped lake, take-offs were spread over seventy-five minutes from 0130. Jim and his crew were among the last group at 0224, although the final two aircraft, piloted by Bill Williams and the Australian, Flying Officer K.S. Arndell, were even later, finally taking off at 0255.

At last, twenty Lancasters from the two squadrons assembled in bombing formation over Torneträsk Lake, Kiruna Municipality, close to the Norwegian border and approximately ninety miles south of Tromsø. Once they were in airspace over neutral Sweden, they again encountered flak when over Abisko, although it seems not to have been particularly accurate. The Luftwaffe base at Bardufoss was only forty-four miles south of where the *Tirpitz* was now anchored and close to their most direct flight path. If they were spotted, enemy aircraft would easily outpace and intercept them long before they even reached the *Tirpitz*. From Torneträsk Lake the Lancasters began the twenty-minute approach.

The final section along the Balsfjorden gave them a clear view of the target. Visibility was excellent, not only for the aircraft but also for the *Tirpitz*. The Lancasters were spotted from the ship while they were still over forty miles away, at about the same distance as Bardufoss and well before the final approach. If they were visible from Tromsø, it seems strange that there were apparently no sightings by the Luftwaffe. On a crystal-clear day, with no wind noise, the sound of such a large group of heavy bombers might well have travelled over a considerable distance, although Jim did comment that there was a westerly wind, which would have tended to have blown the sound away from Bardufoss. For whatever reason, no fighter aircraft were seen. 'Everything went off exactly as planned,' wrote Phil Tetlow:

> 'Ten miles away from Tromsø we left the formation and found our wind (a tricky business) which was then radioed in to the leader. Our timing was perfect and we joined the second force just as they were jockeying into position to start their run up. But something was going wrong! We could hear, over the R/T, the leader of No. 1 Force telling his men to go round again. I had been busy with the wireless up to now, but I took a quick look and soon realised the trouble. Patches of cloud were drifting over the ship, hiding her completely except when breaks gave us a glimpse of her guns blazing furiously and rapidly filling the sky with little black puffs.'

Just thirty seconds before the first bombing run, broken cloud at 6,000 feet had begun to drift over the area. Tony Iveson of 617 Squadron was the first to attack. Sightings became intermittent. Egil Lindberg, meteorologist and leading member of the local Norwegian Resistance, noted that, 'You could see the planes dive into the clouds and out, while the anti-aircraft guns exploded around them.'[109] The general feeling was that it was almost impossible to see the *Tirpitz* sufficiently clearly from the air to make a successful attack.

Jim led IX Squadron's attack at 0854, noting that the westerly wind had caused low stratus over the fjord and that the ship had appeared to be beached at one end.

All had been going well with Don MacIntosh's crew until they began their bombing run and encountered increasing cloud cover.

Don described how his bomb aimer Pete Ramwell gave corrections whenever he caught a glimpse of the ship through the layers of cloud:

> 'When still thirty or forty seconds short of our bomb-release line, he got a clear view of her and, brief though it was, it was enough for him to give a last-minute correction. Satisfied, he bombed, though only the bows of the ship were visible. She was completely obscured by the time our missile exploded, so we weaved furiously out of the barrage of flak, came down below the cloud to evade any lurking fighter, and started the long, weary, and uneventful trip back to Scotland. I intercepted a couple of messages from the leaders to base, stating that they had attacked but were unable to ascertain the damage done.'[110]

It is worth noting that the two squadrons used different types of bombsights. Roy Harvey described the techniques:

> '617 had the latest type which was very accurate, but required the bomb aimer to have a clear view of the target, whereas IX Squadron had the standard Mk XIV', (described by Doug Tweddle as 'a sort of geed-up bomb sight') which could use an offset aiming point (normally upwind of the target so that smoke and debris would not cover it). However, an accurate local wind was needed. To obtain this, four aircraft were nominated as wind finders. Each pilot chose a feature on the ground and then flew in a large circle to pass over the same feature on the same course as at the start. The navigator, by noting the air position indicator's readings when crossing the ground feature and the time elapsed then could calculate the wind speed and direction that had affected the aircraft at that point in time. These four winds were then passed to me to average out and produce the false wind settings for the bomb aimers.'

It is at this stage that reports began to be contradictory, and it is difficult to create a detailed account of the attack by collating the information in the ORBs. Some timings were recorded in GMT+1, others in GMT. An analysis of IX Squadron's ORBs suggests that the cloud layer was sufficiently broken to offer glimpses of the target. Jim went in at 15,500ft at 0854, recording that he had arrived late at the rendezvous point. He noted that the battleship appeared to be beached at one end. 'Lucky' Adams' crew report reads:

> 'Primary attacked 0755 hours [GMT]. 15,200ft. Battleship in graticule of bomb sight immediately prior to bombing. Target obscured by cloud at time of release, but position easily estimated.'

The report noted, however, that because only Adams was using oxygen, the results of the bombing could not be accurately assessed. Bill Williams, Deputy CO, making his run at the same time, reported that the centre of the ship was in the bomb sight. His rear gunner saw a direct hit on the ship's bows, followed by a big explosion and a column of brown smoke. Within the same time span, Benny Taylor observed thick brown/yellow smoke coming from amidships. He had also spotted bombs entering the water 'in several directions' about half a mile from the ship. Don MacIntosh, observing the scene during a small break in the clouds, reported that another aircraft seemed to have made a direct hit on the port side aft. It was later learned that this breach had caused 8,000 cubic metres of flooding. Normally, this would have caused considerable problems, but the strong currents in the fjord compensated for the inrush of water, helping to stabilise the ship.[111] If the current had been in the opposite direction, perhaps the results of this second raid might have been very different.

Flying Officer Larry Marsh's report was positive. On his bombing run at 0756, he observed that 'Ship seemed to be hit by one bomb near forward mast and billows of smoke resulted. Guns in forward section of ship then ceased firing'. Flying Officer Williams attacked two minutes later, reporting, 'Two hits seen on battleship, one in centre near superstructure and the other on bows. A third bomb seen to fall very near the bows.' Generally, though, broken cloud prevented detailed observation, even by the Lancaster that was photographing the attack. Flight Lieutenant A.M. Morrison and his crew had made four approaches before finally releasing their Tallboy on the fifth but saw no results because of thickening cloud.

Memoirs have to be treated with caution. Memories recalled decades later are not always totally accurate. Arndell was the only one who reported at the time that he had brought the bomb back because the cloud had completely obscured the ship. Doug Tweddle's report in the ORB reads, 'Primary attacked 0901 hrs 15,000ft. One large yellow flash seen after bombing', making it quite clear that the bomb had been released. However, in his memoirs of 1977, he reminisced:

> 'We had the same problem; he had this smoke cover and these fjords are notorious for their own private weather and when we flew in we couldn't see a damn thing so we just came back, again we brought the bomb back. I see that on 30 October I flew from Kinloss to base in two hours thirty mins to Bardney and brought the bomb back.'

Just as on the first raid, there had been no sightings of German enemy aircraft.

There is also a hidden story that might have had a very different outcome. The ORB shows that, while half the aircraft were back at base by 1445, four later arrivals stand out. Australian 'Jonah' Jones had received facial wounds when flak smashed in the left panel of the pilot's cupola. Jim, along with Doug Tweddle and Flying Officer Laws stayed with Jonah's Lancaster. As was the usual practice, his bomb aimer, who would have had some pilot training, had taken over. Jim, along with Doug Tweddle and Flying Officer Laws, stayed with the Lancaster to monitor the situation and give appropriate advice to the relatively inexperienced pilot. The order in which they landed is probably significant as it meant that he was guided in after the others were down safely: Doug Tweddle touched down at 1523, with the last three landing within the next nine minutes. Flying Officer Laws landed at 1527, Jim, at 1530, and Flying Officer A.F. Jones after another two minutes.

By the time the last aircraft had returned to the UK there could be no doubt that the raid had been unsuccessful in spite of strenuous and taxing efforts to sink 'the Beast'. There were a few who had only just made it with the narrowest of margins. After wireless operator Jack Faucheux sent out an SOS when on the approach to Shetland, a Catalina of Coastal Command guided them in to Sumburgh, where 'Lucky' Adams, the only member of the crew with oxygen, lived up to his nickname and landed just as his engines died. The hydraulic system had suffered damage, too, and they were only a few feet away from a Nissen hut when the Lancaster finally came to a stop.[112]

Jim had been airborne for just over thirteen hours; Doug Tweddle logged his flight as a total of thirteen hours ten minutes, remembering it was 'probably' one of his longest trips.

Tirpitz was still afloat and, according to the Film Unit crew of 463 Squadron, was still firing all her guns, including 'the heavies.' The mood on the return to base must have been dark and despondent. The long, cold, tiring and uncomfortable flight, the apparent invincibility of the German battleship, and the prospect of making yet another raid cast a long shadow over the crews. The only consolation was that all aircraft were back safely and there had been no losses or major injuries.

Chapter 8

13 November – 31 December 1944

Operation Catechism: The final raid on *Tirpitz*, more operations, and a curious incident

There was no time to brood. They were all back at Bardney the following day, with the aircrew making sure that everything was ready in anticipation of a third attempt. Opportunities to pay a return visit were diminishing by the day. After the equinox, the days in the north of Norway shorten by nearly ten minutes every twenty-four hours until the sun finally disappears below the horizon at the end of November. There were six and a half hours of daylight on 1 November but by the middle of the month, only four. Sunrise in Tromsø on 1 November is 0811, sunset 1442 and on 15 November, 0926 and 1329.

There was a day to relax before they were again busy with cross-country flights, practice bombing and air-tests involving seventeen crews. Because of bad weather they were grounded on 3 November but the next day, twenty-three Lancasters left Bardney for Kinloss and Lossiemouth expecting to make the return visit to attack the *Tirpitz*. Conditions proved unsuitable so they were back at Bardney by 6 November. Crews would have been keyed up waiting for more instructions but had to wait another week before twenty aircraft were bound for the north of Scotland again. On Armistice morning they were ordered to proceed post-haste to the advanced base in Scotland. Phil Tetlow remembered wondering inanely how the two-minutes silence affected them. 'That was the condition this target had reduced me to,' he wrote. 'I conjured up visions of the entire Luftwaffe waiting to pounce on us. I prayed for a last-minute cancellation.'

The plans laid out in the October scoping document were put into action for the second time. For whatever reason, the de-icing procedure at Kinloss failed to be completed, which meant that seven Lancasters, including those of Jim and Doug Melrose, whose bomb aimer Sammy Morris was credited with the only successful hit on the Kaafjord raid, were among those that were still in Scotland as they could not take off with the others. Doug Tweddle noted that, just 1,000 feet above them, temperature inversion meant crews saw the ice that had formed between de-icing and take-off melting quickly.

Jim's report of 12 November describes the third and final raid on the *Tirpitz*, masking the deep disappointment that was to stay with him to the end of his life that his aircraft was not de-iced in time to take part in the attack:

> '12/11 Thirteen aircraft took off at between 0300 and 0330 hours from advanced bases to attack the battleship "*Tirpitz*" anchored in Tromso fiord. Seven aircraft were unable to leave airfield being unserviceable through frost. Each of the attacking aircraft carried one 12,000lb Tallboy bomb. Aircraft were modified to carry overload petrol – no mid upper gunner being carried. Two of the aircraft were late on taking off, arriving late at the rendezvous point and subsequently did not proceed to the attack, but returned and brought bombs back. Attack on battleship was made by remaining eleven aircraft at between 0945 and 0948 hours and was made on a predetermined heading. Bombing was carried out from 14,000 to 16,000 feet. Crews reported clear weather conditions over target area and bombing was well concentrated around the target. Hit was observed amidships followed by explosion and fire, and

many near misses seen. One crew reported ship appeared to be listing to starboard with fire amidships. Flak opposition which was heavy at commencement ceased during attack. All aircraft returned to base with the exception of Flying Officer [Dave] Coster's aircraft which sustained engine damage over the target and made a forced landing in Sweden, all the crew being safe. Results were difficult to observe at conclusion of attack owing to smoke, but later reconnaissance photographs indicated that battleship had been sunk.

'Aircraft from 617 Squadron also participated in the attack. *CINE* photographs were taken by an aircraft from 463 Squadron (F/L. Buckham), but as the target was obscured by smoke *PHOTOGRAPHS TAKEN BY AIRCRAFT OF 9 SQUADRON* are not worth inclusion as exhibits.

'Numerous congratulatory messages were received.'

There is so much that is not said in this description, which is as usual couched in standard RAF format. There is no explanation as to why seven of IX Squadron's aircraft were not de-iced; it is simply stated as a fact. Was it perhaps that the task took longer than anticipated? Was it so cold that de-iced aircraft were quickly icing up again? Doug Tweddle remembered that the airfield was exposed and the night, pitch black and freezing, which would almost certainly have led to the task taking longer than anticipated. It was vital that de-icing was carried out with the greatest care. He emphasised that every inch of the runway was needed. Roy Harvey also recalled some of the problems:

'As the heavily overweight Lancasters would never get off the ground with frost on their wings the ground crew had to de-ice them on a bitterly cold night on a very exposed airfield. We finally took off at 0130. Even this was not without its problem for Bill [Williams] had great trouble getting the aircraft airborne... It was my job to call out the airspeed as the aircraft gained speed down the runway and on this occasion I have a strong recollection that we were running out of runway before Bill was able to "bounce" the aircraft off... Due to the weather conditions and the aircraft weight, our rate of climb was affected but we finally made it. We appeared to be affected by air pockets when the aircraft lost height suddenly.'

When interviewed by a journalist from the *Lincolnshire Observer* in 1969, Bob Riches recalled that 'after frantically scraping ice from the wings and control surfaces, we staggered into the air over Findhorn Bay into very rough weather'. He remembered that for the first part of the journey they flew with their navigation lights on, just above the sea, while being battered with rain and hail from the very low cloud base. Occasionally an aircraft ahead of them would drop a small red marker to check their position because of wind drift.

Group Captain McMullen took the difficult decision to break radio silence at this point. As Jim's aircraft would not be joining the raid, Bill Williams now learned he was to lead the squadron in the attack. The news that Jim was not part of the operation caused considerable consternation amongst the men of IX Squadron. Roy Harvey described the impact the message had on Bill Williams' crew:

'About four hours later, as we neared the Norwegian coast, I picked up a message telling our deputy controller to take over the leadership. This caused much speculation amongst the crew. Had our leader ditched? Been shot down? Suffered engine trouble? It was as though an alert had been sounded in our aircraft. Every man increased his vigilance, scouring the skies for the first signs of hostility... We were at least half-a-dozen aircraft short in our squadron! There was no time for questions.'

As they flew steadily towards the Norwegian coast Flight Lieutenant Pete Morgan, Bill's wireless operator, was watching as daylight crept into the winter sky. He was struck by the beauty of the scene. 'The air was so clear, the visibility marvellous, hardly a cloud to be seen and the ground snow-covered. We seemed to be just floating in the air.'[113]

Reality soon kicked in. As the squadrons sorted themselves out, Roy Harvey realised that others were missing and there were only eleven of IX Squadron aircraft preparing to get into formation:

'Not only did the squadrons have different bomb sights but also methods of attack. 617 Squadron attacked in small groups of three or four which I believe was to allow the maximum number to aim their bomb before the ship was covered by smoke from its guns and explosions of the bombs. IX Squadron, however, "in line astern" with the wind-finders joining at the rear.'

Remarkably, there had again been no sighting of enemy aircraft. Doug Tweddle vividly described the view. 'When we flew in over the coast, it was the most glorious day, snow on the hills and sunshine and to an ambitious fighter we would have looked like bugs on a white sheet.' He continued, 'Any two or three determined fighters would have seen off the force. To our good fortune, there were no fighters there.'

After the previous raids, it must surely have been a certainty that the Luftwaffe would have been on the alert for a further attack. Coincidentally, the twelve FW190s based at Bardufoss were 9 Staffel (Squadron), 5 Gruppe (Group). It was commanded by Heinrich Ehrler, one of the most-decorated Luftwaffe pilots, credited with 208 enemy aircraft shot down in over 400 combat missions, most of which were over the Eastern Front. German sources claimed that 'At no time was the commander informed that his unit's sole responsibility was the protection of the ship';[114] he had understood that his role was simply there to assist with training. Roy Harvey, writing over thirty years later, suggested that 'Reading between the lines, it would appear that a decision was made to let the pilots get to know each other over the weekend before they started their flying training on Monday.'

At 0800, word reached Bardufoss that Lancasters had been sighted twenty minutes earlier. Air-raid sirens were sounded at Bodø, some 160 miles to the south; plotting errors indicated the target as Hammerfest, eighty miles north of Tromsø, also contributed to the chaos of misinformation. At 0850, Ehrler entered his command post. He had planned to fly to Alta but was still on the ground forty-three minutes later, when there was another report of aircraft noise. Ehrler took off shortly afterwards just as the attack began on the *Tirpitz*, soon discovering that his radio transmitter was out of action. He then made a critical decision: observing 'to his left [in the direction of Tromsø] a distant mushroom cloud and anti-artillery bursts', he headed west, hoping to cut off the bombers. Curiously, his search of the coast yielded no sightings, so he continued to Alta. Officers on the *Tirpitz* had advance warning of the raid but the air cover that had been requested failed to materialise as the Luftwaffe squadron had been sent to Kaafjord, leaving them insufficient fuel to return to Tromsø and defend the battleship.

The commander of 9 Staffel had finally taken off at 0930 with the other aircraft. It was too late for them to intercept the Lancasters so they returned to Bardufoss. Ehrler was court-martialled, found guilty, relieved of his command, demoted and sentenced to three years imprisonment. The recommendation that had been made for the Iron Cross with Oak Leaves and Swords was withdrawn.

The author of an article on the internet suggests that the sentence might have been politically motivated. Göring, who had ordered the court-martialling of Ehrler, found that his influence had weakened while Dönitz was becoming more powerful. Ehrler's impressive combat record possibly saved him from execution and he was officially pardoned by Hitler, with his sentence commuted and his rank restored.

The six hours or more between the departure of the last aircraft from Scotland and the first message to be received after the raid must have seemed endless to those still on the ground. Uppermost in their minds must have been the knowledge that, with a fighter base so close to Tromsø, there was a high risk of heavy casualties. The minutes must have dragged. There can have been little or no sleep. They had been keyed up for the operation. Quantities of coffee were probably consumed. And, after months of planning, there must have been utter frustration, too, as they had been denied the opportunity of another attack on the ship that had so far resisted all attempts to sink her.

The first news to come through of the successful sinking of the great battleship must have been a huge relief, though tempered with the knowledge that not all the aircraft had been accounted for. Dave Coster and crew were missing. Pilot Officer C.E. Redfern's was the first Lancaster home at 1420 but there was a thirty-five-minute gap until George Camsell appeared. Most, however, were to land as it was beginning to get dark. The last to arrive was Larry Marsh at 1609. Separate accounts gradually formed into a coherent story.

The weather had been clear and 'the pride of the German navy' was completely visible, surrounded by a mass of lighter craft cramming on speed to get out of the target area. Bob Riches remembered being 'rather put off' by the fact that the battleship was firing at them with her main deck armament. 'Fortunately,' he continued, 'the elevation of the guns was limited.' They were soon out of the danger zone and into flak that he said was lighter than they were used to.[115]

German defences had been quickly launched but the artificial smokescreens were late and relatively ineffective. Willy Tait had led

617 Squadron at 0841 and, within the first ninety seconds, nine of their eighteen Lancasters had scored two direct hits and three near misses which fell within thirty metres of the *Tirpitz*. It was then the turn of IX Squadron led, in Jim's absence, by his second-in-command, Bill Williams. He watched the first four bombs, noting that one hit the battleship amidships, stopping the gunfire. Taking a last look, he could see three columns of smoke, indicating that there had been at least three hits. Four minutes after they had dropped their bombs, they were on their way home. In Larry Marsh's Lancaster, there had been a close shave. A fragment from a shell had exploded in front of the Lancaster, piercing the Perspex blister where the bomb aimer, J. Allen Carr, was preparing for the run up. In spite of flak splitting his flying jacket from wrist to elbow, he released the Tallboy but reported that it had undershot, hitting the water near the side of the ship.

Pete Ramwell discovered that his automatic computer box was out of order. He asked Mac if he could go round again to give him time to work out his own computations. As they turned slowly in a wide circle, they had a grandstand view of the action and could watch some of the 12,000lb missiles as they were released. None seemed to have hit the vessel, although all seemed very close. By the time Pete was all set to go, they turned into their bombing run, 'scarcely daring to breathe', in case they disturbed Pete's run up. As the bomb was released, the Lancaster gave a convulsive jerk. The Tallboy sped down to its target almost three miles below. There was a tremendous explosion about twenty yards away from her on the port side. They had missed but wondered if they had inflicted serious damage. Then the rear gunner shouted, 'Skip, she's on fire!' Mac banked and they could see a mighty blaze raging amidships. There was another explosion and then – yes – they watched as she keeled over slowly! They cheered and laughed and sang, then fell to feverishly discussing whether the Germans would be able to repair the so-called 'invincible battleship' or whether they had put her out of action for good.

It took only four minutes for the rest of IX Squadron to drop their bombs on the wounded battleship. Doug Tweddle was among the first to drop his Tallboy at 0945. He reported that it had hit the fjord side of the vessel and that only one flak gun was seen to continue firing. 'We were still over the area,' he noted, 'when we saw the *Tirpitz* start to roll over. I knew before we got back to Lossiemouth when we were shown pictures taken later by a Spitfire that the *Tirpitz* had been sunk.'

As Larry Marsh turned his Lancaster out to sea, Bob Riches spotted a group of four or five twin-engined aircraft circling above the mountains. He thought they might have been Ju88s and was greatly relieved to watch them heading east without attacking. 'It was a lucky break for us,' he wrote. 'Presumably they had been recalled. If they had attacked us,' he continued, 'it would have been a massacre, for those of us who were not shot down would never have made it back to base due to the very small reserve of fuel.'

Within eleven minutes of the first bomb hitting the battleship, she had capsized. Around the wreck was a great pool of burning oil. Rescue was hampered by the torpedo nets that surrounded the ship but as soon as they were cut a swarm of vessels rescued any of the battleship's crew who had been on deck.

Bruce Buckham's crew had filmed the whole raid, flying over the area for nearly thirty minutes. As they were about to leave, his rear gunner, Eric Gierch, called out that the ship seemed to be turning over, so they circled at fifty feet, watching intently as *Tirpitz* heeled over to port, 'ever so slowly and gracefully.'[116] Below was utter chaos. Men leapt from the capsizing ship into the icy waters. One of the sailors, a signaller called Johann Tröger, was on a rescue boat when he saw Bruce Buckham's aircraft overhead. 'There you are', he said to a man standing next to him. 'They've come back to make sure we're really finished and take a picture of us.' Some of those trapped in the hull were rescued but many more died slowly in the bitterly cold blackness as oxygen was gradually used up.

As soon as Bill Williams' aircraft was clear of the coast, wireless operator Pete Morgan sent a message to report that the attack had been accomplished. They then descended to 3,000-4,000 feet above the sea and turned on a southerly course back to Lossiemouth. 'The weather was still beautiful,' he remembered, 'and, as on the previous occasion, we knew that if damaged or low on fuel we could cross over Norway and land in Sweden. In addition, a Royal Navy destroyer was on station about halfway to pick up any crew who by then were running low on fuel and ditched close by.'

With 800 or 900 miles still to go, it was vital to take the most direct course. Roy Harvey commented that normally all members of the crew could now relax. The pilot could use 'George' (the autopilot). The flight engineer could keep a check on his dials to make sure the engines were running correctly and economically. The navigator could get the bomb aimer to take an occasional drift to check that his course was correct before coming into 'GEE' range, and the wireless operator would listen to receive any messages. Finally, the rear gunner could admire the view (water, water and more water) and keep an eye open for any other aircraft. However, there was a major problem – 'GEE' was u/s. 'To check that we were on track instead of an occasional drift,' he noted, 'I needed a regular one every 15-20 minutes.' For the bomb aimer to provide this it was necessary for him to squeeze into his bomb aiming position and, lying prone, to use his bomb sight. In flying kit this was quite difficult and after getting the drift, reversing the procedure. He would just about get settled in the cockpit and 10-15 minutes later would have to go through the procedure again and again. After the third or fourth time, Sandy in the rear turret reminded Roy that he could provide the drifts using his gun sight, so Fred was relieved of the task.

He also described a rather unsettling incident that occurred after they had passed the destroyer. A Lancaster from the other squadron was approaching from behind them:

> 'He caught us up and formatted closely on our starboard side, wing-tip to wing-tip, so close that Bill commented as to what did the pilot think he was doing. (It dawned on me afterwards that he was trying to make Bill break away – it would have been a good story to tell in the mess and worth a laugh when they returned to Woodhall Spa.) When the pilot realised that Bill was not going to oblige, he returned to his original course and moved off to starboard. At this point, bearing in mind that I had no "GEE" and that we were expecting cloud over the last leg of the journey, the thought did go through my mind to suggest to Bill that we follow the 617 aircraft, but my pride wouldn't let me do so. So we plodded on with Sandy continuing to provide me with drifts.'

As they approached the Shetland Islands, Larry Marsh's wireless operator, Ian 'Twitcher' Davis, reported that he had intercepted a message from Wing Commander Tait which roughly said, 'Missed, sorry but we will have to go again.'[117] Bob Riches added that, because of some problems at Lossiemouth, they were diverted to Kinloss where they were bussed to the briefing room for interrogation:

> 'We reported to the interrogation officer of the demise of the *Tirpitz*. The news swept through the room and we were greeted by jeers of derision by the nearby 617 crews. Obviously not one of the 617 crew had reported this observation.'

As 617 Squadron had been in the first wave, Bob Riches added that they would not have seen the end of the attack due to the smoke over the target.

Bill Williams had experienced a difficult take-off twelve and a half hours earlier. On his return to Lossiemouth just before 1600, he was faced with another problem when the throttle on the starboard outer engine had stuck partly open, causing them to veer off the runway. Thankfully, Bill managed to rectify the problem, steadying the Lancaster and landing safely. As they taxied to their dispersal, Roy Harvey remembered that 'a very happy ground crew' told them that news of the success had already been broadcast on the radio.

He went on to recall that the debriefing by Wing Commander Tait and 'Groupy' McMullen was followed by eggs and bacon, greatly welcome as, in spite of the long flight, they had been given only a few extra sandwiches and coffee over and above the usual flying rations.

It was only now that Don MacIntosh learned why aircraft had been left on the ground at Lossiemouth:

> '"Mac", Nigel said. "You know you were worried about not seeing anyone over Norway? Well, half the chaps didn't take off. There was hard frost during the night, and Bazin told the ground engineer to de-ice all the aircraft, but he decided he knew better and thought it wouldn't be necessary. He was last seen walking towards the sea," he said with a grin.'[118]

The administration notes by Flying Officer R.C. Pugh in the ORB leap off the page in a highly individual style, owing more than a little to the Old Testament. The comment describing it as 'the outstanding operation of the month' is, however, rather modest:

> 'As it is now known this operation was completely successful and was in no doubt the outstanding operation of the month, and when it became known at the station great jubilation was evident among the ground crews, the extra work called for being thought well worthwhile.'

The next sentence reverts to RAF reportage. 'Later in the month the aircraft were de-modified (extra fuel tanks removed and mid-upper turrets re-fitted).'

They partied that night. Doug Tweddle remembered that 'it was ol' McMullen (Groupy McMullen) who put a blank cheque on the bar, saying to the boys, "Drink that lot off!".' It was probably memorable although, as Thorburn comments, 'Hardly anyone **could** remember'. Many years later, Phil Tetlow recalled that Jim 'was as drunk as a newt':

> 'In the Mess, pandemonium was raging. Everybody was hopelessly drunk. Eventually we managed to corner our skipper and he explained that the only thing left of the *Tirpitz* was her backside sticking up out of the water! I can remember nothing more of that gloriously chaotic evening.'

The story was not quite over. Back at Bardney on 13 November, Jim, along with Sandy Watts, Bill Williams and Roy Harvey were photographed on the airfield. It was an image that appeared in newspapers around the world.

Congratulations began to arrive. Considering his obsession with 'The Beast', Churchill's telegram was brief but to the point, and simply read, 'Heartiest congratulations to All'. King George was slightly more expansive, conveying congratulations to 'all those who took part in the daring and successful attack on the *Tirpitz*'. Lord Trenchard sent his heartiest congratulations and thanks to all who took part in sinking the *Tirpitz*. The Admiralty telegram was more forthcoming:

> 'Request you will convey our warmest congratulations and thanks to those concerned in this very successful attack on the *Tirpitz* today. It was a good job well done'.

The Norwegians were, of course, particularly delighted as the German defences of the Norwegian coastline had been considerably reduced. The destruction of the *Tirpitz* had also removed the constant threats encountered by the supply convoys. Crown Prince Olaf ended his message of congratulations by sending on behalf of the Norwegian forces their heartiest thanks and admiration.[119]

However, it is the personal message from the Chief of Air Staff that captures the mood of the moment:

> 'I have just heard of the splendid achievement of 9 and 617 Squadrons in sinking the *Tirpitz*. Please pass to them my warmest congratulations and my expression of unbounded admiration which I feel for their skill, courage and perseverance now so happily crowned with full success. Apart from the effect on the war at sea of the permanent removal of the most powerful unit of the German Navy, this exploit will fill the whole German nation with dismay at a critical time and will enhance the fame of Bomber Command and the Royal Air Force throughout the world'.

The feeling was, in Doug Tweddle's words, that it was 'a great weight off our backs.' When Sir Archibald Sinclair arrived at Bardney to congratulate the squadron, many of the crews had already left for a well-deserved forty-eight hours leave:

> 'The station mustered all the other people, all the aircrew and ground crew, who hadn't been on the trip, put them in the big hangar... Sir Archibald Sinclair told them what a wonderful bunch of guys they were and no one was any the wiser. I mean, that's all right: he felt happy and we didn't mind. We were at home.'

The successful destruction of the *Tirpitz* made worldwide headlines. Regional newspapers in Britain and further afield featured many of the airmen who had taken part in the operation. It was described as perhaps the most dramatic achievement of Bomber Command, skilfully planned and courageously executed and likely to have far-reaching consequences. The battleship that survived numerous attacks was now lying on her side in waters in the north of Norway. For the people of Belfast it was a reminder that only a generation before, the Harland and Wolff shipyard had seen the launch of another 'unsinkable' ship, the *Titanic*. Newspapers published in the city were keenly aware of the psychological impact, describing the sinking as a success of the first order. A fortnight after the event, the *Belfast Telegraph* referred to an item in the *Stockholms Nyheter*, describing how a refugee from Tromsø, who had watched the whole attack from a nearby viewpoint, had seen three direct hits on the battleship, one amidships, echoing the words of Bill Williams. There was naturally a technical interest too for their many readers who were employed at the Belfast shipyards. They quoted Swedish reports that described how the battleship's double bottoms had been filled up with concrete in the patching up. 'If this was so,' continued the article, 'it probably affected her equilibrium adversely when the three earthquake bombs hit her fair and square on Monday.'

In spite of the euphoria, it was back to the routine of practice bombing, air tests and air/sea firing and days when the ORB recorded, 'Nothing particularly interesting worth mentioning from a historical point of view'. After the success of the sinking of the *Tirpitz*, the full force of the dark days of November brought bad weather and, no doubt, a sense of great anti-climax. The ground crews were kept busy with the task of restoring the aircraft to their previous specification. Operations did take place, including one to the Dortmund-Ems Canal on 21 November. In spite of briefing five crews for a raid on Trondheim, only three took off with nine 1,000lb bombs. However, no attack took place. The last operation of the month was on 26 November when fifteen crews flew as part of a massed raid on Munich. When conditions allowed, the familiar routine of practice bombing, cross-country and fighter affiliation resumed in the last few days of November.

December 1944

As the weather was generally poor at the beginning of December, the first few days began fairly quietly for most of the crews. Five aircraft returned safely from a large-scale raid on Heilbronn on 4 December when, it is believed, over 6,500 people were killed in the one night. Doug Tweddle remembered that, in spite of the specialised targets, the squadron still had to continue with main force general work, though not always involving the experienced crews. 'The more senior crews were becoming more clued-up about Tallboy dropping,' commented Doug Tweddle, rather modestly. 'New crews were cutting their teeth on the main force targets,' he continued. 'The older boys were more useful for the Tallboy targets.'

As younger crews came in, and they were flying on different raids, they manned the aircraft that were usually allocated on a regular basis to experienced crews. When Flying Officer R. Ayrton, a young Australian, was briefed to fly 'Y' Youngers, Doug Tweddle's response was to give him 'a hell of a briefing' about what he must not do to it:

> 'To be fair to the lad, he got himself as equally devoted to "Y" Youngers as I was myself and he did a good job and kept it out of trouble for which I'm very grateful. Later on, he became someone much more clued-up himself and I'm not quite sure if he in turn didn't get allocated the aircraft. You couldn't

monopolise these. You couldn't say, "That's mine and when I'm not flying and when I'm on leave, no one else can have it."'

In fact, Doug had taken over 'Y' when she had already completed twelve trips. He went on to fly thirty-seven operations on 'Youngers' and he understood that she probably completed over eighty in all.

There were again a number of instances when crews were briefed for an operation, only for it to be cancelled, particularly during the middle of December. Doug was very aware of the problems this created for the armourers:

> 'So you can imagine our armourers had a hell of a rough time, because they would bomb up the kites for the Tallboys; they were so heavy that they used to have a special trolley with hydraulic pumps on the end of it and they would load that up onto the kite and then someone would say, "Oh! That trip's cancelled. Take it down and bomb it up for fifteen ones or a Cookie and something for a general target." And they'd have changed their minds again and down came the armourers. I don't think they got any sleep.'

Jim was obviously conscious of the pressures the ground crews were under. On the occasional weekend stand down, he would go round all the crews and extract 'a quid apiece' from them. 'We're giving the armourers a drink tonight at the "Jolly Sailor",' he would tell them. Doug Tweddle recalled that they would all go into Bardney and get the armourers drunk, because they worked very hard. 'All of them did,' he said, 'but in particular they had a bit of a job.'

It was not just the armourers who had long and hard days. Much of the everyday repair and maintenance by the ground crew was carried out at dispersals, entailing a bicycle ride from the living quarters. A ten-hour day was standard, which did not include other duties such as airfield guard and fire-watch duties.

Five crews from the squadron took part in an attack on the Urft Dam on 8 December with few results. Three days later, on 11 December, Jim led twenty crews on another raid on the dam. Cloud cover restricted visibility and, although actual hits were claimed, several near misses resulted in damage to the spillway. Twenty-nine minutes separated the first and last bombs dropped by the squadron. Jonah Jones reported that he had flown over the target area for twenty-five minutes before releasing his bomb. Thirty seconds later Jim went in at 1533, reporting that their bomb had overshot and no direct hits were seen, although some water was over the dam and 'accordingly believed breached'. 'It was,' recalled Phil Tetlow, 'a very different effort to our last masterpiece'. He went on to explain that the American whirlwind advance was halted at a point near Clochen because High Command had received information that the dam, which was directly in the path of the advance, was to be destroyed once our troops came within range of the pent-up fury of the waters that would be unleashed by the dam's destruction.

Two hundred Lancasters had taken part in each of the two raids, but on both occasions they had encountered problems with scattered patchy cloud. Despite many direct hits, the dam remained intact. Phil Tetlow remembered that, despite this, 'the enemy were so demoralised that we were able to occupy the area before the proposed destruction could be carried out.' He considered that the sortie was one of military tactics rather than air strategy.

The weather intervened yet again. On each of the next five days from 12-16 December crews were briefed, only for operations to be cancelled. For example, on 16 December, twenty-one crews had to deal with a number of delays before they finally received news that they were to stand down. The previous day, the station officers had taken advantage of a thick mist that had formed during the afternoon to hold a Mess party in the evening. However, there was some cheerful news to report in the ORB, which recorded that it was a notable day in the squadron history. Word had been received of the immediate awards of nine DFCs and one DFM, together with the promotion of three officers to the rank of acting flight lieutenant.

Awards to Bill Williams, Doug Tweddle, Don MacIntosh and Ed Stowell recognised four of the seven pilots who had taken part in all three raids on the *Tirpitz*. The DFM was to Flight Sergeant Arthur Horry, the bomb aimer in Bill Williams's crew.

It could be that it was about this time that there was a curious incident when Jim behaved completely out of character and he seems to have broken his leg. Don MacIntosh placed it much earlier, soon after the attack on La Rochelle, but it is unlikely to have been then as Jim had been back in the air three or four days later on the raids on Brest. There is, however, a considerable gap in his logbook between 11 December and 3 February, which could be explained by his being out of action and unable to fly.

According to Don MacIntosh, a mess party had been organised, the hut was decorated with streamers, 'food had been rustled up from somewhere' and everybody wore their best blue:[120]

> '"I'd stand back a bit Mac if I were you," said Nigel and pointed upwards. Across the ceiling of the building were open girders, on top of which a pair of Canadian ex-lumberjacks leapt about, sure-footed like mountain goats, one even balancing a pint of beer on his head while standing up. They came down to great applause and then, to our surprise, the Wingco, Jim Bazin, normally the most serious-minded of men, climbed the girders, saying with spirit that anything the Canadians could do, the Brits could also do. Most of us would have disagreed with him.'

Mac described how Jim swayed slightly onto the girders, remarking that it was in itself a feat for a man of his size, age and agility. The Canadians climbed up again and passed him a pint of beer. 'He stood tall on the narrow girder,' wrote Mac, 'raising his tankard in victory and smiling benignly at us all.' All noise stopped. All eyes were raised upwards. Jim stood poised in triumph for at least five seconds, defying gravity and prudence; then, said Mac, 'slowly, like a giant tree, he swayed, gently at first, then fell, still holding his tankard, with an almighty crash on the floor.' His fall was greeted with loud cheers until the Medical Officer announced that Jim had broken his leg and he was carried off the field 'like a fallen Greek warrior.'

This behaviour was certainly out of character but perhaps had been triggered by childhood memories. During their brief stay in Montreal, Jim and his sisters and brother had been challenged by their Canadian cousins to hockey games on the polished floor of their uncle's hall. If the lumberjacks had been from Australia or New Zealand, the urge to try to equal the feat would perhaps not have been quite so powerful.

According to Don MacIntosh, Jim recovered quickly. A day later he was back in command, complete with sticks and in plaster. 'The Canadians attended him assiduously,' he commented. 'One young gunner stayed in his quarters to keep his fire going and run errands for him when his batwoman went off duty.'

The Bavarian capital of Munich had already been the subject of numerous attacks when, just a week before Christmas, twenty-two crews took part in yet another raid. The route to the target was circuitous as they went the long way round to approach the city from the south. They flew past Mont Blanc and Doug Tweddle remembered seeing it so clearly that it looked like a photograph. They then flew over the northern plain of Italy to Milan before turning north and coming up to Munich via the Brenner.

The route also took them over neutral Switzerland. Unlike their flights over Sweden, they encountered no interference. 'The lights of Zurich twinkled peacefully underneath us on our left', remembered Don MacIntosh. 'Incongruously, I saw the red and green of traffic lights changing in the clear Alpine air.' On such a long flight it was important to stick to the timings to keep clear of night fighters. Fred Whitfield remembered it as 'a nightmare of a trip'. 'The Skipper could not get the Lancaster above 18,000ft in order to clear the snow-capped Alps,' he reminisced. 'Our altitude should have been 22,000ft. It goes without saying that everyone's eyes were constantly on the lookout for anything ahead.' The bombing run had to be made through a line of searchlights about ten miles apart. After all that, the bomb failed to release and had to be jettisoned. The squadron attacked over a period of thirteen minutes, with fifteen of the twenty-two aircraft dropping their bombs between 1001 and 1008. Although three suffered flak damage, all returned safely. Each area was bombed on an individual heading, which Don MacIntosh believed was to make sure that 'each part of the city got its fair share.'

On the flight home, crews reported seeing the city of Ulm on fire after an attack by 4 Group the same night. Don MacIntosh and his crew had just an hour's flying over German territory before reaching friendly airspace. 'I reckon you're well inside our lines', reported Nigel. 'I've got today's *Daily Express* map of the front line and we passed that about ten minutes ago.' Don's crew had found that the information given to them by the Intelligence Officer was often wrong, so his navigator Nigel had come to rely more on maps in newspapers, particularly the *Daily Express*, for information. As Don engaged the autopilot and prepared to have a very welcome coffee, there was a tremendous bang immediately underneath, followed by the 'chain lash' of shrapnel striking the metal skin of the fuselage. They decided it must have been fire from the trigger-happy Americans, who had spotted an aircraft coming from Germany, and had assumed it was an enemy aircraft.

The route to Gdynia the next night was another long flight, taking them over the North Sea, neutral southern Sweden and out into the Baltic. The target was the heavy cruiser *Lutzow*. Doug Tweddle's crew was on wind-finding in the bay off Königsberg (now Kaliningrad, Russia). Doug noted that it was the only occasion when they 'not only got a fixed point in which to orbit [but] my rear gunner got a flame float[121] out on the water and used that as a fixed point.' Six crews took part in another raid on the night of 21-22 December; this time their target was J.G. Farbe's synthetic-oil plant in Pölitz, just north of Szczecin, a target Jim described as very important. As Bardney was fogbound, five of the aircraft returned to airfields at Peterhead, Fiskerton and Lossiemouth, but, tragically, Curly Read's aircraft crashed on landing at Coningsby, with two fatalities, the flight engineer and the bomb aimer. As Bardney was fog-bound, they had been re-routed to Coningsby airfield, which was a FIDO (Fog Investigation and Dispersal Operation) and only ten miles from Bardney, but Curly had asked if it was possible to land at Bardney. On the second approach, they hit a tree and crashed. The rear turret broke and Jack Linaker jumped out into a potato field, about 200yds from the bulk of the wreckage. Curly survived, although with a fractured skull. Before going for a medical check-up, the walking wounded went to the sergeant's Mess for a cup of tea. Jack commented that the WAAF nearly fainted when she saw the state they were in. After a fortnight's leave, Jack was teamed up with Ray Harris's crew.

Bardney was still beset by thick fog over Christmas. A squadron conference was held on 23 December. Christmas Eve saw the beginning of a cold spell with twelve degrees of air frost on 28 December.

Although a briefing was held on 30 December, the operation was cancelled, so the final raid of 1944 had already taken place when five crews were part of a raid on 28-29 December against shipping in the Moss area of southern Norway, a particular target being a vessel near Kambø near the mouth of the Oslofjord. It was believed to have been successful. All returned safely.

This, then, was the sixth New Year's Eve of the war. Most of the crews now flying had only been in their early teens when war had been declared. Jim had turned thirty-one at the beginning of the month and was a decade older than many of the men under his command. His first combat experience over the north-east of England in October 1939 must have seemed in the distant past. Against all the odds, he had survived the Battles of France and Britain and, since May 1944, had carried out twenty-three bombing raids over France, Germany and Norway. Although the future was beginning to look a little brighter, there was still no certainty as to when or how the war was likely to end.

Chapter 9

January and February 1945

A disastrous New Year, a VC for George Thompson, Bergen U-boat pens, synthetic oil refineries, railway bridges and viaducts

1 January 1945

The New Year began badly.

Just as the Mess party was about to begin on New Year's Eve, orders came through that the squadron was 'on' for the next day. The next morning all those who were not flying formed a small group at the take-off end of the runway to wave the crews off in the time-honoured way. The destination was the Dortmund-Ems Canal. As a consequence, it was a regular target as it was a heavily defended major supply route for barges carrying coal, iron ore and other vital raw materials to the factories in the Ruhr. There would always be a line of barges waiting to pass through the canal. As soon as it was repaired, there would be another attack. 'This meant,' wrote Roy Harvey, 'that very little notice could be given to the squadrons.' This was the case on New Year's Day, 1945.

Because of the short notice, only ten crews had been briefed and were ready for take-off. 'The night,' Roy recalled, 'was bitterly cold.' Flying Officer Harry Denton was the first to take off at 0744. Three minutes later, Flying Officer Cliff Newton was away, but Roy noticed that he seemed to be having engine trouble. Almost immediately there was a brilliant flash as the Lancaster crashed and the bomb load exploded. 'There was a huge "Woomph!" and a great flash of fire some distance away,' remembered Flying Officer Dennis Nolan. 'I just said on the intercom what everyone thought. Some poor sod at Woodhall had gone in. Woodhall Spa, base for 617 Squadron, was six or seven miles away. But it wasn't. It was Newton, not that we knew.'[122]

Terry Lintin, a Bardney resident who became an unofficial historian of IX Squadron, remembered the crash. 'The aircraft had been bombed and fuelled up for three days due to bad weather,' he recalled. 'Water had formed in the fuel due to condensation and the plane lost power after take-off.' It seemed that the pilot banked to port to avoid the village and possibly in an attempt to regain the emergency runway. 'He didn't make it and crashed in a field,' he continued. 'The plane caught fire and blew up. There were 12,000lbs of bombs on board. There was one survivor.'[123]

That one survivor was Canadian Flying Officer Paddy Flynn, the bomb aimer.

Three minutes later at 0750 it was Flying Officer Jack Buckley's turn to take off. Just as they were about to leave the ground, Dennis Nolan noticed two red warning lights illuminate, so shouted to Jack, who ordered 'Cut'. Fortunately, Flight Engineer Ken Dawes was very quick to cut all four engines. Dennis commented later that they had only been a couple of seconds away from an almighty prang. Had they been even a few feet higher, it would have been the tip of the wing that would have touched the ground and, in Dennis Nolan's words, they would have been cartwheeling down the runway, 'with bombs and bodies everywhere.' They were not out of trouble, however. He commented that the Lancaster was an aircraft that was keen to get off the ground and they had almost reached airspeed. 'As the speed dropped,' he remembered, 'the ride got bumpier and bumpier, from near-hover to jolting and banging along.' There was a Lancaster at dispersal with her navigation lights on. The two crews watched each other helplessly in mutual horror as they thundered towards the stationary aircraft. On the airfield's border there was a heap of soil about three feet high, which Dennis described as 'a nice launching pad for a speeding Lanc.' The wheels were torn off as they took off again and continued, hitting a line of young trees in Scotgrove Wood, which slowed them down, but caused only minor damage. They waited with bated breath for an explosion, but all was quiet. At last, they stopped and there was silence.[124]

Dennis Nolan climbed out on to the wing but, as it was dark, he could not get his bearings. Other members of the crew were leaping for safety. He remembered the overpowering smell of petrol and the red-hot glow from the engines. The pilot was sitting on the rim of the escape hatch, heaving up Ken Dawes, who 'was shouting like mad' because his leg was broken. Sergeant Copperwaite, the rear gunner, was trapped and someone grabbed an axe to chop him out of the rear turret.

They waited for help, but it was a while coming as all the rescue teams had gone to the other crashed aircraft. 'They never did identify the cause of the engine failure,' reminisced Dennis Nolan. 'Frozen water in the fuel seemed the most likely possibility.' They had had a miraculous escape.

The remainder of the squadron was then put on hold until taking off at intervals of two of three minutes between 0808 and 0819. By that time their engines had been warmed at idle for an extra thirty minutes. Why had Harry Denton managed to take off without any problems? Richard James has suggested his Lancaster may have been at the far end of the airfield so there had been more time to warm up.

Don MacIntosh had been on leave and on his return, heard about it from Alec Ritchie:

> '"It was the cold that did it, Mac," he said, "the aircraft hadn't been flown for a week and we had the coldest weather anyone could remember. Well, at the crash they found ice in the fuel

filters and what must have happened is that a solid chunk broke off and temporarily blocked the flow to engines at full power." He smiled. "Don't worry, it's alright now, they've pushed out a notice about it. I don't think it'll happen again."'[125]

Having lost the two aircraft that had crashed on take-off, a further two Lancasters, piloted by Flying Officer P.W. Reaks and Harry Denton, failed to return from the raid. It was only the next day that they heard that Harry's aircraft had been attacked and seriously damaged over the target at Ladbergen. It was much later that they learned the whole story:

> 'Just after releasing the bombs, they were hit by flak which started a fire inside the fuselage fed by hydraulic fluid being sprayed under great pressure from broken pipes under the Lancaster's floor. Wilf Hartshorn made a futile attempt to extinguish the inferno with a small hand-held extinguisher, but it had no effect. He made his way forward to the escape hatch in order to abandon the aircraft. He was stopped by the Skipper who made hand gestures to indicate that he should hang on as they still had engines running. A second shell blew out all the cockpit glazing, which at least had the effect of clearing the smoke and, eventually, the hydraulic oil reservoir emptied and the fire subsided somewhat.'[126]

Sometime afterwards, Harry Denton recorded his account of the events.[127] The outward flight had been trouble free, and he met up at the pre-arranged rendezvous without any delay. 'The Spitfire escorts,' he remembered, 'were like excited children round their mother.' There had been bursts of flak when they reached the Rhine. The air was so clear that the stretch of water that marked the Dortmund-Ems Canal was visible well before the attack. It was a fairly long run in but, as the bomb was released, things changed dramatically. 'There was a terrific blast,' he recalled, 'the aircraft shook violently and filled with smoke'. Once it had cleared, he realised that the communications had been smashed and could see – and feel – that the canopy was shattered. The starboard engine was on fire, but the flames were doused straightaway by the automatic fire extinguisher. Harry's priority now was to make it safely to Allied-held France or Holland. The three remaining engines were now on full throttle but, because the trimming tabs were damaged, the aircraft was tail heavy, and they were steadily losing height. They limped through the sky for almost an hour with the bomb doors swinging open and both gun turrets ablaze. 'How lucky I had been,' he thought.

His problems were not over. Suddenly he saw three enemy aircraft flying towards him head-on. He thought the end had come. 'To my amazement,' he mused, 'they passed us 200yds to port'. He concluded that they must have run out of ammunition. As they neared Arnhem, they were on the receiving end of more flak mingled with tracer bullets. Harry had to make several more steep dives and changes of course. One of the port engines was also now on fire. When it was extinguished, Harry commented that it balanced the aircraft a little better, but they were still losing height at 500ft a minute, and now only had four minutes flying time left.

Harry Denton, by now badly frostbitten, was desperately trying to keep the aircraft aloft. At this point, as he was trying to identify somewhere he could put the Lancaster down, a flight of Spitfires 'swooped in' to warn him about high-tension cables just ahead. Barely managing to avoid them, he spotted a suitable place, a couple of paddocks close to a Dutch village. By now 'the old aircraft was wobbling badly' and Harry felt that one wheel was still down. Fortunately, it collapsed as he made a pancake landing, slithering along until they hit a bank.

He waited for the aircraft to catch fire or explode and was greatly relieved to see petrol oozing away on the soft ground. Against all the odds, he had made a remarkable landing, which, together with the skill in keeping the Lancaster aloft in spite of all the damage, would earn him a DFC.[128]

While Harry Denton was still fighting to keep the Lancaster aloft, he had believed that fighters were still attacking them. Wireless Operator, Flight Sergeant George Thompson knew differently. The heat was setting off the Lancaster's own ammunition. The events are recounted in the citation for the Victoria Cross that Thompson was awarded posthumously. He saw that the fire in the mid-upper turret was burning fiercely and had fought his way down the fuselage through the exploding ammunition. He was already suffering terrible burns to his face, hands and legs. There had been no other way to extinguish the flames as the blankets supplied as standard equipment to douse fires were themselves burning fiercely. More details emerged once they were on the ground. The VC citation emphasised some of the challenges he faced.

> 'It was difficult enough crawling around a Lancaster when it was stationary. There were obstacles everywhere and no movement was exactly free. It was ten times worse when your space, already confined and awkward, was lit by fire, ventilated by a freezing hurricane and set with traps like exploding machine-gun bullets and a gaping hole big enough to drop through.'

With extraordinary determination, George Thompson had managed to drag the unconscious Mid-upper Gunner, Sergeant Ernie Potts, through the damaged fuselage to a place of relative safety. 'With great difficulty,' notes the VC citation, 'he extricated the helpless Gunner and carried him clear. Again, he used his bare hands, already terribly burnt, to beat out flames on a comrade's clothing.' It was now that he realised that the rear turret was also on fire. Battling his way back through the fuselage, he succeeded in rescuing Sergeant Haydn J.T. Price, the Rear

Gunner, pulling him from his cramped position and, half-lifting, half pulling, managed to get him away from the burning turret. At this stage George knew that he must tell Harry Denton that both gunners were out of action. In spite of his own dreadful injuries, he struggled to the cockpit to make his report. Exhausted and in great pain, he then fought his way back through the burning fuselage, clinging with his badly damaged hands to the sides to get across the gaping hole in the floor. The flow of cold air caused him intense pain and frostbite had developed. Still, at this point, his only concern was for the two men he had left in the rear of the aircraft. He gave them as much care as he could in the time before the crash landing.

'Even now,' mused Harry, 'I can't understand the supreme endurance and the immense strength that enabled George to do what he did'. That George Thompson had continually put out flames with his bare hands, and had then partly dragged, partly lifted, both unconscious men past a large hole in the floor as well as all the obstacles in the fuselage was, Harry marvelled, superhuman. 'I never dreamed,' he said, 'that there had been such a fight for life in the aircraft.' George could have devoted his efforts to quelling the fire and so saved himself but, instead, he had opted to go through the flames to rescue his comrades, knowing the intercom was out of action and he would not be in a position to hear or heed any order which might be given to abandon the aircraft. 'His signal courage and self-sacrifice,' read the citation, 'will ever be an inspiration to the Service.' George Thompson's response to what must have seemed an impossible situation was summed up in the phrase: 'Young in years and experience, his actions were those of a veteran.'

Having landed the Lancaster, Harry struggled out of the smashed aircraft. He met a figure burned beyond recognition. It was not until the man spoke that Harry recognised his wireless operator. In spite of his terrible injuries, George had emerged from the shattered Lancaster to congratulate Harry on his landing. 'Jolly good landing, Skipper,' he said. Harry learned that the crew had been in crash positions and that there had been no further injuries. He managed to get George to a nearby farmhouse. 'He was in a pitiful condition, weak and helpless,' he remembered. He gave him a shot of morphine and dressed his wounds with anti-burns ointment. The Spitfires had notified a nearby airfield of the site of the crash landing and within twenty minutes a Canadian doctor had arrived on the scene. Sadly, and in spite of the heroic efforts to save him, Ernie Potts never recovered consciousness and died from the terrible effect of the flames, leaving a young widow and child.[129] The rest of the crew were, for the moment, still alive. They had started off in the morning in perfect conditions, but the flight had ended tragically, another example of the terrible cost of war.

Flying Officer Ron Goebel was well enough to be sent back to England straightaway where he was treated for frostbite, but the others were taken to the Catholic hospital in Eindhoven. Wilf Hartshorn had some burns and frostbite to his hands but was otherwise unhurt. 'He suffered with tinnitus throughout his life,' his son Phil remembers:

> 'This he attributed to being in close proximity to four Merlin engines with no cockpit canopy or helmet. He was repatriated and spent some time in hospital but never crewed up again. He was given ground duties for the rest of his service, spending some time in the airfield caravan at Bardney during the summer of 1945.'

Harry was able to visit George frequently over the next four days. 'He was not thinking of his pain,' Harry commented, 'he kept asking how the rest of the crew were getting on. I have never seen such bravery'. The doctors wanted to fly George Thompson home to a specialised burns unit, but the weather was bad, aircraft were grounded, and the brave Scot died three weeks later, as a result of pneumonia.

While Harry Denton and his crew were battling for survival over the Low Countries that morning, eight more crews at Bardney were being briefed for another raid that afternoon. The destination was Gravenhorst near Magdeburg and the target was the Düker Aqueduct, where the Mittelland Canal flows over the Hörsteler Aa. Damage had already been repaired by forced labourers and prisoners of war on many occasions after earlier assaults. With the events of the morning still fresh, who knows what went through the minds of the crews as they waited in the growing darkness. Take-off was at 1630. On their return just before midnight, they were able to report that bombs had been seen to burst across the canal. In spite of the fact that it was a very small target, reports showed that craters pitted over half a mile of banking as a result of the attack by the 152 Lancasters that had taken part in the raid. As they had been late taking off, one Lancaster had taken a short cut to catch up with the others over the target. Flight Sergeant Vincent Peace was the Mid Upper Gunner. As they started their run, he saw three bursts of flak. Rear Gunner Geoff Bamforth saw them too, but there was no response from their skipper. As Flying Officer Percy Bates called out that the bombs had gone, there was an explosion in the front of the aircraft, a scream from the pilot, and orders to 'Bale out'. The Lancaster went into a steep dive but only the Navigator, Flight Sergeant Frank Alton, Geoff, the Rear Gunner, and Vincent managed to bale out:

'We three jumped into the German morning. It was around 1115 and I had no idea what to expect. Possibly the Germans would shoot us on the way down. Possibly we would be treated according to the Geneva Convention, like we'd been told we would be. Possibly the German civilians might not accord with Geneva. In any case, I knew the rest of our boys had not survived because I watched our Lancaster go past me in flames and smash into the ground.'

Vincent Peace had got off lightly, with only a sprained ankle. A Luftwaffe corporal arrived on a bicycle. In excellent English, perfected when he had been a student in Hull, he invited Vincent to a nearby army camp, where he gave his name, rank and number to a junior army officer. The German smiled. 'Peace?' he said, 'we have been waiting a long time for you.'[130]

The next week or so there were days when flying was out of the question, others when practice bombing, cross-country and training flights could take place and on 10 January, there was a day spent clearing snow from the runways.

During these winter months convoys were still making the dangerous crossing of the North Atlantic. By 12 January in the winter of 1944/1945, five convoys had already made the hazardous journey to deliver essential supplies from North America to Europe. Attacks by packs of U-boats were an ever-present danger. With the liberation of France and the loss of many U-boat facilities, Germany now had few naval bases along the European mainland. However, they continued to occupy Denmark and Norway, essential coastlines if they were to continue U-boat operations. With its sheltered harbour, the Norwegian port of Bergen was now strategically vital for the Germans. Two Allied attacks on the town had been unsuccessful. The first was a disastrous failure, causing the deaths of 193 Norwegians, including sixty-one children in a nearby primary school. Little damage had been done to the U-boat pens on either raid.

It was then up to IX and 617 Squadrons. There were a series of briefings followed by orders to stand down. By 12 January, sixteen crews from each squadron prepared for a daylight raid. They were told that there were fighter bases around Bergen, but pilots were still undergoing training and had no operational experience.

All the Lancasters carried Tallboys and the thirty-two aircraft were escorted by Mustangs from a Polish squadron. The Mustangs were due to depart sometime after the main force and would then join up with them ready for the last run in to the target. Once the bombing had been carried out, they were to cover the Lancasters' withdrawal. The weather was clear with good visibility. 'We were the designated wind-finder,' noted Ray Harris. As they were early and, in spite of a light haze, bombing conditions were good, Wing Commander Fauquier [617 Squadron and Master Bomber for that day], gave permission for Ray to go first. Jimmy Parson, the Bomb Aimer, ever single-minded, began calling the run, which, remembered Ray Harris, was perfect.[131]

Ray said they had dropped their bomb, were leaving the coast and just about to break out the Woodbines when four Mustangs from the Polish squadron appeared. He wondered what the use was now of an escort, thinking they would be better employed marking the Lancasters that still had to attack the U-boat pens. He lost sight of them, thinking they must be behind him. It was only then that he realised that they were not Mustangs, but FW190s. A salvo of cannon shells crashed into them as he took evasive action. They had been told that there would be no fighter aircraft, but they were being attacked and were hit by ten or more bursts of fire. However battle-hardened and however highly trained, he remembered that being shot at was terrifying.

The attack continued. The trim tabs on the ailerons had gone. Ray believed that they were still there, some of them at least, but he could not shift them. By this time, he thought the Lancaster was so badly damaged that it would probably fall out of the sky. They were still diving straight for the sea when word came that the FW190s were heading for home. They were only saved from crashing into the water when Ray, with the help of Maurice Mellors, the Flight Engineer, successfully managed to level off at 1,000ft, 10,000ft below where they had first been attacked. Harold 'Jimmy' Parsons was in the process of uncoupling his intercom so he could move from his position during the attack:

'Suddenly we were going very fast downhill. It was like being in an express lift in a skyscraper or weightless in space. The thing went down and left me where I was, with a gap between me and where I'd been, which was fortunate because, where I had been, holes appeared simultaneously in both sides of the nose section and a pipe, fractured, started spilling pink hydraulic fluid… We got away somehow and levelled off.'

Only now was Jimmy able to reach Bill Gabriel who had been 'almost as smashed up as his turret', lugging him over the main spar to the rest bed, administering oxygen and morphine to a 'woozy' Bill who was bleeding from wounds in his head and leg. 'The good news,' said Ray Harris, 'was that we still had three-and-a-half engines.' He would manage to fly back across the Norwegian Sea at 1,000ft, making a safe landing at 60mph faster than usual. Their first task was to send Bill off to hospital, where he was operated on by a surgeon who was a German prisoner of war. Then they went to the pub.[132]

While Ray and his crew were under attack, 617 Squadron continued to bomb the U-boat pens. After they had completed their assault, and the smoke had cleared, it was the turn of IX Squadron.

Bill Williams was leader on this occasion. His navigator, Roy Harvey, remembered it well:

'IX Squadron… then bombed and added to the smoke and debris over the target. While this was going on the fighter pilots were chatting away between themselves in Polish, obviously enjoying their "grandstand" view of the attack and the aircraft that had already bombed were circling around.'

As it would be some time before the target would be clear enough for the other aircraft to bomb, the leaders decided that all those who had completed their bombing runs should return to base, leaving the fighter escort to continue giving cover to those remaining. Roy Harvey remembered that it was not the practice to fly in tight formation:

> 'Each aircraft set off individually. Unfortunately, as we left the coast German fighters intercepted us, one of which came in to attack our aircraft. On being warned by our rear gunner, Bill decided that it would be "prudent" to get down to sea level as quickly as possible so, from something like 16,000 ft, he stuck the nose down… Sandy recalls an FW190 coming in dead astern and saying, "corkscrew starboard skipper," as he started firing. But there was no corkscrew, just a dive. The FW190 was on fire and followed us down and went straight into the sea.'

After Bill had pulled back on the column after a 'very rapid rate of descent', the rear gunner's voice came over the intercom. 'Hey Skipper,' he called, 'I nearly got my feet wet then.' Later, when they learned about the losses and damage, Bill's crew came to the conclusion that the fighter that had made to attack them had run out of ammunition.

Gerald Prettejohns, in his vivid memoir entitled '*A Boy from Hackney*', gives an intriguing insight into German tactical misinformation. He explained, '"Lord Haw-Haw" was giving wrong wind vectors but the Squadron Leader spoke on open radio to the crews to ignore these and to use the briefed winds.'

Dennis Nolan watched while the pilots of three FW190s 'stooged' about, trying to decide which aircraft to go for. 'The sods,' he mused, 'were selecting which bomber to go for, us or him. They chose him.' They watched in horror as the Lancaster tried to shake off the attack before the engines caught fire, sealing its fate. There would be no survivors, but the fighters used up all their ammunition as they kept firing into the burning wreckage before turning away and returning to base, helpless to attack any of the other bombers. 'I thought that here were three of the best fighter aircraft of the war,' he said, 'operated by three of the worst or least experienced pilots.'[133]

What was the outcome of this third raid? Was it worth the loss of three crews and the risk that civilians would be killed? There was significant damage to the bunker itself, as well as workshops, stores and offices. Two U-boats and a transport ship received some damage. One of the Tallboys hit a minesweeper that was trying to escape the attack, with the loss of twenty of the crew of thirty-four, possibly the only occasion when a minesweeper was sunk by a Tallboy. Twenty Germans were killed; there were no reports of Norwegian casualties. The bunker survived the war and is now used by the Norwegian Navy to maintain and repair submarines.

On 14-15 January, forty-eight hours after the Bergen raid, six targets were attacked by Bomber Command over a widespread area of Germany. Eleven Lancasters left Bardney between 1610 and 1640 for Leuna, then in Czechoslovakia, on what Phil Tetlow described as one of Bomber Command's 'most perilous tasks ever attempted.' Synthetic-oil refineries were now priority objectives. Jim strongly believed that destruction of military targets was a far more effective means of bringing the war to an end. Each refinery was to be taken out 'savagely and accurately until its output was negligible.'[134] Because of the distance involved, the Germans felt that their oil refineries were reasonably safe from attack, as the site, not far from Leipzig, involved a ten-hour trip, with six of those hours over enemy territory. Two hundred aircraft were involved in this particular attack, carrying mixed loads of incendiaries and high-explosive bombs. Visibility was said to be good but as they approached the target there was some haze. In spite of this, bombing was well concentrated and several large explosions and large clouds of smoke were seen over the refinery. According to Don MacIntosh, the refineries 'made a splendid blaze, the yellow glare lighting up the windscreen, even after we left for home.'

Mac's crew was detailed to go out ahead of the main force in order to find an accurate wind for bombing:

> 'This we did, by dropping a flare and then doing the usual orbit. Luckily we were not molested and so we were one of the first to bomb. "Intelligence" had assessed that there were approximately a thousand AA guns defending the target area and judging by the reception we got, it was a fairly accurate estimate. The sky over the refinery resembled a Crystal Palace fireworks display as we started our run up and the shell bursts were still visible some fifty miles away on the homeward journey. It afterwards transpired that this attack produced the best night bombing of the war. There was no more oil from that source.'

Flying Officer Cook's Lancaster was reported missing – no signals or messages received - but the others were back at Bardney between 0159 and 0259. In his post-war interrogations, Albert Speer[135] described this as one of the most damaging raids carried out during this period. It was a severe setback to German oil production.

Apart from a few training flights and high-level bombing practice, the rest of the month was quiet, often summed up in the ORB with the phrase 'Nothing of importance'. When Jim had a taste of being Station Commander on 29 January, it gave him the opportunity to recommend Flight Sergeant Bob Riches for the immediate award of the DFM. There would have been plenty of activities on the days when flying was out of the question. A journalist from the *Newcastle Journal* reported that squadron members were busy studying and discussing intelligence reports and learning about new equipment.

The ORB noted that DFCs went to Pilot Officer A.F. Jones and Pilot Officer J.A. Peterson, whilst Pilot Officer Cunningham received a DFM. The *Newcastle Journal* also reported that by this time there were nearly thirty members of the crews of IX Squadron who had been awarded either the DFC or DFM.

February 1945

There were no entries in Jim Bazin's logbook between 2 December and 2 February, but he was leading operations again on 3 February, taking part in an attack on the U-boat pens at Ijmuiden, a high-priority target. Although Jim's logbook entry simply reads '"Ops" 2hrs 40'; his report reads, 'Bombsight u/s for this type of target,' so he made no attack. It was a daylight raid, with aircraft taking off at 1410 and all home safely soon after dusk. Visibility was good so bombing was visual, but the wind had caused some slight overshooting of the target. Some of the armour-piercing 12,000lb bombs had fused delays so that they would bore through the 10ft-thick concrete roofs and explode inside, thus ensuring maximum possible damage. Phil Tetlow commented that everything went as planned and several bombs were seen to strike on or near the target, adding that it was only after the war that they learned from first-hand observers just how much damage had been done. Doug Tweddle was wind-finding again. While IX Squadron was tackling the boat pens, there was quite heavy anti-aircraft fire and flak was reported to have been very close. Fred Whitfield remembered it well. 'We began our bombing run well out to sea and the German naval gunners had our range from the start.' He said he always had the greatest of respect for the naval flak as they were very accurate. Back at Bardney, they discovered their Lancaster had been holed in three places. Gerald Prettejohns' memories were also vivid. When shrapnel hit the cockpit window, Bill Williams was hit by shattered Perspex and the bomb aimer had been hit in the chest by shrapnel. Gerald was sworn at as he was removing it, and was told, in no uncertain terms, that it was a new shirt, issued by the store only that morning.

The squadron was now able to penetrate deeper and deeper into Germany. Ground forces were making great progress and the task now was to seal off the battle area by destroying key bridges and viaducts preventing the Germans bringing in reinforcements. Phil Tetlow recalled that utmost precision was required as the targets were practically invisible from 14,000ft. Their next operation on 6 February was the aqueduct at Altenbecken. Jim's logbook shows that he headed eighteen crews and was airborne for 5hrs 35mins. Fred Whitfield recalled the route seemed to be a solid wall of flak stretching for eighty miles from the front line to the Rhine. The whole area within fifteen miles of the target was covered by 10/10ths cloud so the attack was called off and the Lancasters returned to Bardney with their bomb loads. Doug Tweddle commented, '[The bombs] were so expensive. You couldn't throw those away.'

With the developments on the ground, and with Montgomery preparing Allied troops to cross the Rhine, precision bombing was vital. Both IX and 617 Squadrons were tasked with sealing off the battle area. Phil Tetlow remembered that, while some targets were heavily defended, they met no resistance at other sites. 'Accuracy,' he wrote, 'was more difficult with just one bomb,' going on to note that one of the targets was only put out of action after three attacks. Because they were now a highly-experienced crew, Don MacIntosh was given the responsible role of Deputy Controller, which Phil Tetlow considered 'a worthy tribute to his skill and determination.'

On several days, the ORB noted that only small numbers of aircraft took part in raids. This was certainly the case on 7 and 8 February with raids on Ladbergen (one crew) and Pölitz (two crews), where I.G. Farben produced fifteen per cent of Germany's total consumption of synthetic fuel, and again on 13 February, when just one of the Lancasters took part in an attack on Dresden.

The next day seventeen crews were briefed for yet another attempt on the viaduct at Altenbecken, again abandoned because of the heavy cloud cover that had plagued them for much of the winter. Leading the squadron was Bill Williams. His Navigator, Roy Harvey, remembered that they had met heavy anti-aircraft fire as they passed over the front line and saw a plane losing height. 'When you were with the main force and this happened,' he commented, 'you had a feeling of detachment for you didn't know the squadron which it belonged to, and therefore anything about the crew.' When operating as a small force, it was highly likely that they could identify the crew. It became very personal. They watched as the Lancaster lost height in a controlled way so waited to see if the crew would either bale out or crash-land in Allied-held territory.

Tragically, Flight Lieutenant Johnny Dunne and his crew were lost. 'We saw it all,' said Jim Brookbank. Like everybody in his crew, he was shouting, 'Jump, jump, jump, you fools!' But nobody did. The Lancaster had been hit by flak. 'It was just a single shot,' he remembered. They were in a very loose gaggle on the way back from bombing and scattered across the sky. 'One little German flak gun had one pot shot and that was it,' he recalled, noting that the Lancaster went down rather slowly, not in a screaming dive. 'They couldn't all have been killed,' he thought, 'because the Lanc wasn't a mess all over.' 'A mystery, that one,' he concluded. 'It was the end of old "Tosspots" Philpott.'[136]

When Don MacIntosh learned that Johnnie 'the bright star, the young Australian, loved by all' had been shot down, he asked, 'What happened?' 'An unlucky shot, Mac,' was the reply. He was told that no one had actually seen him being hit but they had watched the Lancaster suddenly plunge down. Doug Tweddle thought that it must have been a direct hit which had probably burst inside the cockpit. Johnny had joined the squadron about the same time as Doug and Mac, and their careers had seen them promoted and decorated at the same time. 'I always thought he, Dougie and I were invulnerable,' mused Mac. 'I thought that only other people got shot down.'[137] It was an incident reminiscent of the occasion when there was an explosion in the cockpit of Jim Bazin's aircraft when on the Caen raid on 6 June 1944, and yet another illustration of how it is only a matter of luck that the consequences on that occasion had not been much more serious.

Two crews encountered more 10/10ths cloud on an operation to Rogitz that afternoon. The results were not visible, but the glare of fires could be seen against the clouds.

As events on the ground continued to unfold, there were still more operations. Böhlen in Saxony was a significant industrial town and an important target for the RAF. It was the site of Braunkohle-Benzin AG (Brabag), where vital synthetic aviation fuel and other products were distilled from lignite, extracted from one of the world's largest lignite mines near the town. Towards the end of the war, 800 prisoners worked there as forced labourers, housed in an extension of the Buchenwald concentration camp. The only results observed on this night raid, in which seven crews took part, were bomb bursts seen reflected in the clouds. All were back for a well-earned breakfast.

For once there was good visibility for the two crews briefed on the evening raid on Gravenhorst on 21 February. They reported that bombing appeared accurate and both were back at Bardney by midnight. Jim led a special 'Tallboy' operation against the now familiar target of the Altenbecken Viaduct on 22 February, with bombing 'generally concentrated but slightly overshooting.' He was over the target at 1558. He also reported that his bomb had slightly overshot but added that most of the damage was concentrated on the easterly half of the viaduct. Two days later and thirty miles short of the target, seventeen crews were informed that an attack on Ladbergen was abandoned. All aircraft had returned safely from all three raids.

Flying Officer Harry Denton, who had so skilfully managed to land his burning aircraft on New Year's Day, received the DFC. On 21 February, the press announced the award of the Victoria Cross to Flight Sergeant George Thompson for his superb courage and devotion to duty. He had died of his injuries on 23 January. Headlines ranged from 'VC gave life for crew of burning plane' (*Daily Telegraph*) to 'Quiet Grocer's Boy Won VC in Plane Fire' (*Daily Herald*). The *Newcastle Journal* marked the award in an article headed 'Bomber Squadron that goes on "special missions"', adding that the whole squadron was justly proud of the gallant feat of George Thompson, the tall, heavily-built Scot who was described by his fellows 'as always on the job.'

Chapter 10

March to November 1945

Bombing operations continue, Berchtesgaden, Victory in Europe

On 3 March 1945, twenty crews were briefed for another assault on the canal and aqueducts at Ladbergen. They were part of a large-scale operation by 212 Lancasters and ten Mosquitoes. Take-off was at 1830 and once again they encountered cloud. However, on this occasion, the attack was to prove highly effective, with the destruction of the two aqueducts and 100m of canal bank. As there was 9/10ths cloud cover, bomb aimers depended on the TIs. Limited visibility meant that two of the squadron's aircraft returned with their bombs. It was said that the area had taken on the appearance of a lunar landscape. All were home safely by 0041.

Just about the time most of the Lancasters were on their return approach in the early hours of the morning, there was a surprise attack on Bardney. Bob Woolf was one of those returning to the base after a night at the pub. One of the German attackers swooped in, flying low and clearly visible:

'Full of Dutch courage, we waved our fists at the beast and gave him the full benefit of our extensive different ways of saying, "Go away, you nasty person." To our horror and astonishment, he did a split-arse turn and seemed to come straight back at us. We did our own version of the manoeuvre and dashed into the nearest shelter, which was the toilet block. A Lancaster crew trying to get through the door at once created the kind of comic logjam you see in the films, and we were still in it after our adversary had whizzed past without bothering to stop, whereupon we bravely came out again.'[138]

By the beginning of March, the Luftwaffe no longer had control over their air space and was almost powerless to defend German sites. Göring had approved a suggestion from a number of experienced night fighters that they should resume the intruder operations they had first carried out during the early months of the war. It involved attacking Allied bombers on their return to base, an operation that was known as *Unternehmen Gisela*. While a bomber crew was absorbed in making a safe landing, tired after a long flight, a Lancaster was an easy target for a short burst of cannon fire. Bob Woolf described it as 'a kind of last hurrah by the Luftwaffe'. Two hundred night fighters had been deployed along the east of England. When it was possible, returning bombers could be diverted to airfields where it was deemed to be safer. After the Germans suffered the loss of about twenty-five Ju88s, *Unternehmen Gisela* was abandoned.

There was another major raid on 6 March, this time a return to Sassnitz, an important deep water port on the Baltic. The port was a transport hub, with a ferry terminal and an important rail terminus where different tracks enabled the switch from standard to broad gauge. It was also a seaside resort and the site of Hitler's massive Prora holiday camp that had been built in the 1930s. During the war the camp was used to house German troops. The squadron provided twenty of the 191 Lancasters that had been briefed for the evening attack on shipping. Ironically, the raid was on the same day that the German Commander-in-Chief of the German Navy had reported that an intensification of enemy action in the area would be 'most undesirable.'

After several applications to fly with other crews had been turned down by Jim Bazin and Doug Melrose, Bob Woolf finally had permission to join Ray Harris on the Sassnitz raid. He remembered seeing the vivid lights of the cities of neutral Sweden, 'like diamonds on velvet'. There was some light flak as they passed over the country; they encountered more over the target, though not as much as they had expected. The main problem was the sheer number of Lancasters. As Bob Woolf spotted a Lancaster losing height immediately above them, he shouted, 'Dive!' to Ray Harris, whose reaction was so sudden that Bob was thrown upwards, hitting his head on the astrodome, 'greatly adding to the star count.'

This time there was 7/10ths cloud with tops at 6,000ft. Several sticks of bombs were reported to have straddled shipping and black clouds were seen pouring from a destroyer that had blown up. The destroyer was a Type 1936A: 150 crewmen died. Although those taking part in the raid would not have known it at the time, the port was full of refugees waiting in trains and on ships. Don MacIntosh mentioned such a raid, which could have been this attack on Sassnitz that he described so vividly in his book. After a long but uneventful trip, they arrived at the target on time. On their approach they saw that the harbour was lit up by parachute flares. Bomb aimer Semple relayed a running commentary:

> 'There's a destroyer going at full speed across the harbour! He's leaving a terrific wake – start turning left about 60 degrees. He's going like the clappers, making for the open sea! OK, start slowing up your turn. A couple of minutes to go, I'm going to lay off quite a bit for his speed. Left, left. Steady... Bombs gone! Can you keep straight, I can see the bomb going down. We'll get a terrific picture. He's still charging for the harbour exit, straight as a die. Steady. Christ, that went off alright! Near his port beam, amidships. He's turned over! I can

see all the water and mud churning up, and his stern out of the water. OK, camera finished.'[139]

Once they were on their way home, Semple told Mac that they had hit the ship. 'It'll make a swell photograph for my law office,' he said. When Don was shown the photograph the next day, he had a pang of regret. He felt that the men had not stood a chance. 'The sailors,' he reminisced, 'had clean hands', adding that if the captain had any sense he would not have been in the harbour in the first place. 'It was like shooting fish in a barrel.'

They were still being attacked as they turned for home. Bob Woolf described an incident on the return journey, when they were pursued by an FW190 that Ray managed to shake off as they flew through cloud. Bob paid tribute not only to Ray's skills as a pilot but also to the crew as a whole, adding that it was good to know that there were crews just as good as his own!

The next day, eighteen Lancasters left Bardney for a night raid on Hamburg. The visibility was good and Don MacIntosh remembered that it was too quiet for comfort over the North Sea. Although there was patchy stratus cloud, bombing was well concentrated on red and yellow TIs. Large explosions and fires were observed, with smoke reaching 10,000ft.

New crews were arriving in a steady stream during the month, so there were training exercises on the few days when there were no raids. After a three-day respite, fourteen aircraft were involved in a daytime attack on Essen on 11 March. Bob Woolf was back with Doug Melrose:

'Dense cloud covered the target, so we bombed on PFF (Pathfinder Force) sky markers. Packed in close formation, Ernie [Stalley, Rear Gunner] watched in appalled disgust as a batch of bright yellow 1,000-pounders flashed past our starboard tailfin.

Such a disturbing sight, so obvious in daylight, made us all wonder how often this must have happened on night ops, and how often that was the explanation for the red balls of fire in the darkness that meant another bomber going down.'[140]

In spite of 10/10ths cloud, brown smoke was seen. Roy Harvey had missed out on the raid as he was given leave to attend a wedding in London. Jim Bazin's navigator stood in for him and, on his return, Roy was the target of good-humoured banter, telling him that they had been directed all the way back to Bardney. Normally, Roy left it to Bill Williams to find his way to Bardney once they had reached Lincoln. Roy commented that he was credited with the raid though he had not taken part in it. He had completed a tour of thirty-one operations between 14 June 1944 and 13 March 1945, ten of them with IX Squadron, including two attacks on the *Tirpitz*. He had flown 210 operational hours. At this point, crews were given three options. They could continue flying as a crew and start a second tour, or individuals could opt to stay with the squadron. The third option was to take a rest period from operations, be split up and posted to training units to fly with new crews during their training.

'After much thought and discussion,' he wrote, 'the consensus of opinion was that we had had our share of luck and the end of the war in Europe was in sight.' Only Bomb Aimer Freddie Horry opted to stay with the squadron.

Dortmund was the target the next day. Again, there was thick cloud but there were several reports of yellow-brown staining that had been seen on a circular area of billowing cloud.

The next daylight raid was on the seven-span viaduct at Arnsburg on 13 March, the first of three on successive days. Jim led the fourteen Lancasters that were briefed for the first raid. In spite of making three runs the target could not be identified so their bomb was not dropped.

Although he might not have been aware of it at the time, it was to be Jim's last operational raid with IX Squadron. Wing Commander Fauquier, his opposite number at 617 Squadron, had been ordered not to fly on any more operations, so perhaps Jim had received similar instructions.

In later years, Doug Tweddle felt it was a day that he should have stayed in bed. As he was going down the runway, the Lancaster suddenly swerved and could not immediately be steered back on course:

> 'Down the left-hand side of our runway there were some sodium lights – quite big things – but by really good luck and what-have-you we sort of picked our way between them, but we definitely had the port wing off the runway. I juggled round, got it on again and actually got airborne but obviously with reduced power. I just got up to around 200 or 300ft and then throttled back as you normally would do. We were flying these upgraded Merlins... I remember the Rolls-Royce man who used to live with us at IX, he used to say, "For God's sake, get the revs off because you're really pushing that engine." When I throttled back on this, this flame that had dived out of my starboard inner quietened down, and I felt I could sort of manage.'

Remarkably, he described how he had continued, joining up with the rest of the squadron and completing the sortie. The bomb was not dropped but Doug's troubles were still not over. As he came in to land, the flame reappeared and he had to feather the engine. He was diverted to Waddington. The girl in the control tower asked if he had any hang-ups:

> 'I said, "One." She said, "What is it?" I said, "It's a 12,000lb Tallboy," at which I could hear the consternation by the tone of her voice. She came back, "Go to Carnaby clear." I said,

"I can't go to Carnaby. My engineer tells me we're down to 180 gallons," at which you normally thought about getting out of a Lanc… I tried about three times to line up on the main runway at Waddington and I kept drifting away… So my navigator figured out. "You can go in a straight line to Carnaby. Without any frills, we might just make it." So I said, "Right, we're going. Tell them, by the way, to put all the lights on, the lot, because I'm coming in from the sea and I'm coming in at once"… it was like the Blackpool illuminations. So I came in over the sea on three engines with a Tallboy doing 130 knots. I wasn't going to stall on that one. I used the entire length of the main runway.'

Once he had landed, he 'sneaked in' to the emergency billet. In the darkness he overheard a conversation between two men from 617 Squadron saying, 'Who the hell is this IX Squadron man?' Because of the rivalry between the two squadrons, Doug deemed it diplomatic to stay quiet. The next day he eventually made it back to Bardney, encountering the same problem in spite of reassurance from the engineer at Waddington that there would be no recurrence. Once he had taxied, Jim Bazin quickly darted up the pair of ladders. Doug said he had never seen him move so speedily.

The ORB simply summarised the event in just a few simple words:

'One aircraft piloted by Flight Lieutenant Tweddle was diverted to Carnaby on return as, after leaving the target area, the port outer engine emitted flames. The engine was feathered and a safe landing was made at Carnaby.'

On occasions when the weather had closed in over Bardney, or aircraft were having difficulties, they could be diverted to other RAF airfields such as Woodbridge, Manston (Kent) and Carnaby (Yorkshire) that had been built to accept returning aircraft that were damaged or low on fuel. Phil Tetlow recalled that Woodbridge had about 600yds of undershoot grass, 3,000yds of asphalt which was a lot in those days, and a further 500 or 600yds of overshoot grass at the top end. It was also very wide. He added that if it was a bad weather diversion and it was important to get aircraft onto the ground, two Lancasters could land at the same time. After a night when they slept 'in a big heap somewhere', they would have flown back to Bardney as soon as conditions were suitable.

Jack Linaker recorded an occasion when Ray Harris landed at Woodbridge after bringing back a Tallboy. The American major could not believe that the Lancaster had been flown to Germany, returning with one bomb:

> 'He said, "You mean to say you went all the way to Germany and came back with one bloody bomb and you never dropped it?"
>
> '"Yes!"
>
> '"Bloody hell! With one bomb and you came all the way back?"
>
> '"Yes!"
>
> '"Right. You in that jeep, you in that jeep, we're going to see this."
>
> 'We went to where our kite was. They were just opening up the bomb bay. The American major looked up.
>
> '"Jesus Christ Almighty. You mean to say you sat on that much dynamite!"'[141]

It was Arnsburg again the next day. In spite of haze, they were able to bomb visually with good concentrated results. The last two aircraft to arrive at the target brought back their bombs as the viaduct was by then covered with smoke. All arrived safely at Bardney by early evening.

There was some good news when they learned that Flight Lieutenant L.E. Marsh and Flight Lieutenant W.T.C. Gabriel had each been awarded a DFC for the attack on the Bergen U-boat pens. The citation for Larry Marsh described how he had shown great presence of mind by not feathering his engine immediately, so that he could get the longest possible use from his mid-upper turret. It continued by praising his superb flying skill which had enabled accurate fire from both turrets, preventing the enemy from pressing home their attacks, which lasted in all thirty-two minutes. In spite of being wounded and with a turret put out of action after it had been hit, Bill Gabriel's citation noted that he had 'kept up such a good commentary that the enemy were unable to press home their attack.' Fifteen attacks were made, lasting seventeen minutes. His coolness had greatly contributed to the saving of the aircraft. Flight Sergeant J.B. Riches received the DFM for the same incident and was also commended for his good advice enabling his captain to carry out successful combat manoeuvres.

It was back to Arnsburg for the third time on 15 March. Once again, 11 Group provided Mustangs fitted with long-range tanks. Jonah Jones made a forced landing at Gosselies after his port engine could not be feathered when it caught fire. Four of his crew managed to bale out before the fire was seen to have been extinguished, so Jonah's previous order was countermanded. They hoped to make it back to England but as dusk was falling, Jonah was not happy with the idea of flying over the Channel, so it was thought wiser to land on friendly territory. George Camsell, who was leading the squadron, made for home with the others while Doug Tweddle volunteered to stay with Jonah and his crew:

'I said to Paddy, who [was] after all the wireless ops, the man who sends out the signals and what have you, he said, "O! Let's go to Brussels, Doug. That's a great place." But although we were heading in that direction, I thought we'd better get down sooner, so we came across an aerodrome where the original Fairey Aviation people were. I believe it's called Gosselies. It's near Charleroi and its Somerfelt strip-metal stripping that the Americans laid out on the ground. I gather it's about 11,000yds and there's a church steeple right at one end of the runway. I called up the "D Darkie Dog" button which was common to everywhere in the flying world at that time…

'So the American came out – as a matter of fact I could see him walking out with a trailer mike on to the tarmac in front of the tower. "Have you had a Lancaster down there?"

'He said, "No, we never have."

'I said, "What's that in the corner? A Fortress?" And he said, "That's right."'

If a Fortress could land, there would be no problem with a Lancaster. So Doug landed first in order to talk Jonah down. Jonah made 'a magnificent landing.' The Americans hosted them 'beautifully,' contacting the Belgian Blue Cross to arrange billets for the night and providing them with meal vouchers. Doug noted that the food was 'a great deal better than we had.' Their host's daughter had 'a very nice MG sports car,' so they all trooped off to Charleroi, still in their flying gear, went to a restaurant where there was a seven-piece girls' orchestra. It was pointed out to them that, as they were not in uniform, they could be mistaken for Germans. Once it was established that they were RAF, 'the drinks came flying in.' Next day, they all flew back to Bardney in Doug's aircraft to find that he had been posted as having crashed, and Jonah was listed as being somewhere else. Once they had described their adventures in Charleroi, there was no problem in finding volunteers to go to rescue 'Jonah's kite.'

With the end of the war now in sight, there was more and more pressure on the Germans. All six crews returned safely on 16 March from a raid on the Bavarian city of Würzburg after another assault on enemy morale. Lancasters had dropped 1,207 tons of high explosive and incendiary bombs, killing 5,000 people and flattening 21,000 homes. Ninety per cent of the city's buildings were destroyed, and the imposing eleventh-century medieval cathedral was also badly damaged.

They were again over the north of Germany on 19 March, when the target was a railway bridge at Vlotho. For once, visibility was good, with a cloud base at 14,000ft. Although Doug Tweddle remembered 'nothing particularly exciting', he did make an interesting comment about the fighter escorts. 'They gave you top, middle and bottom cover beautifully until the flak started coming in,' he noted. 'Then they just disappeared high out of the way until it settled down and came back again.' However, he added that at that stage of the game, there was little point in bombers avoiding flak as there was always the danger of steering into something else.

Railway bridges were the targets for the next three operations. The bridge at Nienburg was struck several times on 20 March. It remained intact, although railway tracks on either side of it were damaged. Heavy flak was encountered on 22 March at Bremen and, during their return flight, large clouds of smoke were still visible ninety-five miles from the target. Part of the bridge at the small spa town of Bad Oeynhausen was seen to have collapsed after the raid on 23 March. It was about this time that Me262 jet fighters ('the Swallow') were now able to mount large-scale attacks on Allied bombers. On this occasion, Doug Tweddle commented that members of the squadron believed that one of the Lancasters had been attacked by an Me262 and had to return to base. There had also been heavy flak and another aircraft was damaged, both on the bombing run and afterwards, but managed to land at Seething in spite of both tanks being damaged. By this time, there was generally little opposition. The weather was fine, and there was a large escort of Mustangs. The hydraulics of Doug Tweddle's Lancaster were hit but, fortunately, self-sealed. Flying Officer Follett's aircraft was so badly damaged that he had to fly home with the control column roped back.

In his book on IX Squadron, Tony Mason commented that the last six months of Jim's command saw the squadron reach a peak in efficiency and accuracy, particularly citing the success at Altenbecken Viaduct, adding that Jim had commanded the squadron 'through its most outstanding period' and for having led so many of its successful raids.[142]

He also referred to the attack on Bad Oeynhausen, the seventh attack on vital bridges by IX and 617 Squadrons, considering that it was one of the most concentrated raids carried out by them. Air Vice-Marshal Sir Ralph Cochrane had described it as 'a magnificent feat.'

Although a successful end to the war was obviously within sight, the intensity of the previous months was beginning to tell on everyone in the squadron. It was the end of the winter, living conditions were very basic with little if any heating, food was in short supply and there had been numerous demanding raids. Unsurprisingly, the pressure was beginning to have an impact on general health.

The continuing demands on aircraft and equipment were also having a major effect. It was on the Bremen raid that Doug Tweddle encountered a problem soon after take-off. It could have had very serious consequences:

> 'I was flying with Jim Bazin's engineer… I was busy over Nottingham or thereabouts, climbing in sector when my port inner CSU packed up. Just all I can remember was a howl and this temporary engineer of mine got it feathered. It was really remarkable. He just shot up and put his finger on the feather button and fortunately for us he got it stopped because we were

there with a Tallboy right over Nottingham. Normally, if you didn't get a runaway engine stopped, well, it seized and burnt because you had virtually unlimited revs and then, if you got a fire, things were serious, you know. So, I was grateful to Jim's engineer. He did a good job there.'

There was yet another challenge. Doug was supposed to be leading the operation but could not break radio silence to warn George Camsell that he was now in charge. So, Doug made the decision to drop the Tallboy on the emergency dropping zone in the Wash, just off King's Lynn, which meant he could get back to Bardney in time to brief George with the news that he was on his own. When he was over Bremen, George Camsell was hit and lost an engine, losing a second one when the Lancaster was attacked again over the Frisian Islands on his return to Bardney. He was now flying with two engines on the same side. They made it back to England, landing on the first clear area that they spotted in Norfolk. George ended up by going through a hedge at the far end of the field, finishing up 'a-straddle' a road. A local bobby got off his bike, uttering the classic words, 'Hello, you lads! What's going on?'

There was time to enjoy some more fine weather before the next operation, which was a daylight attack on the oil-storage unit at Farge on 27 March. The ORB gives little detail, apart from the information that the operation was generally considered successful. One aircraft did not attack as the bombsight was unserviceable. All returned safely by mid-afternoon.

It was not until the early evening of 7 April that the squadron was involved in another operation, again on an oil refinery. Twelve aircraft took off for a night attack on a benzol plant at Mölbis, Saxony. Because the winds were much stronger than the forecast had indicated, some were late reaching the target. However, bombing was accurate and concentrated. The Lancaster piloted by Flying Officer A.E. Jeffs was on the homeward journey from Mölbis when it caught fire, crashing way off course four miles NNW of Wantage with the loss of all the crew. The next evening, eighteen aircraft, including seven crews from the previous night's operation, were part of a major raid involving seventeen Mosquitoes and 231 Lancasters (including some from Jim's old 49 Squadron) on the Leuna-Werk der I.G. Farben, Lützendorf. Seventeen of the eighteen aircraft were back at Bardney by 0315 but Flying Officer Woolstencroft and his crew had been lost over Germany. They are buried in the 1939-1945 War Cemetery in Berlin. This was the last reported loss for IX Squadron in the Second World War, just four weeks before VE Day.

All fourteen aircraft from the squadron returned from a scheduled joint raid with 617 Squadron on 13 April. The target was to have been the heavy cruiser *Prinz Eugen* but thick cloud over the River Elbe meant no bombs were dropped. The cloud tops were at 17,000ft; Dave Coster reported seeing vapour trails 1,000ft above them but no further explanation was offered.

They were more successful a few nights later when huge explosions were seen after bombing the Skoda munitions factory at the historic Bohemian city of Pilsen on the early morning of 17 April. It was an operation conducted at the request of Allied troops. Some reported yellow flames, others saw red flames with black smoke. Most of the crews commented on the clear, concise instructions they had been given by the controller, which resulted in concentrated bombing. The area was being cleared for ground forces to move in. Three weeks later, Pilsen's German commander surrendered to US troops on 6 May.

The attacks on the aqueducts, bridges and oil refineries had made it increasingly difficult for the Germans either to move their ground forces or for the Luftwaffe to take to the air.[143] It was now obvious that the war was coming to an end. Some of the long-established members of the squadron were completing their tours and were leaving for other roles.

Among them was Bill Williams, leader of so many successful raids, who was posted to No 1654 Heavy Conversion Unit RAF Swinderby and Wigsby on the day of the Pilsen raid. Roy Harvey moved to 84 OTU RAF Desborough two days later. The departure from the squadron must have been as difficult for those who were leaving as well as for those who remained. For some, though, it was now possible to begin thinking of life beyond the war.

For those remaining at Bardney there was still the likelihood of more operations. It was crystal clear by now that further raids on the Reich were likely to have little effect on the outcome of the war. However, on 19 April, sixteen Lancasters from IX Squadron and twenty from 617 Squadron made a Tallboy raid on coastal batteries on Heligoland. The two tiny islands in the North Sea, just forty miles from Cuxhaven at the mouth of the Elbe, had been attacked by nearly 1,000 aircraft the previous day, one of the final massed raids of the war. The island's inhabitants were in the process of being evacuated on 19 April as the area was deemed to be unsafe after suffering devastating damage.

The squadron's final operation was controversial. On the dark and cold morning of 25 April, eighteen crews who had been selected for the raid were told of the day's target. The briefing was being recorded by the BBC, which confirmed that this was to be a very special event. There was also a growing sense that this could also be the last operation of the war. No doubt there would have been much speculation as to the destination, only resolved when Jim Bazin, with a half smile, announced, 'The target, gentlemen, is Berchtesgaden.'[144] He paused. There was a gust of unforced laughter from his audience, probably helping them to be able to relax a little and concentrate on the details that were to follow. Jim Brookbank described Jim Bazin's way of speaking as a 'slow, drawn-out posh drawl,' while Patrick Bishop described 'a cultured, amused accent', more like the speech of a university professor than a warrior.[145]

Don MacIntosh remembered that 'a trip to B' had been a standing joke for years. The War Correspondent for the *News Chronicle* wondered if the target really was Hitler, but Jim continued, 'That's the house where the gentleman lives. If he doesn't happen to be there, there will still be plenty of SS men around.' Jim emphasised the challenges that awaited the crews. 'The target,' he explained, 'is very, very small indeed.'[146]

The Berghof, deep in the heart of Bavaria, Hitler's retreat, where he often spent up to four months of the year, was the nerve centre of the redoubt, headquarters of any final resistance by the enemy. This made it a politically sensitive target, likely to be heavily defended. Visitors described it as an observation post perched 6,000ft up on the crest of a mountain, approached by a winding road cut through rocks. They would then be ushered into a large copper-plated lift and carried 300ft up to the top to Hitler's home. Looking out from it, visitors described it like being in an aeroplane in flight.

Berchtesgaden was imbued with layers of political meaning for both Germans and the Allies. Guests had included David Lloyd George, the Duke and Duchess of Windsor, and Mussolini. It had also been the site of an assassination attempt on Hitler in March 1944. The Berghof itself was where Hitler had entertained Chamberlain before the Munich peace talks. Many of the highest-ranking Nazi figures, including Göring and Bormann, had holiday homes in the area. It was believed that many had already moved there from Berlin. Hitler, in the bunker in the Reich Chancellery, was living out his last days in the German capital. If the stronghold in Bavaria remained intact it could become an Alpine fortress for senior members of the German government. There was also always the risk that it could become a place of pilgrimage for neo-Nazis after the war. Although Thorburn commented that many aircrew came to regard the operation as 'a PR exercise, a needless risk and a potential waste of good men,'[147] many of the senior members of the Allied forces felt it was vital that both Berghof and Berchtesgaden should be completely destroyed.

Whether a massed aerial raid was the right way to go about it was another question. The snow-covered target of Berchtesgaden was small and difficult to locate from the air. Berghof was also heavily camouflaged.

It would be a long flight, around 1,250 miles in total with the final approach of 250 miles over German-occupied territory. BBC commentator Brian Bliss was also there at Bardney, perhaps adding a little extra colour to his account. As the first Lancaster swung into position at the end of the runway, he reminded listeners that 'this was the squadron that sank the *Tirpitz*'. He went on to say that 12,000-pounders would be taking the attack to Hitler's doorstep. 'It's a really clear evening,' he enthused. 'We can see her shape silhouetted against the evening sky, A – Able is off! Everyone here is waving! A marvellous sight as she rushes by.' It was 0419 when the first aircraft took off. It was piloted by Jack Buckley. Don MacIntosh and Pete Morgan were the last to leave at 0436.

The flight on that clear spring morning was uneventful. Don remembered that there was no smoke from the factories below and that the escorting Mosquitoes 'buzzed along the stream like policemen, ready to take the number of any strays.'

Many crews would log well over eight hours in the air. Destruction of the German oil refineries meant that there would probably be little cover by the Luftwaffe although flak was anticipated. With such a specific target, this would have seemed to be a perfect operation for IX and 617 Squadrons to do on their own but, surprisingly, this was to be a massed raid. The crews were to discover that the danger now would not be from German defenders but from other Allied bombers. It was usually 617 Squadron that went in first, but on this occasion Doug Melrose was to lead the attack. Bob Woolf described the moment when they were on their run with a Lancaster from 617 Squadron directly above them:

> 'We were moments from release time and I saw the 617 aircraft had his bomb doors open. I watched in utter horror as the bomb was released and began its curving flight. It was heading absolutely straight for us. I had no alternative, even though we were on our run. "Starboard, Skip, a touch starboard," I shouted. The bomb missed our port wingtip by nothing at all. I could read the word Torpex on it as it went past, the name for the explosive inside it. Well, the run up was spoiled and we couldn't make another, so we brought the Tallboy home for the last time.'[148]

Doug Melrose and his crew were not the only ones having problems. Flying Officer Williams had been forced to turn back when he was over the Rhine on the outward journey. While the Tallboy was being selected and fused, some sort of fault, possibly electrical, caused it to drop off the aircraft. It was seen to explode in a wood. Once at Berghof, Flying Officer Arndell reported that he had not been able to attack the target owing to 'interference from other aircraft.' For the same reason, Flying Officer Laws had to make a second run. Ten who did manage to drop their Tallboys did so within two minutes and Flying Officer Laws went in for his second run three minutes later. Of the seventeen who had left Bardney, only eleven had been able to attack the primary target, although there had undoubtedly been considerable damage. Five Lancasters returned with their Tallboys.

In a BBC interview later that day at Bardney, Doug Melrose described his approach. These broadcasts would have almost certainly been carefully prepared and scripted, to be read over the air rather than allowing interviewees to be spontaneous. This was common practice at the time and would also have been important to avoid broadcasting sensitive material. He told the listeners of how everything was carefully checked as they neared the Bavarian Alps. 'There were to be no mistakes on this attack!' he said. They had arrived on time and were met by flak that was pretty accurate and fired 'in real anger', though it was not as heavy as they had anticipated. Because Doug was leading the formation he had not been able to observe the results immediately, but by the time they turned for home, he was able to see that there was smoke and dust covering most of the target. With some satisfaction, he added that most of it was over Hitler's hideout.[149] It is worth noting, however, that this account contains nothing about the fact that they had been unable to release their Tallboy!

Jack Buckley's Australian Bomb Aimer, Flight Lieutenant C.J. Campbell, was in an ideal position to observe the scene as it was unfolding. As the target nestled in a valley, he recalled that it was hard to identify, adding that the approach over a hill 3,000ft above it was tricky. The run up had been perfect, though, and the house was 'dead in the sight' as he released the Tallboy. Because it was delayed action, he did not have the pleasure of seeing the explosion. Once the bomb had been released, they circled the target and saw several bombs hit the SS barracks next to the house.

On his return, Rear Gunner E.J. Cutting was also interviewed by the BBC. He was flying with Flight Lieutenant Harry Watkins and it is an interesting exercise to compare the formal language of the ORB with his lively account:

'PRIMARY ATTACKED. Clear. Slight haze. Bombs appeared to be overshooting but one bomb was seen to hit. 0900. 030T. 14,500ft. 150 knots. We were caught in a slipstream as bomb left A/F. Tallboy fused thirty secs. Raid marred by higher squadrons crowding above first and lowest squadrons, thus spoiling the bombing run.'

Of course none of this information would have been of interest to the BBC listeners. They only wanted to hear the good news!

'I saw a 12,000-pounder land about 100 yards from Hitler's house. There was a terrific flash and, even though we were flying pretty high, we could hear the explosion above the roar of our own engines and the whole plane seemed to rock. Great piles of earth came shooting up into the sky. I thought to myself, well, even if that's a bit short it must have done damage to the place. But just at that moment, there was another flash followed by a huge explosion. One of the other aircraft had planted their bomb right on the target.'

War Correspondent Vernon Brown's description took the drama of the raid into the homes of the readers of the *News Chronicle*:

'Six Lancasters headed towards it. I saw their bombs fall as we flew alongside to drop our load. It was horrific. Into this scene below, which had the prettiness of a Victorian picture postcard, burst the 12,000lb earthquake bombs. Below, the ground spewed rocks and earth and bricks, and even trees were uprooted and thrown like straws into the sky.

'Planes were above, below and alongside us. The huge bombs went down at regular intervals. Said the engineer, Pilot Officer L. Harrison of London, "Not one must be wasted. We've either to be certain to hit the target or bring them back." I saw thirty bombs go down – there may have been more – on the target area, which included the large SS barracks where

Hitler's storm-troopers were stationed. There were at least two direct hits on the "Eagle's Nest." The force of the explosions tossed our plane upwards. I saw others shudder.

'As I write, great clouds of smoke roll to the sky. All the target is now covered in smoke and you can smell it inside the plane. There are no enemy fighters. Even the flak which bursts around is not so heavy as anticipated.'[150]

* * *

'Springtime in the Alps, fellahs. Have a look,' Don said as they completed their run. Flying home, they saw the ruins of Munich and Stuttgart 'peaceful and shattered beneath us, all their terrors gone':

'I had a mental picture of Chamberlain arriving back from Berchtesgaden to a hero's welcome in England, waving a piece of paper and saying, "I believe I have brought peace in our time." A communications gap? Perhaps something was lost in translation.'[151]

As they approached the English coast, Vernon Brown described his feelings about the operation, adding that two aircraft had been lost on the raid:

'We are nearing our English base. We have been in the air for almost nine hours and flown 1,600 miles. Below us lies English landscape in spring but I keep thinking of that mountain grandeur we have just visited. 'Hitler's home, "like an aeroplane in flight," will soar no more on its mountain top.'

They probably gave vent to their feelings on their return to Bardney. Don MacIntosh noted that 'there was no particular elation.' This had not been the grand finale that they might have hoped for and expected. Frustration and anger must have been mixed with relief that there would be no more night raids on cities, or daylight attacks on aqueducts and oil refineries. Considering how chaotic the operation had been, it was remarkable that there had been few losses. After the months or, for some like Jim, years of action, there was probably a sense of anti-climax too. All they could do now was wait for the announcement that the war was over – at least in Europe.

Members of the squadron – aircrew and ground crew alike – probably anticipated that there would be a chance to relax but this, of course, was not Jim's way. Typical April weather intervened and the next few days saw cloud, fog, wintry showers and there was no operational flying. 'Nothing of importance to report today' was a recurring entry in the ORB. On the first days of May, though, in spite of occasional rain and sleet, there were exercises: practice bombing, fighter affiliation, cross-country and air-to-sea firing. On 4 May, there was a welcome entry which read, 'Five aircraft set off for special duty mission'. This was Operation Exodus, a welcome change, bringing prisoners of war back to Britain. Men were involved in rescue and repatriation rather than attack and destruction. Doug Tweddle remembered it well:

> 'We pushed off and landed in this French field, taxied round and over the horizon came these big American open lorries with ex-PoWs that had been coming out of camps. They were broken up into groups of twenty-four and then marched round. We stuffed them into a Lanc and we climbed in. You can imagine how tight it was. You had to get them all over the main spar for the sake of take-off. After that they could sit about.'

On landing at Dunsfold there were so many aircraft that they just taxied round the peri track before coming to a halt. Members of the

WVS were out in force. Not all PoWs had been taken prisoner in Europe. The group that Doug Tweddle ferried back had been captured in North Africa:

> 'We had picked up a bunch of Sikhs and there they were, bless them, they had no material apparently to have a proper Distar (Patka) or whatever it's called, so they had a piece of rag tied in their hair. All marched over, put up a cracking salute [and were] obviously top-class soldiers.'

Doug went on to say, 'These men were in a strange land, surrounded by strange people. They had no idea what to do.' The last image he remembered was that people came out, took hold of them and led them away 'just as if they were children.'

The ORB notes that there was a further special duty mission two days later. Then, in a curiously low-key entry, on 8 May, which described the weather - Intermittent thundery rain. Thunderstorms at dusk - and the information that one aircraft had been detailed for a cross-country exercise. Only then, in block capitals and underlined, came the statement: <u>VE DAY (VICTORY IN EUROPE)</u>.

'On VE night', wrote Don MacIntosh, 'One of the hangars was cleared for the party.' The WAAFs had been busy making decorations and the electricians had festooned the girders with dim blue electric bulbs. Don recalled that there was a memorable pathway of flares lighting the road leading up to the hangar. There was no longer any blackout! There was beer and soft drinks and the group captain had invited Bardney residents, possibly in recognition of their endurance of many nights of broken sleep during the departure and return of the Lancasters. Don likened the procession of the 'motley' crowd of civilians and airmen to the pilgrims on their way to Canterbury (the film *The Canterbury Tale* had been released the previous year). It was then that he realised how isolated they had all been at the camp. 'Everyone was half-cut,' recalled Jack Linaker, 'as the Officers' and Sergeants' Messes had pooled their resources and everything was free. It was a great night.' He continued, 'Everyone was half cut and there were blown-up condoms floating round like balloons. When I woke up I was in such a state that I never got like that again.'

One woman was looking slightly dazed. 'You know,' she said, 'We've lived with it so long. It seems strange that it's all over.' She had brought her two boys so that they would be able to remember the occasion. Not everyone had stayed in Bardney. 'Most of the bright sparks,' recalled Don, 'had made a bee-line for London, where all the action was.' Reaction set in. He suddenly felt depressed and went back to the Mess to think and drink alone. Although it was ostensibly a time for rejoicing, it was also a time to remember all those who had not made it to VE Day, as well as those like Gerald Prettejohns, who had already been posted to other units.

Jim's son Michael, by now coming up to his fourth birthday, and James, nearly two, were taken to meet their father, who was coming home on leave. The only entries in Jim's logbook that fit the occasion are 20 April or, more likely, 7 May. For young Michael it was an amazing experience that made a huge impression on him, mainly due to the sheer volume of the engines:

> 'My mother drove us to an airfield in an open car to meet him. To me the sight and sound of the Lanc was overpowering. She parked where he was due to arrive. The aircraft landed and taxied towards us. Dad was the pilot: I could see him as I was in the back seat. As the aircraft came closer and closer, the noise of the four Merlin engines grew louder and louder and my Mum was getting really worried. Dad was sitting there roaring with laughter as the Lanc got closer and closer to the car.'

Jim obviously thought it very amusing, Michael was greatly intrigued but Elizabeth did not enjoy it at all!

The next couple of weeks saw the squadron involved in a wide variety of occupations. A real sign that the war was over manifested itself in the disposal of incendiaries, which were, as Doug Tweddle said, 'getting rather ripe and were dangerous'. There must have been huge quantities. Between 9 May and 18 May, fifty-three aircraft were detailed to fly out and drop them over the North Sea. There were 'Cook's Tours' as well, when members of the hard-working ground crews were given the opportunity to see the results of the raids. Eight took place during the week of 13 May. Don MacIntosh flew on one:

'I took half-a-dozen WAAFs from the motor pool as passengers. We flew across the Channel and over Northern Germany, while two or three took it in turns to crouch in the bomb-aiming compartment in the nose. I descended to 500ft over Essen, Bremen and Emden to give them a better view of the eerie spectacle. Not a single building had a roof and the cities were completely gutted. I didn't see how any human beings could exist, let alone help to fight a war, in them. From the air, it looked impossible that life of any kind could be carried out among the ruins. What did they do for food, water and sanitation? How on earth did they keep going for so long?'[152]

It was a relief for them to return to Bardney and to leave behind them the 'moonscape of destruction.'

There were more mercy flights, too, with nine aircraft taking part in Operation Exodus on 15 May.

Jim's days at IX Squadron were now numbered. Reading the accounts of the men who served under him in IX Squadron, a picture emerges of a man who was comfortable in his command and who communicated easily with everyone in the squadron. Jim seems to have been very conscious of how men were reacting to stress. Don MacIntosh summed it up:

> 'Fear, like a trickle in the wall of a dyke, quickly became a flood, breaching the barriers of the mind and stomach and communicating itself to the whole crew. Expecting trouble, their already taut nerves stretched to every bang and flash, drastically lowering their efficiency. I'd seen it happen, though we didn't talk about it. Near the end of their tour, Bazin tried to shield them and finish them early. Nobody in our squadron had been sent LMF (Lack of Moral Fibre) that I knew about.'

Sadly, and for whatever reason, the handover to the new CO does not appear to have gone smoothly and seems to have had a lasting effect on Jim. Something had obviously happened in the last few hours of his command that affected him profoundly. Doug Tweddle referred to the handover to Jim's successor, Wing Commander Dupont, suggesting that it could have been about a disagreement over citations that had been recommended. Instead of staying in the room after he had introduced the new CO, Jim had stormed out, clearly very upset. Doug added, 'We knew this was a bad sign.' Several members of the squadron commented in later life that they could not understand why he had never attended a reunion of IX Squadron. His relationship with 607 Squadron was quite different. He rejoined it as soon as he could and eventually became CO.

It was announced on 21 September that Jim had been awarded the DSO. The citation read:

> 'After completing a tour of operations with Fighter Command, during which he was awarded the DFC, this

officer volunteered for operations with Bomber Command. Whilst in command of his present squadron he has completed many hazardous sorties. He has led his squadron on nearly every one of its daylight attacks, many of them against highly defended targets, including shipping at Brest and two attacks on the *Tirpitz*.

'Since Wing Commander Bazin assumed command of his squadron, he has trained it in the operation of new equipment, and the very high operational standard reached has been largely due to his untiring work and devotion to duty.'[153]

There were still five months to go before Jim was to finally return to civilian life. His next posting to 3 Group 31 Base was in a supervisory role, then five days later, on 30 May, he was appointed to Air Staff. He was at Bomber Command HQ on Operations (General Duties) until 2 November, when he stepped into the world of post-war Britain.

It was just two weeks short of the sixth anniversary of 607 Squadron's move to France.

It had been a long war for him and, considering what he had experienced, it was remarkable that he was still alive and in one piece. Patrick Bishop commented that Jim 'seemed indestructible,' continuing by saying that, at least on the face of it, the war had not seemed to have affected him.[154]

After the initial exhilaration of the first weeks of September 1939, there had been the stark reality of the winter in France, culminating in the desperate days of May 1940, when the RAF was struggling to keep back the advance of the German land forces. Within just a few weeks of their return to England and the news that their squadron had been depleted of many of its men, Jim was in the air again, this time defending the skies over England in the Battle of Britain, first in the north-east of England, then at Tangmere.

There followed some months training controllers in the new Ground Control Interception before being posted as a controller to Scotland. By the time Jim arrived at Inverness at the end of February 1942, all but nine of the heavy raids on Scotland were over, although there continued to be a series of smaller incidents until the end of April 1943, all but one over the east coast, and mostly on the area nicknamed Hellfire Corner.

For the last eighteen months of the war, eleven of them as CO of IX Squadron, he took part in bombing raids over France, Belgium, the Low Countries, Germany, eastern Europe and Norway, usually on specialist daylight operations.

There might have been no outward sign, but the man just short of his thirty-third birthday must have been a very different person from the 26-year-old who had been called up for service a week before war was declared in September 1939.

The transition to civilian life was to be another challenge.

Chapter 11

Postwar

1946-1951, a return to 607 Squadron, and his civilian career

Jim's last day of service was on 2 November 1945. Because he was an engineer, he could have applied for early release but, for whatever reason, he chose to stay on. He resumed his engineering career and was also appointed to the Board of Durham Chemicals. Like millions of men and women during this period, Jim, Elizabeth and the two boys had to try to adjust to family life together in a bleak post-war world, where even bread was rationed.

Meanwhile, 607 Squadron was still serving in the Far East, where it had been stationed since March 1942 as a Hurri-bomber unit. Then, in January 1945, it was one of the first squadrons to fly Spitfires in Burma. It was not until 10 May 1946 that it was once again based at Ouston, reverting to its earlier role as an auxiliary squadron. Joe Kayll, now back in England after nearly five years as a prisoner of war, was appointed commanding officer. He had been awarded the OBE for his part in the arduous and dangerous task of organising many escape attempts, including the 'Wooden Horse' exploit with Dudley Craig as his No. 2 and Aidan Crawley as Intelligence Officer.[155]

Although Jim is listed as being back with 607 Squadron on 5 December 1946 as a Flight Commander, the first entry in his logbook dates from three weeks earlier, when he went up as a passenger in a Harvard flown by Flight Lieutenant Collingridge. The heading on the page simply reads

'607 Sqdn', heavily underlined. He was flying Harvards from January until 12 April when an entry in the 'Duty' column simply states, 'Spitfire 1st Solo'. It was a curious entry as he had already flown Spitfires on six occasions between April and July 1943, when he was based in Inverness. He spent ninety minutes in the air but with no indication whether it was a local flight or whether he went further afield. For the next few years, many Saturday mornings saw him at Ouston, sometimes taking his two young sons with him. The boys would watch take-offs and listen to what was going on in the Control Tower, before adjourning to the Mess, then down the road to 'Old Ma Murray's' to tuck into bacon and eggs, a memorable treat in the days of post-war austerity.

> 'Clipped wings of Spitfires swooping in the sunlight over the beaches and golf courses of St Andrew's tell holidaymakers at one of Scotland's most exclusive resorts that the invaders from over the Border are at work.'

This dramatic description in the *Sunderland Echo* of 19 July 1947 marks the first post-war Summer Camp which was held at Leuchars. The headline announced that the seventy members of the squadron were working hard and playing just as hard. Six Spitfires and two Harvards were airborne on training exercises and refresher courses, beginning at dawn and no doubt disturbing the sleep of holidaymakers trying to have a lie-in.

Among the busy ground crew were men who had been with the squadron from pre-war days. Sergeant R.E. Gibson BEM had joined the squadron at the same time as Jim in 1935. Other Wearsiders mentioned by name were Leading Aircraftmen George Greenfield and F. Petch, who, along with several other members of the ground crew, had all served in the Battles of France and Britain before spending the rest of the war with the squadron in India and Burma. It was also noted that Leading Aircraftman Harold Campion had played in the team that won the RAF Shield at Abbeville in 1940. It was not all work, however. They were also treated to a coach tour taking in some of the magnificent scenery of the Perthshire Highlands.

In spite of concern over the highly sensitive political situation in Germany, the annual Summer Camp in 1948 went ahead at Lübeck, at an airfield very close to the border with Soviet-controlled East Germany. Jim flew there via West Raynham, Manston and Eindhoven, territory familiar from his days with IX Squadron. Four weeks before they were due to leave, Soviet troops blockaded all West Berlin's road, rail and water access, prompting the US and UK to airlift supplies to the section of the city held by the Allies. A few days later, US B-29s capable of carrying nuclear weapons arrived in England. So it is hardly surprising that the forty ATC cadets from Northumberland and Durham who were to have accompanied the squadron learned a few weeks before they were due to leave for Germany that they were to spend their summer camp in Kent instead.

Back at Ouston, routine flights and training exercises continued at weekends throughout the year, whenever the weather permitted. July 1949 was particularly busy. At the beginning of the month, the squadron took part in Exercise Foil at Church Fenton. Then a couple of weeks later, squadron members flew in formation to Horsham St Faith now Norwich International, for the Summer Camp.

With Joe Kayll's retirement from the squadron at the end of September 1949, Jim took over as CO on 1 October. The memorial tablet to 607 Squadron on the wall of the south transept in Durham Cathedral was dedicated two months later.

It is interesting to note that the number of entries in Jim's logbook diminishes dramatically over the next eighteen months, partly because of his new duties, but possibly as an indication that his interests outside the squadron were beginning to take up more of his time.

On 1 December 1950, the *Newcastle Journal* reported that Jim had been adopted as the Conservative candidate for the West Newcastle constituency. His career had been blossoming as he is now described as chief engineer of a number of engineering companies and managing director of the headquarters at Hebburn. In spite of the increasing demands made on the time he needed to devote to the election campaign, Jim continued as CO of 607 Squadron for another three months, now assisted by Doug Tweddle, who had 'felt the yen' to fly again. He had got in touch with Jim, who had given him a warm welcome and appointed him as his Auxiliary Adjutant. Finally relinquishing command on 1 March 1951, Jim transferred to the Reserve. A month later, he joined 300 others at a gala dance, where he was described as the former CO of 607 Squadron. At some point, perhaps marking his retirement from the squadron, Jim had donated the Bazin Shield to be awarded to the best cadet squadron of the seventeen units in Northumberland and Durham that were attached to RAF Ouston.

His sixteen years with the RAF were behind him and his focus now was on his engineering career and his political interests. With just a slim majority of five seats, and the proposed prolonged absence of King George VI on a Commonwealth tour that was being planned for 1952, Attlee called a snap election for 25 October 1951. Although his elder son Michael was at school on Election Day, he occasionally accompanied Jim during the campaign and has vivid memories of seeing wet roads through a large hole in the floor of the car and hearing his father rallying potential supporters through a megaphone. Jim was now facing the sitting MP, Ernest Popplewell, a railwayman with the 'air of a trade unionist', and a veteran from the First World War who had been awarded the Croix de Guerre. In the 1945 election Popplewell had won the seat from the Conservative William Nunn, who had been elected unopposed in 1940. From a debate reported in the same paper in October 1951, we learn something of Jim's political ideas. Strongly believing in the United Nations, he warned the audience that the greatest military threat would be from Russia, where the Communist dictatorship was busily rearming. 'We must realise,' he continued, 'that we are no longer the leading nation in the world,' adding that the new super-states were now the Soviet Union and the USA. He emphasised that it was only the development of sufficient quantities of atom bombs and aircraft to deliver them that had prevented an attack by the Russians. 'At the end of the war,' he stated, 'we were ahead of the world in the development of the jet engine. Now,' he continued, 'we have to buy 200 or more aircraft from America.' The debate ranged over a wide variety of subjects with Jim challenging Popplewell's statement that countries should be given independence even if they weren't sufficiently prepared. Jim was doubtless aware of the violent events that had taken place in Kashmir, the land of his childhood, after the partition of India in 1947. It seems to have been a very lively discussion and gives us a rare insight into Jim's views on world politics, which drew on his own experience, both from his childhood in India and his service in the RAF.

Elizabeth gave birth to their daughter Anthea in January 1952. Because Jim's focus was on developing his career, he spent less and less time with his family so, during school holidays and occasional weekends, Elizabeth, with Anthea and the two boys, would join her sister Toni and her two sons at Beanley Southside, not far from Alnwick, where the cousins were free to roam the surrounding hills in the company of shepherds and rabbit catchers – but only after they had carried out their designated morning chores!

Although he was not generally enthusiastic about attending reunions, Jim did travel south to RAF Binbrook in October 1956 for the presentation of a new standard to IX Squadron, meeting up with some of the former COs. Doug Tweddle, who had first met him when they shared an instructor at OTU, mused on Jim's break with IX Squadron.

'He doesn't come to reunions,' he said, 'I'm not sure why. He's getting on a bit, but I think there is something deeper than that.

By this time, Jim's marriage to Elizabeth had ended and he had married Nan Boston, moving with her three children to Acombe House, near Hexham, where their daughter Miranda was born. Later they were to move south to Surrey. For most of their married life they lived at Breton East, in a wing of the house in Weybridge that had been part of the German Embassy's pre-war country retreat. It had been taken over by the army during the war, inevitably resulting in considerable wear and tear. Among many other projects to restore the house to its original state, Jim spent much of his spare time painstakingly renovating the handsome staircase. He also supervised the construction of a deep swimming pool, making it known that only those who had helped to build it would be allowed to use it!

An examination of some of his passports shows that from the 1950s he was travelling the world, initially selling atomic energy to countries including Japan and negotiating sales contracts in Algeria (1951), Australia, Europe, the Far East (1957), Thailand, Belgium, Switzerland, Hong Kong, Nigeria and Ghana (1958), and Romania and Yugoslavia (1961). As a result of this work, a national newspaper named him 'Supersalesman of the Year.' When he joined the Adams Group in the mid-1960s, much of his work involved travel to countries behind the Iron Curtain. It was about this time that he acquired the nickname 'Dangerman', a popular television series that ran from 1960-1962.

In 1980, Jim was one of the Battle of Britain pilots invited to a party held during the eightieth birthday celebrations of Queen Elizabeth the Queen Mother, an event that he greatly enjoyed. Now in his late sixties, he was still commuting to his office in central London, usually leaving home before six o'clock to avoid the traffic jams. However, his health was beginning to deteriorate and he eventually had to retire. One evening, Nan received a call from the wing commander who administered the

Battle of Britain Association. He had been asked to supply details to the *Surrey Herald* of any remaining 'Few' in the area but had only been able to provide Jim's name. It took considerable and well-timed persuasion by Nan, but she prepared the ground carefully and Jim grudgingly agreed to be interviewed.

Not long before Jim died, he stayed with his son Michael on the Isle of Man. On the parade ground of the former RAF station at Jurby, which had been used during wartime cross-country exercises, and the only place on the island that he expressed an interest in visiting, he stood stock-still in total silence, lost in deep thought.

He died on 9 January 1985 after a long illness, and a full life that he felt had been lived on borrowed time. The funeral cortège made its way to the crematorium through heavy snow, a poignant reminder of the bitter winters of the war. The service was attended by representatives from the Battle of Britain Association, and it was there during the eulogy that the family heard, often for the first time, some of the highlights of his RAF career. Back at Breton East, when only close friends and family remained at the end of the afternoon, Nan signalled to a neighbour, a member of the Magic Circle, who reappeared a short time later and treated everyone to a superb magic show. All agreed that Jim would have enjoyed it!

Because of his deep involvement with Tangmere, it was Jim's wish that his ashes should be interred in the churchyard where friends from 607 Squadron were buried. Members of the family travelled down from Weybridge in two cars. Stopping at a pre-arranged pub for lunch, it was some time before the car with Nan arrived. Apparently, they were already some distance into the journey when they suddenly realised they had forgotten Jim's ashes. The urn had been kept in the drinks cupboard. It was felt by some that perhaps Jim would have been more comfortable alongside a whisky bottle! That day there had been some problems with the Battle of Britain Memorial Flight, so, disappointingly, the promised tribute could not take place. During the service his elder son Michael read John Magee's powerful poem 'High Flight'.

The memorial tablet at Tangmere simply reads:

> James Michael Bazin
> DSO DFC
> 607 Sqn
> 1913–1985
> Sunward I've Climbed

Another line from Magee's moving poem reads 'and done a hundred things you have not dreamed of.' For a man who spoke little and wrote nothing of his life story, these words seem to be a particularly appropriate epitaph for his extraordinary career.

Four months after Jim's death, the RAFA Commemorative Issue of May 1995 marked the 50th Anniversary of VE Day. Jim's medals were featured on the cover, along with the Battle of Britain Memorial Flight's Lancaster, Spitfire and Hurricane. On pages 28 to 31, a four-page article by Stan White summarised Jim's RAF career.

It was simply headed *'A Long War for Some.'*

Appendix

Jim Bazin's operations with 49 and IX Squadrons and the men who flew with him

Sergeant A. Bell	(AB)	2
Flight Lieutenant C.J. Campbell	(CJC)	5
Sergeant C. Cameron	(CC)	26
Sergeant R. Collins	(RC)	21
Flying Officer D. Cooper	(DC)	4
Sergeant S.E. Evans	(SE)	24
Flying Officer Fitzgerald	(DF)	3
Sergeant J.R. Gran (Canadian)	(JRG)	21
Flight Lieutenant Edgar F.A. Jones	(EFAJ)	3
Flight Sergeant K.L. Lewis	(KLL)	21
Pilot Officer R.F. Lewis	(RFL)	2
Sergeant W.C. Lewis	(WCL)	3
Sergeant H. McDonnell	(HMcD)	17
Sergeant G.E. Parkinson	(GEP)	1
Flight Lieutenant A.M. Ritchie	(AMR)	5
Flight Sergeant K.I. Rogers	(KIR)	1
Squadron Leader F.G. Rumbles	(FGR)	1
Sergeant T.G. Williams	(TGW)	1

49 Squadron

May 1944
24	Vector bombing	HMcD	KLL	RC	CC	JRG	SE
27	Morsalines	HMcD	KLL	RC	CC	JRG	SE
29	H2S	HMcD	KLL	RC	CC	JRG	SE
31	Coastal batteries	HMcD	KLL	RC	CC	JRG	SE

June 1944
2	Wimereux	HMcD	KLL	RC	CC	JRG	SE
5	La Pernelle	HMcD	KLL	RC	CC	JRG	SE
6	Caen Bridges	HMcD	KLL	RC	CC	JRG	SE
8	Pontaubault	HMcD	KLL	RC	CC	JRG	SE
9	Étampes Marshalling yards	HMcD	KLL	RC	CC	JRG	SE

IX Squadron

June 1944
21	Gelsenkirchen	AB	KLL	JRG	RC	CC	SE

July 1944
19	Creil Day	AB	KLL	JRG	RC	CC	SE
26	Givors E/R	WCL	KLL	JRG	RC	CC	SE
31	Rilly-la-Montagne	WCL	KLL	JRG	RC	CC	SE

August 1944
4	Étaples Day	HMcD	KLL	JRG	GEP	CC	SE
9	La Pallice Day	WCL	KLL	JRG	RC	CC	SE
13	Brest Day	AMR	RFL	JRG	RC	CC	SE
14	Brest Day	AMR	RFL	JRG	RC	CC	SE

September 1944
11	Archangel	AMR	EFAJ	JRG	RC	CC	SE
15	*Tirpitz*	AMR	EFAJ	JRG	RC	CC	SE
16	Archangel-Base	AMR	EFAJ	JRG	RC	CC	SE

October 1944
15	Sorpe Dam	HMcD	KLL	JRG	RC	CC	SE
28	*Tirpitz*	HMcD	KLL	FGR	RC	CC	SE

November 1944   No operational flights recorded in Jim's logbook
Two return flights from Bardney to Kinloss

December 1944
11	Urft Dam	HMcD	KLL	CJC	DC	TGW	SE

January 1945   No entries in Jim's logbook

February 1945
3	Ops (Ymuiden [sic])	HMcD	KLL	CJC	DC	CC	DF
6	Altenbeken	HMcD	KLL	CJC	DC	CC	DF
22	Paderborn	HMcD	KLL	CJC	DC	CC	DF

March 1945
13	Arnsberg	HMcD	KLL	CJC	KIR	CC	SE

Bibliography

Arthur, M., *There shall be Wings: vivid personal accounts of the RAF from 1918 to today*, Hodder and Stoughton, Great Britain 1993.

Bennett, T., *617 Squadron: The Dambusters at War*, Patrick Stephens Ltd, England 1986.

Bickers, R.T., *The Battle of Britain: the greatest battle in the history of air warfare*, Salamander Books Ltd, New York 1990.

Bishop, E., *Book of Airmen's Obituaries*, Grub Street, London 2002.

Bishop, P., *Air Force Blue: the RAF in World War Two*, William Collins, London 2017.

Bishop, P., *Target Tirpitz*, Harper Press, London 2012.

Bond, S and Forder, R., *Special Ops Liberators*, Grub Street, London 2011.

Bowyer, C and van Ishoven, A., *Hurricane Messerschmitt*, The Promotional Reprint Company, USA 1977.

Braddon, R., *Cheshire VC: A Study of War and Peace*, Evans Brothers Limited, London 1954.

Brookes, A., *Fighter and Bomber Squadrons at War*, The Promotional Reprint Company Ltd, Leicester 1995.

Cooper, A., *Beyond the Dams to the Tirpitz*, Goodall Publishing, London and St Albans 1991.

Cornwell, P.D., *The Battle of France Then and Now*, Battle of Britain International Ltd, Essex 2007.

Cull, B, Lander, B and Weiss, H., *Twelve Days in May*, Grub Street, London 1995.

Dixon, R., *607 Squadron: A Shade of Blue*, The History Press, Stroud, Gloucestershire 2008.

Dixon, R., *The Diary of a Hurricane Pilot in the Battle of France*, Fonthill Media Ltd, UK 2015.

Eriksen, H.K., *World War II in the Borderland*, Borderland Museum Kirkenes, Norway.

Fife, M., *RAF Acklington: Guardian of the Northern Seas*, Fonthill Media Ltd, UK 2017.

Forsgren, J., *Sinking the Beast: the RAF 1944 Lancaster Raids against Tirpitz*, Fonthill Media Ltd, UK and USA 2014.

Gretzyngier, R., *Poles in Defence of Britain*, Grub Street, London, 2001.

Hastings, M., *Bomber Command: Churchill's Epic Campaign*, Simon and Schuster, New York 1979.

Hooten, E., *Eagle in Flames: The Fall of the Luftwaffe*, Arms and Armour, London UK 1999.

Hunt, L., *Twenty-one Squadrons: The History of the Royal Auxiliary Air Force*, Crécy Publishing Ltd, Manchester, 1992.

Iliff, J., *Airmen's Obituaries Book Two*, Grub Street, London 2007.

Iveson, T., *Lancaster: The Biography*, André Deutsch, London 2009.

Johnson, J., *Wing Leader*, Chatto and Windus, England 1956.

Lewis, B., *Air Crew: the story of the men who flew the bombers*, Cassell, London 1991.

MacIntosh D., *Bomber Pilot Donald MacIntosh: A Veteran's First-hand Account of Surviving World War Two as a RAF Bomber Pilot*, Amazon Book. First published privately in paperback by Donald Macintosh in 2006. Now out of print.

Mason, T., *9 Squadron*, Beaumont Publication, Great Britain 1965.

Mayo, J., *D-Day – Minute by minute*, Short Books, London 2014.

McKinstry, L., *Hurricane: Victor of the Battle of Britain*, John Murray, Great Britain 2010.

Milton, G., *The Ministry of Ungentlemanly Warfare*, John Murray, Great Britain 2016.

Mombeek, E., *Eismeerjäger-Zur geschichte des Jagdgeshwaders 5 – Band 4 (Fighters in the Arctic Sea – The History of the 5th Fighter Wing – Volume 4)*, Linkebeek, Belgium 2011.

Nichol, J., *Lancaster: the Forging of a Very British Legend*, Simon and Schuster UK Ltd, London 2020.

Parrott, R., *The Pilot in the Poster: Peter Parrott*, Brown Dog Books and The Self-Publishing Partnership, Bath 2020.

Plummer, R., *The ships that saved an army*, Patrick Stephens, England 1990.

Probert, P., *Bomber Harris: his Life and Times*, Greenhill Books, London 2001.

Ray, J., *The Battle of Britain: Dowding and the First Victory, 1940*, Cassell Military Paperbacks, London 1994.

Richey, P., *Fighter Pilot*, The History Press, Gloucestershire 2016.

Sarkar, D., *The Last of the Few*, Amberley Publishing, Stroud, Glos. 2010.

Saunders, H. StG., *Royal Air Force 1939-1945 Volume III 'The Fight is Won'*, HMSO, London 1954.

Schuck, W., *Luftwaffe Eagle: from the Me109 to the Me262*, Hikoki Publications, Manchester 2009.

Stewart, A., *They Flew Hurricanes*, Pen and Sword Aviation, Barnsley, South Yorkshire 2005.

Sweetman, J., *Bomber Crew: Taking on the Reich*, Little, Brown, Great Britain, 2004.

Taylor, L., *Luftwaffe over Scotland*, Whittles Publishing, Caithness 2010.

Thorburn, G., *Bombers First and Last*, Robson Books, London 2006

Thorburn, G., *A Century of Air Warfare with Nine (IX) Squadron RAF: Still Going Strong*, Pen and Sword Aviation, Barnsley, S. Yorkshire 2014.

Thorburn, G., *Luck of a Lancaster*, Pen and Sword Books Ltd, Barnsley, S. Yorkshire 2013, 2015.

Townshend Bickers, R., *The Battle of Britain*, Salamander Books, London 1990.

Tulloch, B., *Terror in the Arctic*, Matador, Leicestershire 2011.

Ward, C., *Squadron Profiles Number 14: 49 Squadron*, C. Ward, Berkshire 1998.

Webster, C. and Frankland, N., *The Strategic Air Offensive against Germany, 1939-1945, Vol. 3*, 'Victory' Naval and Military Press, England 2006 (Reprint).

Whitfield, F., *We sat alone*, Independently published. Reprinted 2019 and issued as an eBook.

Wood, D. and Dempster, D., *The Narrow Margin: The Battle of Britain and the rise of air power, 1930-1940*, Tri-Service Press Ltd, London 1969.

Wright, R., *Dowding and the Battle of Britain*, MacDonald and Co. Ltd, London 1969.

Wynn, K.G., *Men of the Battle of Britain*, Gliddon Books, Norwich 1989.

Zetterling, N. and Tamelander, M., *Tirpitz: The Life and Death of Germany's Last Super Battleship*, Casemate Haverton, Pennsylvania 2009.

Bibliography

Archives
National Archives, Kew CAB 23/9, 117; CAB 23/87; 607 Squadron AIR 27/2093, 2-24; 49 Squadron AIR 27/129; 9 Squadron AIR 27/128 (1944); AIR 27/129 (1945); AIR 39/128; AIR/50/170; WO 291/392

Journals, magazines and newspapers
Aeroplane Monthly, Key Publishing Ltd, England October 2019.
Battle of Britain: Parts 1, 2 and 3, The *Sunday Telegraph*, London June 1990.
Battle of Britain Souvenir Book 1963, RAF Benevolent Fund, London 1963.
Bomber Command: The Air Ministry Account of Bomber Command's Offensive Against the Axis September 1939-July 1941, HMSO, London 1941.
FlyPast, Kay Publishing Limited, England, May 2012.
Reyrolle Monthly Letter, Oct-Nov 1944.
TABS Annual publication of IX Squadron 2015, 2018, 2019, 2021.
The Battle of Britain: August-October 1940, HMSO, London 1940.
VE Day, The Royal Air Forces Association Commemorative Issue May 1995.

Manuscripts
Darlow, S., *'Bang' – The Jack Linaker Story*, TABS 2017, 28-30.
Grant, Malcolm, Typescript, 9 October 1992.
Harman, E.S., *Report on Operation Paravane: Operational Diary of Numbers 9 and 617 Squadrons*, Monday 11 September-27 September 1944, IX Squadron Archives.
Harvey, Roy., Extracts reproduced courtesy of Roy Harvey, navigator, IX Squadron.
Macintosh, Donald, *A veteran's first-hand account of surviving World War Two as a RAF Bomber Pilot*, Typescript interview from the IX Squadron Archives.
Prettejohns, Gerald., *A boy from Hackney*, Extracts from IX Squadron archives are reproduced by kind permission of his son Jono Prettejohns.
Riches, Flight Sergeant, Extracts from IX Squadron archives are reproduced by kind permission of his son Larry Riches.
Tetlow, Phil, *Wartime Diary of Sergeant Phil Tetlow, 9 Squadron, RAF*, Typed and transcribed by 9 Association Secretary, Squadron Leader Richard James in December 2010.

Tweddle, William Douglas, DFC, Extracts from the transcript of a tape of memories from his Wartime Flying Logbook including the three Tirpitz raids. 4 July 1944-15 September 1977, Reproduced courtesy of John Tweddle.

White, Stan, Typescript notes on a conversation with Jim Bazin. Bazin Family Archive.

Websites

Arctic Convoys of World War II - Wikipedia
Glossary of WWII RAF Slang & Terminology (natureonline.com)
http://en.wikipedia.org/wiki/Heinrich_Ehrler
https://ecrivelo.eu Search Givors
https://experts.umn.edu/en/publications/warfare-dendochronology-trees-witness-the-deployment-of-the-germ
Battle of Britain London Monument, *The Airmen's Stories*
https://wikipedia.org/Allied siege of La Rochelle
https://en.wikipedia.org/wiki/Ijmuiden
https://en.wikipedia.org/wiki/Lorient
www.battlefieldsww2.com/Bergen-u-boat-bunker.html
www.bomberhistory.co.uk/canal_raids/gravenhorst

Endnotes

1. *Reyrolle Monthly Letter* October, November and December 1944, 30.
2. Dixon, R., *607 Squadron: A Shade of Blue,* The History Press, Stroud, Gloucestershire, 2008, 19.
3. Johnson, J., *Wing Leader,* Chatto and Windus, England, 1956, 17.
4. Lord Londonderry's main record at the Air Ministry included the preservation of the core of the RAF at a time when it was under threat from the Treasury. He had encouraged the planning of vital new fighter aircraft such as the Hurricane and Spitfire and it was with his support that radar was developed for use by the RAF. It was during the final part of his time as Air Minister that the Staff College at Cranwell came into operation. However, he is also remembered as a minister who underestimated the strength of the Luftwaffe in 1934–35. Alvin Jackson, 'Stewart, Charles Stewart Henry Vane-Tempest, Seventh Marquess of Londonderry (1878-1949),' *Oxford Dictionary of National Biography 2004; online edn January 2008.*'
5. National Archives CAB 23/9, 117.
6. 13 Group, formed in 1939 was responsible for the area from fifty miles north of York as far as the Firth of Forth, with isolated sectors at Scapa Flow, Orkney, and Northern Ireland. A major role during the war was to provide recuperation space for exhausted members of squadrons operating from the south of England, as well as safer training aerodromes for new pilots.
7. Fife, M., *Acklington: Guardian of the Northern Seas,* Finthill Media Ltd, UK 2017, 32.
8. In correspondence with Geoff Simpson, 10 July 2020.
9. Hunt, L., *Twenty-one Squadrons: The History of the Royal Auxiliary Air Force 1925-1957,* Crécy Publishing Ltd, Manchester 1992, 166.
10. Jim Bazin's Combat Report, 17 October 1939, page 2. *National Archives Reference AIR 50/170/5.*

11. Dixon, 2008, 76.
12. Townshend Bickers, R., *The Battle of Britain,* Salamander Books, London 1990, 13.
13. Dixon, R., *The Diary of a Hurricane Pilot in the Battle of France,* Fonthill Media Ltd 2015, 94-104.
14. Dixon 2008, 78.
15. Dixon 2015, 92-103.
16. Hunt, 167.
17. Dixon 2015, 106-124.
18. Bazin, Combat Report 10.5.40 National Archives AIR/50/170.
19. Cull, B., Lander, B. with Weiss, H., *Twelve Days in May,* Grub Street, London 1995, 53-56.
20. Dixon 2008, 89.
21. Parrott, R., *The Pilot in the Poster, Peter Parrott,* Brown Dog Books, Bath 2020, 57.
22. National Archives AIR/50/170, Image reference 101, Combat Report 10 May 1940.
23. Cull, Lander and Weiss, 37-44.
24. Dixon 2015, 126-127.
25. Stewart, *They Flew Hurricanes,* Pen and Sword Aviation, Barnsley, South Yorkshire 2005, 31-32.
26. Cull, Lander and Weiss, 109-141.
27. Dixon 2008, 134.
28. Cull, Lander and Weiss, 149.
29. Dixon 2015, 130.
30. Cornwell, P.D., *The Battle of France Then and Now,* Battle of Britain International Ltd, Essex 2007, 292.
31. Cornwell, 319.
32. Dixon 2015, 129.
33. 607 Squadron, 82 National Archives AIR 27/2093ORB.
34. Cull, Lander and Weiss, 294-295.
35. Dixon 2015, 131.
36. 607 Squadron ORB, 82-3 National Archives AIR 27/2093ORB.
37. Cull, Lander and Weiss, 307.
38. 607 Squadron ORB, 83 National Archives AIR 27/2093ORB.

39. Stewart, 31.
40. Dixon 2015, 132.
41. Lenehan was based at 55 OTU at RAF Usworth. He was killed on 5 December 1941. When flying over Pelton, Co. Durham, he was seen steering his Hurricane Mk 2 away from the village to crash into a potato field to avoid civilian casualties.
42. Welford, Blackadder and Vick all survived the war, but Gore was to be shot down and reported missing over the sea on 28 September 1940, Parnall was killed over Mayfield on 9 September and Bowen went missing on 1 October.
43. Wood, D., and Dempster, D., *The Narrow Margin: the Battle of Britain and the Rise of Air Power 1930-1940*, Tri-Service Press Ltd 1969, 204.
44. Geoff Simpson in email correspondence July 2020.
45. Hunt, 169.
46. *Newcastle Journal*, 16 August 1940.
47. Taylor, L., *Luftwaffe over Scotland*, Whittles Publishing, Caithness, 2010, 60.
48. White, S., Manuscript notes on a conversation with Jim Bazin 1988.
49. Wright, 184.
50. Wood and Dempster, 272, 273
51. In correspondence with Geoff Simpson, 9 July 2020.
52. White 1988.
53. White 1988.
54. Stewart, 147.
55. White 1988.
56. *The London Gazette*, p.6193.
57. bbm.co.uk/?s=richard+darre
58. Taylor, 70-71.
59. https://www.bbc.com/historyofthebbc/100-voices/ww2/d-day
60. The role of the Beach Units was to assist on the landings, assembly and onward dispatch of RAF personnel, stores and equipment across the beaches so tactical support could be provided from the beachhead as quickly as possible.
61. Arthur, M., *There shall be Wings: vivid personal accounts of the RAF from 1918 to today*, Hodder and Stoughton, Great Britain 1993, 319.

62. Thorburn, G., *Bombers First and Last*, Robson Books, London 2006, 162.
63. Probert, H., *Bomber Harris: his Life and Times*, Greenhill Books, London 2001, 289-295.
64. See Appendix.
65. Mason, T., *9 Squadron*, Beaumont Publications, Great Britain 1965, 68.
66. Thorburn, G.A., *A Century of Air Warfare with Nine (IX) Squadron: Still going strong*, Pen and Sword Ltd, Barnsley, S. Yorkshire, 2014, 179.
67. Braddon, R., *Cheshire VC: A study of war and peace*, Evans Brothers, London 1954, 87.
68. Prettejohns 'A Boy from Hackney'. Ms from Jono Prettejohns, 9 February 2021.
69. MacIntosh, D., *Bomber Pilot Donald MacIntosh: a Veteran's first-hand account of Surviving World War Two as a Bomber Pilot*, Amazon, First published in 2006 by Browsebooks through Bookforce, plc. Bookforce (orderbooks), 1550 Albemarle Street, London 2006, 204.
70. Whitfield, F., *We sat alone* Published independently and republished 2019 as an eBook.
71. Flight Sergeant Riches. Extracts from the archives are reproduced by kind permission of his son Larry Riches.
72. Tweddle William Douglas, DFC. Extracts from the transcript of a tape of memories from his wartime flying logbook including the three *Tirpitz* raids. 4 July 1944-15 September 1977. Reproduced courtesy of John Tweddle.
73. Thorburn, G., *Luck of a Lancaster*, Pen and Sword Books Ltd, Barnsley, S. Yorkshire 2013, 146.
74. Tetlow, Phil., *Wartime Diary of Sergeant Phil Tetlow, 9 Squadron, RAF*, IX Squadron Archives. Tetlow joined the RAF in August 1942, completing 42 operations, including all three raids on *Tirpitz*.
75. MacIntosh, 198.
76. Thorburn 2013, 158.
77. From the *Frank Sowerby Archive*, reproduced with kind permission of his daughter Caryl Carr.
78. Thorburn 2014, 156.
79. Bomber Pilot MacIntosh, *Interview by unidentified interviewer*, IX Squadron Archive.

80. Cooper, A., *Beyond the Dams to the Tirpitz*, Goodall Publications, London and St Albans 1991, 80.
81. Thorburn 2014, 194-5.
82. Ibid, 21.
83. MacIntosh, 242.
84. Research at the University of Minnesota published in September 2019 showed that many of the trees in the Kaafjord area took thirty years to recover from the effects of the smoke screen. https://experts.umn.edu/en/publications/warfare-dendrochronology-trees-witness-the-deployment-of-the-germ.
85. Ray Harvey manuscript, IX Squadron Archives.
86. Senior Engineering Officer Squadron Leader Eric McCabe's Official Report, IX Squadron Archives.
87. MacIntosh, 250-51, 265.
88. *Aeroplane*, October 2019, 54.
89. Sweetman, J., *Bomber Crew: Taking on the Reich*, Little, Brown, Great Britain 2004, 210.
90. White, S., in *RAFA Commemorative Issue*, May 1995, 30.
91. *Aeroplane*, 55.
92. MacIntosh, 262.
93. Bishop, P., *Target Tirpitz*, Harper Press, London 2012, 333.
94. *Report on Operation Paravane: Operational Diary of Numbers 9 and 617 Squadrons, Monday, 11 September-27 September 1944*, in TABS 39/2021, 22.
95. MacIntosh, 287-8.
96. Webster, C. and Frankland, N., *The Strategic Air Offence against Germany, 1939-1945, Vol. III*, 'Victory' Naval and Military Press, England 2006 (reprint), 194.
97. Forsgren, 95.
98. Thorburn 2006, 292.
99. MacIntosh, 292.
100. Forsgren, 100.
101. Bennet, T., *The Dambusters at War*, Patrick Stephens Ltd, 1986, 159.
102. *Aeroplane Monthly*, Key Publishing Ltd, October 2019, 57.
103. The Frank Sowerby Archive.

104. *TABS* 2021, 22.
105. Darlow, S., 'Bang' in *TABS* 2017, 28-30.
106. *TABS* 2018, 25-26.
107. MacIntosh, 335.
108. Eriksen, H.K., *World War II in the Borderland*, 'The Litza Front and Trench Warfare', Borderland Museum Kirkenes, Norway.
109. Thorburn 2006, 304.
110. *TABS* 2015, 23.
111. Thorburn 2006, 305.
112. Whitfield, 26.
113. *TABS* 2015, 24.
114. Zetterling, N. and Tamelander, M., *Tirpitz: The Life and Death of Germany's Last Super Battleship*, Casemate, Havertown, Pennsylvania 2009, 308.
115. Bob Riches interviewed in the *Lincolnshire Observer*, 6 November 1969.
116. Thorburn 2006, 308, 309.
117. *Horncastle News*.
118. MacIntosh, 330.
119. Sweetman, 145.
120. MacIntosh, 231, 235, 373-374, 376.
121. Glossary of RAF Slang: A Flame float is a small incendiary device that would float after being thrown out down the flare chute. The rear gunner would centre the 'pip' on his reflector sight on the point of light and then read off the degree of deviation from a scale on his turret ring – this would provide the navigator with the degree of wind drift blowing the aircraft off track.
122. Thorburn 2014, 198.
123. Malcolm Grant, typescript, 09/10/92. Malcolm Grant, who was four when his father Percy was killed in the New Year's Day accident, visited Bardney and met Terry Lintin, who had been a child at the time of the crash.
124. Thorburn 2014, 198.
125. MacIntosh, 389.
126. Information from Phil Hartshorn about his father, 22.9.21.

127. The following section is based on our personal transcription of a track from the audio CD, *Lancaster at War*, issued by Aviation Classics CD41, 2009.
128. Thorburn 2006, 323. In 1995, during the naming ceremony of Sergeant Thompsonstraat in the centre of Heesch, the village near the crash site, Harry Denton and Ted Kneebone described their experience to Joop Thuring, who was a child at the time. Both men remembered the Spitfire as belonging to 411 Squadron RCAF, although Thuring was not convinced by the identification, feeling that under the stress of the situation, it was an attribution that might have evolved over the subsequent twenty-five years.
129. Phil Hartshorn.
130. Thorburn 2014, 181-2.
131. Thorburn 2014, 134.
132. Sweetmen, 228.
133. Thorburn 2014, 199.
134. *TABS* 2019, 25.
135. Minister of Armaments and War Production in Nazi Germany during most of the Second World War. A close ally of Adolf Hitler, he was convicted at the Nuremberg trials and sentenced to twenty years in prison.
136. Thorburn 2006, 339.
137. MacIntosh, 394-5.
138. Thorburn 2014, 163.
139. MacIntosh, 396.
140. Thorburn 2014, 164.
141. *TABS* 2017, 28-30.
142. Mason, 75.
143. Saunders, H. St.G., *Royal Air Force, 1939-1945 Volume III 'The Fight is Won'*, HMSO, London 1954, 267.
144. Vernon Brown, *News Chronicle*, War Correspondent, 26 April 1944.
145. Bishop, P., *Air Force Blue*, Wm Collins, London 2017, 12.
146. *Aviation Classics*, Issue 1, October 2016, Morton's Media Group Ltd, Horncastle, Lincolnshire. Audio CD, Track 10.
147. Thorburn 2006, 348-9.

148. Thorburn 2006, 350.
149. *Aviation Classics*, Audio CD track 10.
150. Vernon Brown.
151. MacIntosh, 403.
152. MacIntosh, 406-7.
153. *The London Gazette*, 18 September 1945, issue 37277 dated 21 September.
154. Bishop 2017, 12.
155. *Daily Telegraph*, 21 March 2000.

Index

Abbeville, 20–2, 29, 203
Alta, 104, 113, 135

Bardufoss, 124–5, 134–5
Battle of Britain Association, 207
Battle of Britain Memorial Flight, 207–208
Bazin, Anthea, 205
Bazin, Elizabeth, xiii, 6, 43, 54, 59–60, 65, 80, 83, 197, 201, 205–206
Bazin, James Michael,
  BBC recordings,
    October 1944, 110
    June 1945, 187
  Berchtesgaden briefing, 187
  Controller:
    Catterick, 59–60
    Inverness, 61, 64, 122, 200, 202
  conversion to bombers, 68
  education and career, 2
  Exercise Spartan, 63, 71, 219
  GCI, 61
  moves south, 206
  parliamentary candidate, 204
  607 Squadron:
    attacks on north-east August 1940, 11–12, 40–5
    Battle of Britain, vii, 4, 19, 27, 39–59, 199, 206
    Battle of France, vii, xiv, 1, 20, 22–36, 55, 58
    ground crews, 14, 16–17, 27, 31, 33–4, 52
    Firth of Forth, 11–12
    move to France and Phoney war, xiv, 17–22
    post-war return, 201–204
    pre-war flying experience, 3–9
    re-building 607 after Battle of France, 38–9
    relinquishes command, 204
    takes command, 203
    Tangmere 1940, 4, 35, 40, 45–8, 54–5, 60, 65, 199, 207–208
  49 Squadron,
    crews, 210
    D-Day operations, 63, 66, 69–71, 73
    hit by shell in cockpit, 71
    Normandy landings, 71–7
  IX Squadron:
    appointed CO, 73
    behaves out of character, 148–9
    Camrose Trophy, 89
    crew, xiii, 209–10
    ground crews, 87, 100–102, 141, 144, 146, 197
    handover to successor, 198
    intensive practice, 79, 89
    list of operations, App., 209
    takes on specialist targets, 82, 200
    Tirpitz, see under *Tirpitz*
Bazin, May, xiv–xv
Bazin, Michael J.C., 29, 59–61, 65, 196–7, 204, 207–208
Bazin, Miranda, x, 206
Bazin, Nan, 206, 207
Bazin, S. James, 65, 196
Bazin, Walter C., xv, 2

Bennett, Tom, 97
Berchtesgaden, 187–93
Bergen, 162–6, 181
Blackadder, Francis, 6, 10, 15–21, 23, 25–6, 29–30, 32–3, 35, 37–8, 42, 50, 56, 58
Bliss, Brian, 189
Blomeley, Dave, 35
Bowen, 'Chatty' ('Bow-wow'), 20, 35, 39, 55
Bremen, 116, 183–5, 197
Brest, 72, 83–6, 88, 148, 199, 210
Brookbank, Jim, 68, 89, 170, 187
Buckham, F/L, 106, 132, 138
Buckley, Jack, 154, 189, 191

Campion, LAC H., 203
Camsell, F/L, 98, 136, 181, 185
Churchill, Winston, 17, 23, 28, 30–1, 62, 93, 114, 120, 142
Cochrane, Sir Ralph, 90–1, 120, 184
Craig, Dudley, 8, 18, 20, 35, 43, 58, 201
Crawley, Aidan, 201

Dawes, Ken, 154–5
D-Day landings,
  Caen, 71, 77, 171, 210
  Cahagnes, 78, 80, 210
  La Pernelle, 71, 210
  Lorient, 72, 83, 210
  Maisy, 70, 210
  Omaha, 71
  Pontaubault, 72, 210
  Wimereux, 70, 210
Denton, Harry, 153, 155–9, 161, 172
Dimbleby, Richard, 63
Dönitz, Admiral, 136
Dortmund Ems Canal, 113, 144, 153, 156, 177
Dowding, Lord, 19, 30–1, 43, 46, 48, 60

Dunne, F/L Johnny, 170
Dupont, W/C, 198

Ehrler, Heinrich, 134–6
Étaples, 82, 210
Exercise Spartan, 63, 71

Fauquier, W/C, 163, 178
Flynn, Paddy, 154

Gabriel, Bill, 164, 181
Gibson, Sgt R.E., 202
Glover, Alan, 8, 12
Goebel, Ron, 160
Gomme, W/O, 34
Gore, W.E., 28, 38, 54, 219
Göring, Hermann, 37, 40, 45, 51, 135, 174, 188
Greenfield, LAC John, 202
Ground crews, 27, 31, 33–4, 52, 87, 100–3, 141, 144, 146, 197

Harris, Sir Arthur, 69
Harris, Ray, 97, 163–4, 175, 180
Hartshorn, Wilf, 156, 160, 222
Harvey, Roy, 99–100, 108–109, 124, 126, 132–5, 139, 141–2, 153, 164–5, 170, 177, 187
Hawkins, Nigel, 96, 141, 148, 150
Heligoland, 187
HQ 11 Group, 45, 46, 181
HQ 13 Group, 9, 41, 64–5, 217
HQ 14 Group, 61–4, 217
HQ Bomber Command, 4, 69, 106, 115, 143–4, 166, 199
HQ Fighter Command, 40, 46, 55–6, 61, 198

Ijmuiden, 87, 168
Iveson, Tony, 66, 125

Jay, P/O Trevor, 20
Jones, F/L Edgar, 98–9, 209
Jones, F/O A.F., 104, 128–9, 147, 167, 181

Kaafjord, 92, 102–104, 106, 119, 131, 135, 221
Kayll, Joe, 5, 28, 32, 38, 201, 203

La Pallice, 84, 87, 210
Lintin, Terry, 154, 222
Londonderry, Lord, 4, 7, 217
Luftflotte 5, 41, 47
Lützow, 151

Macintosh, Don, 75, 79, 86–7, 91, 93–7, 99, 103–104, 106–107, 119–20, 125, 127, 137, 141, 148–50, 155, 166–7, 169, 170–1, 175–6, 188–9, 193, 195, 197–8
Marsh, Larry, 127, 136–8, 140, 181
McMullen, Gp Capt, 133, 141–2
Melrose, Doug, 74, 81, 98, 104–105, 116, 131, 175–6, 189–91
Merville, 13, 35
Morris, F/O Sammy, 105, 131
Morsalines, 70, 210
Munich, 145, 149, 188, 193

Newton F/O Cliff, 153–4
Nolan, Dennis, 154–5, 165
Norrent-Fontes, 29–30, 32, 34
Norwegian Resistance, 92, 113, 125

Operation Exodus, 194, 197
Operation Overlord, viii, 69, 87
Operation Sealion, 48, 51–2

Park, AVM Keith, 45
Parrott, Peter, 20–3, 35

Parsons, H. Jimmy, 163
Peace, Vincent, 161–2
Petch, LAC F., 202
Pilsen (Skoda), 186–7
Popplewell, Ernest MP, 204–205
Porter, W/C E.L., 73, 89, 186
Potts, Sgt, 158, 160
Prettejohns, Gerald, 99–100, 103, 108, 165, 168–96

RAF Abbotsinch, 8, 58
RAF Acklington, 10–11, 13, 39
RAF Bardney, 71, 75, 81, 86, 88, 94, 98, 102, 106–11, 115–19, 122, 128, 130, 142–3, 146, 151, 154, 160–1, 166–9, 171, 173, 176–7, 179–82, 185, 187, 190, 193, 195–7, 211
RAF Catterick, 40, 57, 59–60
RAF Croydon, 13, 34, 38
RAF Drem, 11, 13, 57
RAF Fiskerton, 69, 71–2, 151
RAF Hendon, 4, 8, 34–5, 48
RAF Jurby, 207
RAF Kenton, 41
RAF Lossiemouth, 106, 122–3, 130, 138, 140–1, 151
RAF Ouston, 59, 61, 108, 201–204
RAF Peterhead, 62, 64–5, 151
RAF Prestwick, 38–9
RAF Sumburgh, 64, 129
RAF Tangmere, 4, 35, 40, 45–8, 54–5, 60, 65, 199, 207–208
RAF Turnhouse, 4, 57–8, 62, 64–5
RAF Usworth, 2, 4, 6, 8–10, 38–40, 42–3, 45–6, 48, 52, 57, 60
RAF Warmwell, 5
Ramwell, Pete, 126, 137
Ribbentrop, von, 8
Riches, Bob, 76, 133, 136, 138, 140, 167, 181, 215

Royal Navy, 11, 91, 93, 106, 139
Runciman, S/L Leslie OBE, AFC, 5, 8, 19, 39

Sample, F/L Johnny, 14, 20, 25, 38
Sassnitz, 174–5
Savage, Bert, 85, 166
Seaham Harbour, 42–4
Smith, Launce, 8, 28, 35, 38
Sorpe Dam, 113, 115, 118–19, 211
Speer, Albert, 167
Squadrons:
  IX Squadron, viii, ix, xiv, 66, 69–70, 73–88, 89–201, 203, 205, 209
  41 Squadron, 41
  49 Squadron, 67, 69–72, 74, 83, 186, 210
  72 Squadron, 41
  79 Squadron, 41
  152 Squadron, 10
  213 Squadron, 48, 52
  315 Squadron, 118
  463 Squadron, 94, 98, 106, 129, 132
  602 Squadron, 11
  603 Squadron, 11
  605 Squadron, 41
  607 Squadron, vii, viii, 1–4, 6–7, 10–11, 22–3, 27, 31, 35–6, 38, 40–3, 45–8, 52, 57–8, 61–2, 66, 74, 198–9, 201–204, 207–208
  609 Squadron, 10
  615 Squadron, 13, 28, 35
  617 Squadron, viii, xiv, 66, 82, 84–6, 88–9, 91–2, 97–8, 105, 107, 109, 111, 113, 115, 118–19, 122–3, 125–6, 132, 134, 137, 140, 143, 154, 162–4, 169, 178–9, 184, 186–7, 189–90

Stavanger (Sola), 40
Summer camps:
  Abbotsinch, 58
  Horsham St Faith, 203
  Leuchars, 202
  Lübeck, 201
  Tangmere, 4
  Usworth, 6
  Warmwell, 5
Synthetic oil plants:
  Bohlen, 171
  Farge, 185
  Gelsenkirchen, 74, 210
  I.G. Farben, 169, 186
  Leuna, 166, 186
  Mölbis, 185–6
  Pölitz, 151, 169
Szczecin, 151

Tait, W/C, 92, 100, 105, 107, 136, 140–1
Tetlow, Phil, 79–83, 86–9, 91–2, 95, 102–104, 107, 117–20, 123, 125, 130, 142, 147, 166, 168–9, 180
Thompson, George VC, 158–60, 172, 223
Tirpitz,
  Operation Paravane, 91–102, 221
  the attack, 102–106
  Operation Obviate, 120–9
  Operation Catechism, 131–42
Tromsø, 131
Tweddle, Doug, 77–8, 84–7, 90, 97, 99, 104, 109, 116, 123, 126, 128–9, 131–2, 134, 138, 142–3, 145–6, 148–9, 151, 168–70, 178–9, 181–5, 194–5, 197–8, 204–5

Urft Dam, 147, 211

V1 sites:
  Creil, 77, 210
  Mont Candon, 81
  Prouville, 75–6
  Rilly-la-Montagne, 81, 210
Viaducts/aqueducts:
  Altenbecken, 169–71, 184
  Arnsberg, 211
  Gravenhorst (Duker), 161
  Ladbergen, 156, 169, 171, 173
Vitry-en-Artois, 14–17, 21–3, 26, 29, 31–2

Walcheren Campaign, Flushing, 116, 119–20
Welford, Harry, 39, 45, 47, 52, 58–9
Westkapelle, 117, 119
Whitty, Will, 25, 33, 35, 48, 58–9, 66
Williams, Bill S/L, 99, 108, 124, 127, 133, 137, 139, 141–2, 144, 148, 164, 168, 170, 177, 187, 190
Woolf, Bob, 68, 83, 86, 173–6, 189

Yadognik, 92–104, 105–108